Starlight Noel

Starlight Noel

Matthew Petchinsky

Starlight Noel: A Cosmic Journey through Christmas Mysteries
By: Matthew Petchinsky

Introduction: "The Celestial Spirit of Christmas"

As the year draws to a close, people around the world unite to celebrate the season of Christmas, a time imbued with warmth, generosity, and a spirit of reflection. While many are familiar with the traditional narratives and customs surrounding the holiday, fewer recognize the rich celestial patterns and astrological influences woven through December, lending a cosmic depth to this cherished season. This guide, *Starlight Noel: A Cosmic Journey through Christmas Mysteries*, explores how the skies above shape our experiences, moods, and festivities during Christmas, offering readers an intimate view into astrology's age-old relationship with the holiday season.

Astrology's Relationship with the Holiday Season

Astrology has long illuminated the interactions between earthly experiences and the cosmos, bridging humanity with the stars, planets, and lunar rhythms. During Christmas, this connection is amplified as the year's darkest days invite introspection, unity, and celebration under the winter sky. The season's ancient pagan origins—rooted in the Winter Solstice—highlighted the rebirth of light as the days grew longer. This symbolism of renewal and light pervades Christmas today, encouraging people to look to the heavens with a sense of wonder and gratitude.

Astrology, especially around this time of year, reflects the holiday's themes. Zodiac signs that dominate December, particularly Sagittarius and Capricorn, embody qualities resonant with the season: Sagittarius brings expansion, optimism, and exploration, while Capricorn grounds us in tradition, responsibility, and long-term planning. By observing these energies, astrology offers a blueprint for navigating the holiday season's joys and challenges, aligning us with celestial rhythms to deepen our experience of the season.

The Importance of Celestial Events During the Christmas Period

December hosts an array of celestial events, from meteor showers to notable planetary alignments, making it one of the most active and enchanting months astronomically. The Winter Solstice, a pivotal event, marks the transition into longer days, symbolizing hope and a new beginning. The arrival of meteor showers like the Geminids fills the December skies with flashes of light, reminding us of the beauty of both earthly and cosmic realms. Additionally, planetary conjunctions often occur around this period, adding a layer of mystique and significance to the holiday's underlying spirit of unity and interconnectedness.

These events are not only spectacular to witness but also hold symbolic meaning in astrology. Eclipses, which occasionally align with the holiday season, serve as moments of transformation and heightened awareness, inviting individuals to release old patterns and embrace fresh perspectives. Solar flares, though less visible, can also impact our energy levels, influencing moods and interactions. For those aware of these celestial occurrences, these natural phenomena offer ways to tap into the holiday season's energy on a profound level, creating a harmonious balance between inner reflection and outer celebration.

The Influence of Zodiacs, Lunar and Solar Activity, and Cosmic Alignments in December

December's zodiac influences—spanning the outgoing, optimistic Sagittarius and the practical, grounded Capricorn—provide a cosmic framework for navigating the holiday season. Sagittarius, ruling the first three weeks of December, brings a sense of adventure and expansion. Its fiery energy inspires individuals to reach out, seek connection, and explore the world around them, perfect for holiday gatherings and new experiences. As the Sun moves into Capricorn just before Christmas, the energy shifts towards reflection, tradition, and family, inviting a sense of grounding and stability that aligns well with the closing of the year.

Lunar phases also play a vital role during December, subtly influencing moods, energy, and overall atmosphere. A December New Moon encourages setting intentions for the upcoming year, while a Full Moon offers a peak of energy—ideal for gathering with loved ones or engaging in festive activities. Meanwhile, solar activity can influence individuals more subtly; while not always predictable, heightened solar activity may bring increased energy, vitality, or even minor disruptions, adding a unique touch to the season's overall vibrancy.

Additionally, cosmic alignments often intensify during December, with key planetary aspects emphasizing themes of harmony, conflict, or introspection. For example, conjunctions between planets can bring about unity and collaboration, making it an opportune time to foster relationships and strengthen bonds. Retrogrades, on the other hand, can encourage self-reflection, inviting people to revisit past choices and make peace with lingering issues. These cosmic influences lend the Christmas season a depth and complexity that makes the holiday both personal and universal, connecting individuals through shared experiences of growth, reflection, and celebration.

Enhancing the Holiday Experience through Astrology

This guide aims to help readers harness these celestial energies to enrich their holiday experience, offering insight into the rhythms and movements of the heavens as they unfold. Each chapter provides guidance on how specific astrological events—such as planetary alignments, meteor showers, and lunar phases—impact our emotions, relationships, and interactions throughout the season. By understanding these influences, readers can plan festivities, reflect on the past year, and prepare for the next with greater awareness and intention.

For instance, exploring how Sagittarius energy affects family gatherings can help readers infuse their celebrations with enthusiasm and warmth, while Capricorn's grounding presence supports reflection on the past year's accomplishments. The guide's coverage of solar and lunar events allows readers to align personal traditions with nature's cycles, enhancing the sense of renewal that Christmas brings.

Ultimately, *Starlight Noel* provides readers with a toolkit for attuning to the celestial spirit of Christmas, offering a path to engage with the season more deeply and meaningfully. Whether one is observing the phases of the moon, marveling at a meteor shower, or feeling the subtle effects of a retrograde, astrology offers a rich and insightful way to celebrate Christmas with greater presence and connection to the world beyond. As we journey through this guide, may we not only celebrate the holiday season but also discover the celestial tapestry that makes it truly magical.

Part 1: Zodiac Insights

Chapter 1: Aries - Christmas Energy and Holiday Dynamics

As the first sign of the zodiac, Aries brings a fresh, pioneering energy to everything it touches. Although Aries' typical season is in early spring, its influence is still felt around Christmas, especially by those who fall under this sign. This chapter explores how Aries' bold, fiery qualities come to life during the holiday season, infusing it with excitement, enthusiasm, and a touch of spontaneity. By understanding the Aries energy during Christmas, readers can better navigate the holiday dynamics and harness the courage and enthusiasm that this sign brings.

Aries Energy: Boldness, Action, and Enthusiasm

Aries, ruled by Mars, embodies a spirit of courage, initiation, and independence. Represented by the ram, Aries naturally charges forward, breaking down barriers and pushing through any challenges that arise. At Christmas, these qualities can manifest as a desire to take charge of festive activities, a tendency to infuse celebrations with high energy, and an enthusiasm for trying new things. Aries individuals, or those influenced by Aries in their natal charts, often bring a palpable liveliness to holiday gatherings, encouraging others to step out of their comfort zones and engage with the season's magic.

This energy can be both exhilarating and intense. Aries is known for its strong opinions and competitive spirit, which can sometimes lead to heated exchanges or bursts of frustration, especially during the high-stress holiday season. Yet, when channeled positively, Aries' confidence and drive make it the perfect sign for sparking holiday cheer, motivating others to get into the festive spirit, and encouraging a sense of togetherness and shared excitement.

Navigating Holiday Dynamics with Aries Influence

During the Christmas season, Aries energy can affect family dynamics in both positive and challenging ways. On one hand, Aries' leadership qualities make it natural for those influenced by this sign to take the reins in planning and organizing holiday events. They're often the ones initiating ideas for family activities, suggesting bold new traditions, or motivating everyone to join in on festive preparations. This proactive energy brings a fresh, exciting quality to the season, making it ideal for families looking to shake up their usual routines and create lasting memories.

However, the Aries tendency towards impatience and competitiveness can sometimes create friction in holiday settings. Aries individuals may feel the urge to do things their way, which can lead to tension if others prefer a different approach. Recognizing this, those with strong Aries influences can work to temper their intensity, practicing patience and collaboration, and remembering that the holiday season is about shared joy and togetherness.

For families and friends with Aries energy in their midst, embracing an open, flexible approach can help accommodate Aries' need for excitement while maintaining a harmonious environment. Encouraging everyone to contribute ideas or share responsibilities can foster a sense of unity, giving Aries individuals the freedom to lead in a way that enhances the holiday experience for all.

Embracing Spontaneity and Adventure: Aries' Unique Approach to Holiday Traditions

Aries thrives on novelty, making them the ideal sign to explore new ways of celebrating the holidays. Rather than sticking rigidly to tradition, Aries energy encourages spontaneity and experimentation, inviting everyone to try something different this Christmas season. Whether it's planning an impromptu winter adventure, adding an unconventional twist to the traditional holiday dinner, or exploring new, exciting gift ideas, Aries individuals bring an open-minded approach that can infuse the holidays with a sense of excitement and surprise.

For those looking to honor the Aries spirit this Christmas, consider embracing a more flexible holiday schedule, leaving room for last-minute activities and impromptu gatherings. Aries thrives in environments where they can make decisions in the moment, acting on inspiration as it arises. By creating space for spontaneity, families and friends can enjoy a holiday experience that feels fresh, dynamic, and alive.

Incorporating new traditions or blending unconventional elements with classic ones can also be a wonderful way to channel Aries energy. This might mean introducing adventurous activities, like an outdoor hike, a sledding trip, or a spontaneous road trip to see holiday lights, appealing to Aries' love for action and physical movement. For Aries, a holiday isn't complete without some level of excitement and novelty, so seeking out unique experiences can help make the season memorable.

The Aries Approach to Gift-Giving: Thoughtful, Bold, and Direct

Gift-giving under the influence of Aries is a lively affair. Known for being decisive and direct, Aries prefers gifts that reflect their enthusiasm and appreciation for action, adventure, and practicality. When selecting gifts, Aries individuals tend to choose items that will inspire excitement or encourage the recipient to take on a new activity. They favor gifts that are practical yet bold, often reflecting their love for adventure and self-expression.

Ideal gifts from an Aries might include high-energy items like sports equipment, adventure gear, or experiences like tickets to an exciting event or a surprise weekend getaway. Aries appreciates the thrill of a surprise, so they are more likely to enjoy giving experiential gifts that create lasting memories. For Aries, gift-giving isn't just about the item but the excitement it brings, making them natural gift-givers for those who enjoy a bit of thrill in their lives.

However, Aries gift-givers should remember that not everyone shares their love for action-packed experiences. By considering the recipient's preferences and focusing on gifts that blend excitement with a personal touch, Aries can balance their desire for bold choices with the thoughtful consideration that makes a gift truly memorable.

Managing Holiday Stress with Aries Strength

The holiday season can be a time of high emotion, and Aries, with its fiery nature, may find itself easily stressed when things don't go as planned. For Aries individuals, holiday stress can manifest as impatience, frustration, or even feelings of burnout from pushing themselves too hard to create a "perfect" holiday experience. To manage these feelings, it's important for Aries to embrace self-care practices and to find outlets for their abundant energy.

Physical activities are especially beneficial for Aries, helping to release pent-up energy and prevent holiday tension. Incorporating exercise, whether it's a brisk winter walk, a gym session, or a festive outdoor activity, can be an excellent way for Aries to recharge. Additionally, practicing mindfulness and allowing for moments of rest can help balance Aries' natural inclination for constant action, creating a more relaxed and fulfilling holiday experience.

For friends and family, understanding Aries' need for independence and occasional alone time can be a valuable way to support them during the holidays. By giving Aries individuals the space to recharge in their own way, loved ones can help them maintain their energy and enthusiasm throughout the season, fostering a positive and joyful environment.

Final Thoughts: Celebrating Christmas the Aries Way

Aries brings a powerful and invigorating energy to Christmas, encouraging all to embrace the season with courage, enthusiasm, and a readiness for adventure. Their bold approach to the holidays transforms traditional festivities into dynamic experiences, making them the life of any holiday gathering. By embracing the Aries spirit of action and excitement, families and friends can enrich their celebrations, blending tradition with a refreshing touch of spontaneity.

As you move through the holiday season, let Aries energy inspire you to approach Christmas with an open heart, a fearless spirit, and a willingness to try something new. With Aries' boldness lighting the way, this Christmas has the potential to be a memorable celebration full of joy, connection, and unexpected delights. Whether it's through dynamic gatherings, thoughtful yet adventurous gifts, or simply finding new ways to connect, Aries reminds us all that Christmas is a time to embrace life with enthusiasm and to let our true spirit shine.

Chapter 2: Taurus - Festive Stability and Grounding Traditions

Taurus, the second sign of the zodiac, is renowned for its dependable, steady energy and a love for all things comforting and beautiful. Ruled by Venus, the planet of love, luxury, and pleasure, Taurus is associated with an appreciation for the finer things in life, a preference for routines, and a penchant for creating cozy, welcoming environments. This chapter delves into the qualities Taurus brings to the holiday season, particularly through grounding traditions and cultivating a sense of stability amidst the season's excitement.

By understanding Taurus energy, individuals can enrich their Christmas experiences with intentional practices that promote a calm, harmonious environment where loved ones feel cared for and connected. The following insights illuminate how Taurus's traits of loyalty, patience, and a deep appreciation for tradition shape a memorable holiday experience rooted in warmth and stability.

Taurus Energy: Steadiness, Patience, and a Love for Comfort

As an earth sign, Taurus brings a grounding energy that can be particularly beneficial during the bustling holiday season. While festivities can often feel chaotic or overwhelming, Taurus provides an anchoring influence, encouraging a focus on meaningful traditions, long-lasting rituals, and creating a calm, luxurious atmosphere that enhances everyone's enjoyment of the season. Taurus energy is naturally slow-paced and patient, fostering an environment where each moment can be savored rather than rushed.

Taurus individuals are often the stabilizing force in any group, offering a sense of reliability and warmth. They enjoy taking the time to decorate their surroundings, ensuring that their home or holiday gathering space is beautifully adorned and full of comforting touches. For Taurus, the holiday season is about indulging the senses and creating an experience that feels rich and fulfilling on multiple levels. By embracing Taurus energy, we can find balance amid the excitement and chaos of the holidays, choosing to celebrate the season with intention and mindful appreciation.

Building and Honoring Holiday Traditions with Taurus Energy

For Taurus, traditions hold a special significance, embodying a sense of continuity and emotional security that resonates deeply with their loyal, steadfast nature. Whether it's a beloved family recipe passed down through generations or an annual tree-decorating ritual, Taurus thrives in the familiarity of holiday customs that bring people together. In a world that is constantly changing, these traditions offer a sense of comfort and predictability, reminding us of the timeless value of shared experiences.

Taurus energy inspires us to cultivate holiday traditions that are both meaningful and enduring. This might mean creating a family cookbook of favorite holiday recipes, organizing an annual gathering that brings friends and family together, or decorating the home with cherished ornaments that have personal significance. By investing time and energy in these rituals, Taurus energy creates a foundation of emotional stability that makes the holiday season feel deeply rooted in love and togetherness.

For those with Taurus influences, sharing these traditions with loved ones is a powerful way to express care and loyalty. When families and friends participate in these customs, they reinforce bonds that endure beyond the holiday season. Taurus energy reminds us that traditions are not merely about repetition but about celebrating the things that connect us across time, space, and generations.

The Sensory Delights of Taurus: Creating a Cozy, Indulgent Holiday Atmosphere

Ruled by Venus, Taurus is inherently drawn to sensory pleasures and aesthetics, bringing a love for beautiful, comforting environments to holiday celebrations. Taurus individuals are known for their attention to detail, especially when it comes to creating a visually and atmospherically appealing space. During the holiday season, Taurus's desire for comfort and luxury inspires them to adorn their homes with warm lighting, plush textures, and rich, earthy colors, transforming their surroundings into a cozy haven that invites relaxation and joy.

For Taurus, holiday décor goes beyond mere appearances—it's about creating an experience that engages all the senses. Soft blankets, twinkling lights, seasonal scents like cinnamon and pine, and thoughtfully chosen decorations all contribute to an ambiance that feels welcoming and harmonious. Those wishing to channel Taurus energy this Christmas might invest in high-quality decorations, candles, and other sensory elements that enhance the space's warmth and appeal, inviting guests to feel at ease and cared for.

Food is another essential component of a Taurus-inspired holiday. Known for their love of indulgent, delicious fare, Taurus individuals are often drawn to the kitchen, where they can prepare dishes that bring people together. Whether it's a traditional holiday feast, a spread of seasonal treats, or simply a comforting hot drink by the fireplace, Taurus energy encourages everyone to slow down and savor the flavors of the season. Hosting a holiday meal with Taurus energy means prioritizing quality, flavor, and a leisurely dining experience that allows everyone to connect deeply.

Gift-Giving with Taurus: Thoughtful, Practical, and Luxurious

Gift-giving under Taurus's influence is characterized by thoughtfulness, practicality, and an appreciation for quality. Taurus individuals approach gifts with a deep consideration of what would bring comfort and joy to the recipient, often selecting items that reflect their love of beauty, luxury, and usefulness. Taurus tends to avoid fleeting trends, opting instead for timeless gifts that can be cherished and enjoyed for years to come.

When selecting gifts, Taurus appreciates items that provide a sense of comfort or indulgence. Think cozy blankets, high-quality teas, artisanal chocolates, or even luxury skincare products—items that allow the recipient to experience a moment of relaxation and self-care. Taurus also values practicality, so items like a well-made leather bag, a set of durable cookware, or a beautiful but functional journal could be ideal choices. For those looking to channel Taurus energy in their gift-giving, choosing gifts that emphasize quality over quantity and are rooted in practicality, comfort, or luxury will resonate deeply.

In addition, Taurus is known for its loyalty and personal touch. A hand-written note, a family heirloom, or a gift that acknowledges a shared memory can make a present feel particularly meaningful, expressing Taurus's desire to connect on a heartfelt level. Ultimately, for Taurus, the best gifts are those that reflect the recipient's tastes and needs, showing a level of care and attention that makes the exchange a memorable experience.

Managing Holiday Stress with Taurus Patience and Calm

While the holiday season can be exciting, it can also bring about moments of stress, especially for those who feel pressured by time constraints or family dynamics. Taurus, with its patient and grounded nature, offers a reminder to slow down and approach the holidays with a sense of calm and mindfulness. Rather than rushing from one event to another, Taurus encourages a focus on quality over quantity, choosing activities and gatherings that truly resonate with the spirit of the season.

To manage holiday stress, Taurus individuals can benefit from embracing practices that keep them centered and relaxed. This might mean setting aside time for quiet reflection, indulging in a favorite hobby, or engaging in grounding activities like yoga, meditation, or a simple nature walk. By reconnecting with the natural world or taking moments for self-care, Taurus can maintain their steady composure and avoid the overwhelm that sometimes accompanies the holidays.

For families and friends, understanding Taurus's need for a calm, stable environment can help create a harmonious holiday experience. By avoiding last-minute changes or high-stress gatherings, loved ones can help Taurus individuals feel at ease, allowing them to enjoy the holiday with their signature steadiness and warmth. Celebrating in a way that respects Taurus's preference for calmness and tradition can create a holiday atmosphere that feels both relaxed and fulfilling.

Final Thoughts: Celebrating Christmas the Taurus Way

Taurus brings a comforting and luxurious touch to the holiday season, reminding us to appreciate the simple joys of tradition, togetherness, and sensory indulgence. Through their love for beauty, stability, and quality, Taurus energy transforms Christmas into a season of grounded celebration, inviting all to relax, savor, and appreciate the richness of life. By focusing on enduring traditions, creating cozy spaces, and giving gifts that reflect love and thoughtfulness, Taurus energy adds a layer of depth and meaning to the festivities.

As you celebrate Christmas this year, let Taurus energy inspire you to slow down, connect with loved ones, and create a holiday experience that feels both comforting and rejuvenating. Whether through time-honored traditions, thoughtful gifts, or a beautifully curated home, Taurus reminds us that the holidays are an opportunity to nurture ourselves and each other, celebrating in ways that are lasting and meaningful. By grounding yourself in the spirit of the season, you can enjoy a Christmas that truly resonates with the heart, creating memories that endure for years to come.

Chapter 3: Gemini - The Duality of Christmas Spirit

Gemini, the third sign of the zodiac, is known for its dynamic, versatile, and intellectually curious nature. Represented by the Twins, Gemini brings a sense of duality to all it encounters, embracing both sides of every experience and often embodying more than one perspective at a time. During the holiday season, this Gemini duality translates to a unique blend of joy and introspection, excitement and reflection, and the mingling of tradition with innovation. This chapter delves into the ways Gemini energy enhances the holiday spirit, encouraging flexibility, social engagement, and a refreshing approach to Christmas traditions.

Gemini's influence during Christmas invites us to explore both the lighthearted and profound aspects of the season. Known for its curious mind, communicative style, and playful energy, Gemini reminds us that the holidays are not just about tradition but also about connecting with others, exchanging ideas, and celebrating the multiplicity of life. By understanding Gemini energy, individuals can embrace a Christmas spirit that balances joy with introspection, novelty with nostalgia, and sociability with personal growth.

Gemini Energy: Curiosity, Communication, and Adaptability

As an air sign ruled by Mercury, Gemini is associated with intellect, communication, and an insatiable curiosity about the world. Gemini individuals are naturally sociable, eager to engage in conversations, and drawn to the exchange of ideas. This makes them excellent hosts, conversationalists, and connectors during the holiday season, when gatherings and festivities often revolve around social interaction. Gemini's influence encourages openness, adaptability, and a willingness to explore different ways of celebrating, blending the old with the new and traditional customs with fresh ideas.

Gemini's duality, however, extends beyond social adaptability. This sign embraces the coexistence of opposites, finding meaning in both joy and melancholy, excitement and quiet reflection. During Christmas, this can manifest as a desire to engage fully with festive gatherings while also seeking moments for personal reflection. Gemini's unique approach to the holidays involves embracing both the external festivities and the internal meaning of the season, making it a time for laughter, connection, and thoughtful introspection.

The Dual Nature of Christmas: Balancing Festivity with Introspection

For Gemini, the holiday season is a time to explore the duality of Christmas—the simultaneous joy of celebration and the deeper significance of the season's traditions. On one hand, Christmas is a lively, sociable time filled with parties, gatherings, and shared experiences. On the other, it is also a season for reflection, when many consider their past year, set intentions for the next, and reconnect with the values they hold dear. Gemini energy effortlessly embraces this duality, encouraging individuals to engage with both the festive and reflective sides of Christmas.

Those with strong Gemini influence may find themselves switching between roles at holiday gatherings, moving fluidly from the life of the party to a reflective observer. This versatility allows Gemini to fully enjoy the season's dynamic energy while appreciating its quieter, introspective moments. Friends and family of Gemini individuals can support this duality by creating spaces and opportunities for both lively interaction and peaceful retreat, allowing Gemini to thrive during the holidays without feeling restricted to a single mode of celebration.

To embody Gemini energy during Christmas, individuals can explore ways to bring balance to their festivities. This might mean setting aside time for a personal holiday tradition, like journaling or reflecting on the year, before engaging in the season's social events. Gemini reminds us that Christmas is a season of both giving and receiving, of connecting outwardly with others while also looking inward, finding fulfillment in the harmonious interplay between the two.

The Spirit of Social Connection: Gemini as the Life of the Party

Gemini's natural sociability makes this sign a magnetic presence at any holiday gathering. With a talent for storytelling, humor, and engaging conversation, Gemini individuals often light up the room, inspiring laughter and connection among family and friends. They have a unique ability to bridge different social circles, ensuring that everyone feels included and appreciated. Gemini's charm lies in its openness and curiosity about others, making Gemini individuals fantastic listeners and conversationalists who can connect deeply with people from all walks of life.

During Christmas, Gemini energy encourages everyone to celebrate the season through shared experiences and meaningful interactions. For those hosting a holiday gathering, embracing a Gemini approach can involve creating interactive elements like group games, icebreakers, or storytelling rounds that invite people to share memories and laughter. Gemini thrives in environments where people are engaged and ideas are flowing, making it the ideal sign for hosting a festive atmosphere that feels lively, inclusive, and dynamic.

Gemini individuals may also be drawn to holiday traditions that involve communication, such as writing personalized holiday cards, creating a family newsletter, or sharing heartfelt stories around the table. Gemini's influence reminds us that Christmas is not just about giving material gifts but also about the gift of words, connection, and time spent with loved ones. By prioritizing quality conversations and meaningful exchanges, Gemini energy enhances the sense of community that lies at the heart of the holiday season.

The Gemini Twist on Holiday Traditions: Embracing Novelty and Innovation

As a mutable sign, Gemini thrives on change and variety, often bringing a fresh perspective to holiday traditions. While Taurus cherishes stability and routine, Gemini seeks to keep things interesting, adding an element of surprise and innovation to the season's rituals. For Gemini, the holiday season is a time to experiment, to blend new ideas with old traditions, and to approach Christmas celebrations with an open, creative mindset.

Gemini's approach to holiday traditions might involve tweaking existing customs to reflect contemporary interests or introducing new activities that keep the spirit of the season alive. For example, instead of a traditional gift exchange, Gemini might suggest a "Secret Santa" with a twist, where participants have to guess the gift-giver based on clues. Similarly, Gemini individuals might incorporate modern elements into their holiday décor, blending classic and contemporary styles or opting for a color scheme that breaks from the traditional red and green.

For those looking to infuse a bit of Gemini-inspired novelty into their holiday, consider finding unique ways to approach gift-giving, decorating, or even celebrating. This could mean organizing a virtual gathering for faraway friends and family, planning a spontaneous holiday outing, or hosting a themed holiday dinner with an unexpected twist. By keeping things fresh and exciting, Gemini energy reminds us that tradition does not have to mean rigidity, and that the holiday season can evolve to reflect the ever-changing dynamics of family, friendship, and culture.

Gemini and Gift-Giving: Thoughtful, Unique, and Versatile

When it comes to gift-giving, Gemini shines through thoughtfulness and creativity. Gemini individuals enjoy the process of finding a gift that reflects both their own personality and the interests of the recipient, often choosing items that are unique, conversation-starting, or intellectually stimulating. Gemini gifts are typically versatile and reflect the sign's love for variety, often incorporating elements of learning, exploration, or humor.

Ideal gifts from a Gemini might include books on a subject the recipient loves, tickets to an event that inspires curiosity, or a personalized item that holds special significance. For friends or family members who enjoy conversation and connection, a board game, puzzle, or interactive activity can also make a fantastic Gemini-inspired gift. Gemini individuals are known for their curiosity and love of learning, so they may also gift items that inspire discovery, like a new hobby kit, a language-learning subscription, or a set of travel guides for future adventures.

To embody Gemini's spirit in gift-giving, choose items that encourage interaction, inspire curiosity, or offer a unique twist on a classic gift. By finding presents that spark interest and engage the mind, Gemini reminds us that the best gifts are those that invite connection and inspire conversation, adding a memorable touch to the season's festivities.

Managing Holiday Stress with Gemini Flexibility and Humor

The holiday season can be overwhelming, especially for those who thrive on variety and mental stimulation like Gemini. With so many gatherings, expectations, and obligations, it's easy for Gemini individuals to feel stretched thin or, conversely, bored by repetitive routines. To manage holiday stress, Gemini can benefit from embracing their natural flexibility, maintaining a sense of humor, and prioritizing activities that keep them mentally engaged.

A helpful approach for Gemini is to keep the holiday schedule flexible, allowing room for spontaneous outings, changes of plan, or breaks from tradition. Gemini individuals can also practice self-care by balancing social events with moments of personal downtime, such as reading, writing, or reflecting on the year's highlights. For Gemini, variety is essential to avoid feeling overwhelmed, so planning a mix of large gatherings, small intimate dinners, and solo time can help create a balanced and enjoyable holiday experience.

For friends and family, supporting Gemini's need for adaptability and mental engagement can be key to ensuring a harmonious holiday. Encouraging open communication, offering flexible options, and being receptive to new ideas can create an environment where Gemini feels appreciated and free to express their dynamic energy. With a little planning, Gemini's sense of humor and adaptability can help them navigate the season with grace, turning any potential holiday mishap into a memorable story or a chance for laughter.

Final Thoughts: Celebrating Christmas with the Gemini Spirit

Gemini brings a refreshing, joyful duality to the Christmas season, inviting us to embrace both the lighthearted and meaningful aspects of the holidays. Through their love for communication, curiosity, and adaptability, Gemini individuals inspire those around them to celebrate in a way that feels lively, thoughtful, and true to the dynamic nature of the season. By balancing tradition with novelty, festivity with introspection, Gemini encourages us all to approach Christmas as a season of discovery, connection, and shared joy.

As you celebrate this year, let Gemini's spirit of curiosity and versatility guide you to try something new, engage deeply with loved ones, and appreciate the myriad ways in which the holiday season can unfold. Whether it's through a heartfelt conversation, a thoughtful gift, or a new twist on an old tradition, Gemini reminds us that Christmas is a time to celebrate both the known and the unknown, creating memories that resonate with laughter, insight, and a sense of wonder.

Chapter 4: Cancer - Nurturing Family Bonds in December

Cancer, the fourth sign of the zodiac, is known for its nurturing, protective, and deeply emotional nature. Ruled by the Moon, Cancer is profoundly connected to family, home, and memories, bringing a unique sensitivity and warmth to everything it touches. During the holiday season, Cancer's influence shines brightly as it emphasizes the importance of familial connections, traditions, and heartfelt togetherness. This chapter explores how Cancer's energy enriches the holiday season, creating a nurturing atmosphere that fosters closeness, security, and love.

Cancer reminds us that Christmas is more than just a festive celebration—it's a time to honor the bonds that unite us with our loved ones and to create lasting memories rooted in care and compassion. By embracing Cancer's nurturing spirit, individuals can deepen their holiday experience, transforming December into a season of connection, emotional warmth, and meaningful family interactions.

Cancer Energy: Sensitivity, Loyalty, and Emotional Depth

As a water sign, Cancer is deeply intuitive and sensitive, often attuned to the needs and emotions of others. Known for their compassion and empathy, Cancer individuals prioritize relationships, creating spaces where everyone feels valued and understood. This emotional intelligence allows Cancer to bring a rare depth to family gatherings, fostering an atmosphere that is safe, welcoming, and emotionally fulfilling. Cancer energy is also characterized by a strong sense of loyalty, making it the perfect influence for family-oriented traditions and holiday rituals.

During the holiday season, Cancer's focus on family and emotional security is especially relevant. While other signs might focus on social gatherings or festive activities, Cancer's approach to Christmas is rooted in a desire to protect, nurture, and strengthen familial bonds. Cancer individuals often go above and beyond to ensure that everyone feels comfortable, cherished, and included, imbuing the holiday with a sense of intimacy and heartfelt connection that lingers long after the season ends.

Creating a Warm, Welcoming Home: Cancer's Gift for Hospitality

Cancer is closely associated with the concept of "home," and for Cancer individuals, the home is more than just a physical space—it's a sanctuary where family and friends can gather, relax, and feel safe. During the holiday season, Cancer's natural hospitality shines, encouraging them to create a cozy, welcoming environment that feels like a true retreat from the outside world. From carefully chosen decorations to comforting meals, Cancer's attention to detail ensures that everyone who enters their home feels embraced by warmth and love.

Cancer's gift for hospitality is grounded in their intuitive understanding of others' needs. Cancer individuals are often attuned to subtle cues, allowing them to create spaces that cater to both physical and emotional comfort. This might mean setting up a quiet corner for introspective family members, preparing favorite dishes that evoke cherished memories, or simply adding personal touches that make guests feel at ease. For those inspired by Cancer energy, focusing on small, thoughtful details—like soft blankets, ambient lighting, or meaningful holiday décor—can create an environment that resonates with warmth and security.

Creating a welcoming home also involves Cancer's dedication to tradition. Cancer individuals value continuity and often incorporate family heirlooms, handmade decorations, or items with sentimental significance into their holiday decor. By blending past and present, Cancer connects their loved ones to a lineage of memories and shared experiences, grounding the holiday season in a sense of history and belonging.

Family Traditions and the Heart of the Holiday Season

Family traditions hold special meaning for Cancer, as they represent the enduring connections that link one generation to the next. During Christmas, Cancer's appreciation for tradition is heightened, inspiring them to preserve and cherish the customs that make the holiday feel uniquely special. Whether it's baking a traditional holiday treat, gathering for a favorite movie, or decorating the tree together, Cancer finds joy in rituals that foster closeness and bring people together.

For Cancer, holiday traditions are more than just activities—they are emotional anchors that provide comfort and stability. By participating in these rituals, family members can experience a sense of continuity that transcends time, reminding them of the love and support that underlies the holiday season. Cancer individuals often take on the role of tradition-keeper, encouraging loved ones to participate in annual customs and preserving family stories that add depth and meaning to the celebrations.

Those who wish to channel Cancer's appreciation for tradition during the holidays might consider reviving an old family custom, creating a new ritual, or sharing stories that highlight the family's unique history. By focusing on activities that bring everyone together, Cancer energy transforms the holiday season into a sacred time of remembrance, bonding, and emotional healing. This emphasis on tradition nurtures the family as a whole, strengthening connections that endure beyond the festivities.

The Art of Giving with Cancer: Thoughtful, Personal, and Heartfelt

Gift-giving under Cancer's influence is a deeply personal experience. For Cancer, the best gifts are those that express love, consideration, and genuine thoughtfulness, often choosing items that reflect the recipient's personality or hold sentimental value. Cancer individuals are known for their sensitivity and intuition, which helps them select gifts that resonate on an emotional level, making the exchange feel particularly meaningful.

Cancer-inspired gifts are often practical yet personal, items that add warmth, comfort, or convenience to the recipient's life. Ideal Cancer gifts might include cozy blankets, family photo albums, personalized mementos, or even a handcrafted item that holds special meaning. For Cancer, a gift is an opportunity to show appreciation, celebrate shared memories, and convey the depth of their care for loved ones.

Those looking to give gifts with Cancer energy can focus on items that have personal significance or create shared experiences. This might involve giving a framed photo from a meaningful moment, preparing a handmade holiday treat, or organizing a family activity that brings everyone together. By choosing gifts that reflect a deep understanding of the recipient's interests, Cancer reminds us that the true value of a present lies in the intention and love behind it.

Strengthening Family Bonds: Cancer's Approach to Holiday Gatherings

Cancer's love for family and nurturing instincts make them natural hosts for holiday gatherings. They thrive in environments where they can care for others, ensuring that everyone feels comfortable, valued, and included. During holiday gatherings, Cancer individuals often take on the role of emotional caretakers, checking in with family members, offering support, and creating a space where people feel safe to express themselves.

Cancer's influence encourages us to approach holiday gatherings with sensitivity and compassion, recognizing that family dynamics can be complex and that not everyone experiences the season with the same emotions. For Cancer, the holiday season is an opportunity to bridge divides, mend old wounds, and create an environment of acceptance and empathy. By offering a listening ear, showing patience, and fostering open communication, Cancer helps family members connect on a deeper level, transforming gatherings into opportunities for healing and understanding.

To channel Cancer's approach to holiday gatherings, consider creating a space where everyone feels heard and appreciated. This might involve setting up areas for quiet conversation, encouraging family members to share memories or stories, or simply offering words of affirmation and encouragement. Cancer reminds us that the holidays are a time to honor the bonds that hold us together, making each interaction a chance to express love and gratitude for one another.

Managing Holiday Emotions with Cancer's Sensitivity and Self-Care

While the holiday season is often joyful, it can also bring up complex emotions, especially for those with Cancer's heightened sensitivity. Cancer individuals may feel deeply affected by the highs and lows of family gatherings, and their empathetic nature can make them more susceptible to holiday stress. To navigate these emotions, Cancer benefits from prioritizing self-care, setting boundaries, and creating time for personal reflection amidst the festivities.

Cancer's connection to the Moon makes them highly intuitive and in tune with their emotional needs. During the holidays, Cancer individuals can benefit from taking regular breaks to recharge, whether through quiet reflection, journaling, or engaging in a calming activity. For Cancer, self-care is essential to maintaining their inner balance and enabling them to offer their best self to loved ones.

Friends and family can support Cancer's emotional needs by respecting their boundaries, offering gentle encouragement, and providing reassurance when needed. Cancer energy is at its best when it feels secure, loved, and appreciated, so creating an environment where Cancer individuals feel supported can help them enjoy the holiday season to the fullest. By embracing self-care and honoring their sensitivity, Cancer reminds us that nurturing oneself is a vital part of being able to care for others.

Final Thoughts: Celebrating Christmas with Cancer's Nurturing Spirit

Cancer brings a profound depth and warmth to the holiday season, transforming Christmas into a celebration of love, family, and emotional connection. Through their focus on family bonds, tradition, and heartfelt giving, Cancer individuals remind us that the true magic of the season lies not in material gifts or elaborate festivities, but in the moments of genuine connection and care that make the holidays meaningful. By embracing Cancer's nurturing spirit, we can create a Christmas experience that feels both comforting and transformative, enriching our relationships and building memories that will last for years to come.

As you celebrate this holiday season, let Cancer's influence inspire you to prioritize family, cultivate a welcoming environment, and approach each interaction with compassion and sensitivity. Whether through cherished traditions, thoughtful gifts, or heartfelt gatherings, Cancer reminds us that the holidays are a time to honor the bonds that define us, filling the season with a sense of love, warmth, and belonging.

Chapter 5: Leo - Holiday Celebrations and Creative Flair

Leo, the fifth sign of the zodiac, is known for its bold, charismatic, and expressive nature. Ruled by the Sun, Leo embodies the warmth, vitality, and creativity that light up any room, bringing joy, excitement, and a sense of grandeur to all it encounters. During the holiday season, Leo energy radiates brightly, encouraging us to embrace the celebratory spirit of Christmas with enthusiasm, confidence, and a touch of theatrical flair. This chapter explores how Leo's dynamic energy influences holiday gatherings, from hosting unforgettable celebrations to incorporating creative and personal touches that make the season truly memorable.

Leo's approach to Christmas is marked by an openness to celebration and a desire to spread happiness and cheer. With a natural flair for the dramatic, Leo individuals take pleasure in creating memorable moments, whether through thoughtfully decorated spaces, imaginative gift-giving, or their charismatic presence at social gatherings. By understanding Leo energy, we can embrace a holiday season that is not only festive and lively but also rich in creative expression, warmth, and generosity.

Leo Energy: Confidence, Warmth, and Expressive Creativity

As a fire sign ruled by the Sun, Leo is associated with qualities of self-expression, creativity, and a natural leadership ability that makes them magnetic at any gathering. Leo's warmth and charm make them wonderful hosts, and their enthusiasm for celebration inspires those around them to let loose and enjoy the festive season to the fullest. With a penchant for luxury, attention to detail, and a love for all things beautiful, Leo energy often brings a sense of grandeur and excitement to holiday festivities.

Leo's confidence is infectious, creating a joyful atmosphere that encourages everyone to express themselves freely and celebrate without reservation. This holiday season, Leo energy reminds us to let go of inhibitions, take pride in our unique qualities, and approach Christmas with a sense of playfulness and positivity. Leo encourages us to view the holiday as an opportunity to shine, share joy, and create an experience that leaves a lasting impression on our loved ones.

Hosting with Leo Energy: Creating a Show-Stopping Celebration

Leos are known for their hosting skills, and they bring a theatrical touch to holiday gatherings that makes every event feel like an occasion. For Leo, hosting is an opportunity to share their love of life with others, using their natural leadership skills to organize a memorable and cohesive celebration. Leo's style of hosting combines luxury with a personal touch, often blending classic holiday elements with innovative ideas that make their gatherings stand out.

Those who wish to host with Leo energy can focus on creating a visually stunning and welcoming atmosphere. Leo gatherings are often characterized by bold décor, vibrant colors, and dramatic lighting that sets a festive mood. Gold, red, and warm tones are especially Leo-friendly choices, as they reflect the sign's association with the Sun and add a sense of warmth and elegance to the celebration. Luxurious touches—like elegant table settings, rich fabrics, and striking centerpieces—enhance the space, making guests feel they've entered a magical, festive world.

Leo also thrives on entertainment, so incorporating interactive elements into the gathering can add excitement and engagement. A holiday talent show, karaoke session, or even a mini awards ceremony for family and friends can bring a lighthearted sense of fun to the evening. Leo's love for performance and storytelling can also be reflected through curated playlists, holiday-themed games, or a dramatic reading of Christmas stories. With Leo energy, the focus is on creating an event that is both entertaining and emotionally resonant, encouraging guests to relax, enjoy, and leave with cherished memories.

Creative Flair in Décor and Presentation

Leos have an innate eye for beauty and a knack for design, making them naturally gifted at creating visually captivating holiday settings. Rather than sticking strictly to tradition, Leo enjoys adding a personal, creative twist to their décor, incorporating elements that reflect their bold personality and unique style. This creativity can be seen in every aspect of the holiday setup, from color schemes and lighting choices to table arrangements and tree decorations.

For those inspired by Leo energy, holiday décor can be an opportunity for self-expression. Consider choosing a distinct theme for the season—such as "Winter Royalty," "Celestial Christmas," or "Golden Wonderland"—that captures Leo's love for grandeur and artistic flair. Leo-inspired décor might feature dramatic lighting arrangements, statement ornaments, or lavish displays that blend elegance with festive charm. Personalized touches, like monogrammed stockings or custom table place cards, add a sense of exclusivity and thoughtfulness to the setup, making each guest feel special.

Incorporating elements of luxury and drama is a hallmark of Leo, so don't hesitate to go big with details like a beautifully decorated tree, a sparkling centerpiece, or intricate holiday displays. By infusing the home with warm, welcoming, and creative touches, Leo energy turns holiday décor into a work of art that enhances the joy and magic of the season for everyone who enters.

The Art of Gift-Giving with Leo: Thoughtful, Luxurious, and Memorable

Gift-giving is a natural talent for Leo, who enjoys choosing presents that make recipients feel seen, appreciated, and indulged. Leos are generous by nature, often drawn to gifts that are high-quality, luxurious, or infused with a touch of extravagance. For Leo, a gift is an expression of affection and a way to share joy, so they are likely to select items that reflect both their own taste and the recipient's personality.

Ideal gifts from a Leo might include items that encourage self-expression, beauty, or creativity, such as designer accessories, luxurious home items, or personalized jewelry. Leos also enjoy experiential gifts, so tickets to a concert, an art show, or even a glamorous night out might be the perfect choice. Leo's love for the dramatic extends to the presentation of the gift as well, often choosing elaborate wrapping, ribbons, or custom tags to make the unboxing experience special and unforgettable.

When giving gifts with Leo energy, focus on items that convey warmth, thoughtfulness, and indulgence. Personalized items—like a framed photo, a custom piece of art, or a monogrammed accessory—carry the Leo touch of exclusivity and show that you took the time to make the gift meaningful. With Leo's influence, gift-giving becomes an opportunity to express admiration and affection, celebrating the unique qualities of each person in a way that feels heartfelt and luxurious.

Embracing Joy and Playfulness: Leo's Approach to Family and Social Gatherings

Leo's love for life is contagious, making them the heart and soul of any social gathering. During the holiday season, Leo's warmth and enthusiasm bring a sense of joy and spontaneity to family gatherings, encouraging everyone to let loose and celebrate without inhibition. Leo individuals often bring humor, playfulness, and an inclusive energy to holiday events, making others feel comfortable and appreciated.

Leo's approach to gatherings is centered around creating a joyful, relaxed atmosphere. Whether it's leading a group game, telling entertaining stories, or simply making sure everyone has a drink in hand, Leo individuals are skilled at ensuring that each person feels valued and included. For those looking to channel Leo's spirit of joy, incorporating playful elements like party games, photo booths, or even a costume theme can add a lively touch to holiday events, encouraging guests to embrace the festive spirit and connect with one another.

Leo also appreciates tradition but adds their unique twist to it, breathing new life into classic holiday activities. They might introduce new games to a family gathering, start a fun countdown to New Year's, or find creative ways to incorporate storytelling and performance into holiday festivities. By balancing tradition with playfulness, Leo energy ensures that holiday gatherings are both meaningful and entertaining, fostering connections that make each person feel a part of the celebration.

Managing Holiday Stress with Leo's Optimism and Self-Care

The holiday season can be busy and even overwhelming, especially for Leo, who often takes on the role of host, organizer, and entertainer. To prevent burnout, Leo can benefit from practicing self-care and setting aside time to recharge, allowing them to approach the season with their usual positivity and zest. For Leo, self-care often involves activities that affirm their self-worth and creativity, like spending time on a personal project, enjoying a favorite hobby, or simply taking a moment to relax and reflect.

For those with Leo energy, it can also be helpful to delegate tasks, allowing others to contribute to the festivities and lighten the load. Leo's natural leadership ability makes them inclined to take on multiple roles, but sharing responsibilities can prevent stress and ensure a more enjoyable holiday experience. Friends and family can support Leo by acknowledging their efforts, offering assistance, and encouraging them to take time for themselves when needed.

By balancing their social commitments with moments of self-care, Leo individuals can avoid holiday stress and stay energized throughout the season. Embracing Leo's optimism, focusing on joy, and allowing for moments of rest can help them navigate the holidays with ease, turning each gathering into a celebration of life, love, and creativity.

Final Thoughts: Celebrating Christmas with Leo's Creative Spirit

Leo's influence brings a vibrant, joyful energy to the holiday season, encouraging us to approach Christmas with confidence, generosity, and a creative flair. Through their love for beauty, warmth, and social connection, Leo individuals transform the season into a grand celebration that touches hearts, inspires laughter, and creates lasting memories. By embracing Leo's spirit of self-expression, we can enjoy a holiday season that feels both exhilarating and deeply fulfilling, filled with moments of shared joy and personal growth.

This Christmas, let Leo's influence inspire you to express yourself fully, celebrate boldly, and embrace the holiday season with warmth and creativity. Whether it's through a beautifully hosted gathering, thoughtful gifts, or personal touches that make each moment memorable, Leo reminds us that the true magic of Christmas lies in the connections we make, the joy we share, and the creativity we bring to our celebrations.

Chapter 6: Virgo - Organizing the Perfect Christmas

Virgo, the sixth sign of the zodiac, is known for its meticulous, organized, and thoughtful nature. Ruled by Mercury, Virgo combines a sharp intellect with a love for detail, making them the ultimate planners and problem-solvers. During the holiday season, Virgo's energy can be a true gift, as it brings structure, efficiency, and a deep sense of purpose to Christmas preparations. This chapter delves into how Virgo's practical approach influences holiday planning, gift-giving, and family gatherings, transforming Christmas into a well-organized and meaningful celebration.

Virgo's approach to the holiday season is marked by attention to detail, a focus on thoughtful gestures, and a drive to create a seamless, enjoyable experience for everyone involved. Virgo energy encourages us to embrace the art of preparation, prioritize meaningful moments, and infuse each holiday task with care and intention. By channeling Virgo's grounded approach, individuals can plan a Christmas celebration that feels harmonious, organized, and fulfilling.

Virgo Energy: Precision, Practicality, and a Heart for Service

As an earth sign, Virgo is grounded, detail-oriented, and highly practical, bringing an analytical perspective to all aspects of life. Known for their commitment to excellence, Virgo individuals are natural organizers who thrive on structure and purpose. During Christmas, Virgo's influence encourages us to prioritize preparation and efficiency, allowing for a smoother, more intentional holiday experience. Virgo energy also has a strong element of service and thoughtfulness, often going out of its way to ensure others feel cared for and valued.

Virgo's analytical mind enables them to anticipate potential challenges, making them skilled at handling holiday logistics. Whether it's planning a holiday meal, organizing gifts, or creating a festive atmosphere, Virgo's dedication to detail ensures that each element of the celebration is carefully considered and executed. This energy extends beyond practicalities, as Virgo's thoughtfulness allows them to approach the season with a genuine desire to bring joy and comfort to loved ones, making each moment of Christmas both meaningful and memorable.

Planning with Precision: Virgo's Approach to Holiday Preparations

When it comes to holiday preparations, Virgo's skills are unparalleled. Virgo thrives on creating order, setting schedules, and making lists, which can be invaluable during the often-chaotic holiday season. For Virgo, preparation is key, and they take pride in organizing every aspect of the celebration to ensure a seamless and stress-free experience for everyone. From managing a holiday budget to crafting the perfect holiday menu, Virgo energy shines in its ability to transform planning into an art form.

To plan with Virgo's precision, start by creating a comprehensive checklist that outlines each aspect of the holiday season. This could include everything from shopping lists and meal planning to a gift-giving schedule and a calendar of holiday events. By breaking tasks into manageable steps, Virgo's methodical approach allows for a smoother, more organized holiday that minimizes last-minute stress and ensures nothing is overlooked.

Virgo individuals also excel at budgeting and managing expenses, making them skilled at balancing quality with cost-effectiveness. For those inspired by Virgo's approach, creating a holiday budget can help keep spending in check, allowing for a season that feels abundant without unnecessary extravagance. Virgo's practical nature encourages thoughtful planning, reminding us that the holiday season doesn't have to be extravagant to be meaningful. By setting clear priorities and focusing on essentials, Virgo energy enables us to create a holiday celebration that feels balanced and purposeful.

Decorating with Virgo's Eye for Detail and Simplicity

Virgo's approach to holiday décor is understated yet elegant, focusing on quality, simplicity, and attention to detail. Unlike more flamboyant signs, Virgo prefers a subtle, refined aesthetic that emphasizes natural beauty and thoughtful arrangements. For Virgo, holiday decorations should enhance the space without overwhelming it, creating a harmonious environment that feels both festive and calming.

To decorate with Virgo's influence, consider a minimalist approach that incorporates earthy tones, organic textures, and natural elements like pinecones, evergreen branches, or candles. Virgo is drawn to clean lines, neutral colors, and décor that serves a purpose, so each element should be intentional and cohesive. For example, a well-curated centerpiece, a neatly arranged wreath, or a few beautifully wrapped presents under the tree can create an inviting atmosphere without clutter.

Virgo's attention to cleanliness and order is also reflected in their décor style. Virgo-inspired holiday decorations are organized, symmetrical, and meticulously placed, creating a sense of balance and tranquility. This approach encourages a focus on quality over quantity, using fewer decorations but ensuring each one adds meaningful value to the space. For Virgo, simplicity is key, and by focusing on well-chosen, thoughtfully placed pieces, they create an ambiance that feels serene, sophisticated, and effortlessly festive.

Gift-Giving the Virgo Way: Thoughtful, Practical, and Personalized

Gift-giving under Virgo's influence is characterized by practicality, thoughtfulness, and attention to detail. Virgo individuals excel at choosing gifts that reflect the recipient's interests and needs, often opting for items that are useful, high-quality, and aligned with the person's personality. For Virgo, the ideal gift is one that is both meaningful and functional, demonstrating a deep consideration for the recipient's preferences.

Ideal gifts from Virgo might include items that promote wellness, productivity, or personal growth, such as a high-quality planner, a favorite book, or a self-care kit. Virgo's eye for quality also makes them likely to choose gifts that are durable and well-made, valuing items that have lasting value. For example, a Virgo might gift a beautifully crafted kitchen tool, a luxurious skincare product, or an eco-friendly item that reflects their commitment to sustainability.

Virgo also appreciates the power of personalization in gift-giving. Whether it's a monogrammed accessory, a custom-made piece, or a handwritten note, Virgo enjoys adding a personal touch that makes each gift feel unique. By selecting items that align with the recipient's values and lifestyle, Virgo energy reminds us that the best gifts are those that demonstrate genuine thoughtfulness and care. To give with Virgo's influence, focus on items that bring value to the recipient's life, showing that you took the time to consider what would truly make them feel appreciated.

The Perfect Holiday Gathering: Virgo's Approach to Hosting with Care and Attention

Virgo's approach to hosting holiday gatherings is marked by careful planning, attention to detail, and a genuine desire to create a comfortable experience for guests. Unlike signs that may focus on extravagance or entertainment, Virgo hosts with an emphasis on comfort, order, and meaningful interaction. Virgo's goal is to create an environment where guests feel at ease, knowing that every detail has been thoughtfully prepared.

When hosting a gathering, Virgo's influence can be seen in the careful planning of the menu, seating arrangements, and overall flow of the event. Virgo individuals often take the time to plan a balanced meal that accommodates various dietary preferences, ensuring that each guest feels welcomed and cared for. They are also known for their knack for organization, often creating a schedule that allows for a smooth progression of activities and minimizes any potential stress.

Virgo's desire for cleanliness and order is also evident in their approach to hosting. They ensure that the space is tidy, organized, and comfortable for guests, paying attention to small details like setting the table, arranging seating, and creating a clutter-free environment. For those inspired by Virgo energy, hosting with care means focusing on the guest experience, attending to practical needs, and ensuring that each person feels valued and comfortable. By prioritizing meaningful connections and creating a well-organized atmosphere, Virgo transforms holiday gatherings into an experience of true warmth and hospitality.

Managing Holiday Stress with Virgo's Practicality and Self-Care

The holiday season, with its many tasks and expectations, can be overwhelming, even for Virgo. While Virgo excels at planning and organization, the pressure to achieve perfection can sometimes lead to stress or burnout. To manage holiday stress, Virgo benefits from practicing self-care, setting realistic expectations, and taking breaks to recharge.

For Virgo, self-care often involves activities that restore order and peace, such as organizing, journaling, or spending time in nature. Virgo individuals can benefit from creating moments of quiet reflection amidst the holiday busyness, allowing themselves to step back, breathe, and regain clarity. Simple self-care practices, like a daily walk, a few minutes of meditation, or a calming tea ritual, can help Virgo maintain their inner balance during the hectic holiday season.

Friends and family can support Virgo by appreciating their efforts, offering assistance, and encouraging them to take time for themselves when needed. Virgo's dedication to creating a memorable holiday experience is admirable, but reminding them that perfection isn't necessary can relieve some of the pressure they place on themselves. By balancing their love for planning with moments of rest and reflection, Virgo individuals can approach the holiday season with their usual grace, turning each task into an opportunity for joy and fulfillment.

Final Thoughts: Celebrating Christmas with Virgo's Organized and Caring Spirit

Virgo's influence brings a sense of order, purpose, and thoughtfulness to the holiday season, transforming Christmas into a celebration that is both harmonious and deeply meaningful. Through their dedication to detail, practical approach, and genuine care for others, Virgo individuals remind us that the true magic of Christmas lies not in extravagance but in the intention behind each gesture. By embracing Virgo's energy, we can create a holiday experience that feels both balanced and fulfilling, centered around meaningful connections and thoughtful planning.

As you celebrate Christmas this year, let Virgo's influence inspire you to approach the season with a heart for service, an eye for detail, and a focus on creating lasting memories. Whether it's through careful preparation, thoughtful gift-giving, or a beautifully organized gathering, Virgo reminds us that the holiday season is an opportunity to show our love through action, care, and the small touches that make each moment special. By infusing the holiday with Virgo's grounded and compassionate energy, we can create a Christmas celebration that feels both joyful and truly complete.

Chapter 7: Libra - Harmony and Balance in Festive Gatherings

Libra, the seventh sign of the zodiac, is known for its appreciation of harmony, beauty, and balance. Ruled by Venus, the planet of love and aesthetics, Libra brings a refined sense of elegance and a natural charm to everything it touches. During the holiday season, Libra's influence can be especially powerful, guiding us to create gatherings that foster connection, unity, and peace. This chapter explores how Libra's energy enhances holiday gatherings, blending elegance and inclusivity to create a festive atmosphere where everyone feels welcomed and valued.

Libra's approach to Christmas is marked by a desire for togetherness, aesthetic appeal, and balanced interactions. With a strong sense of justice and a love for connecting with others, Libra individuals have a gift for hosting gatherings that make everyone feel at ease. By channeling Libra energy, we can create holiday experiences that not only look beautiful but also promote a deep sense of harmony and unity among loved ones.

Libra Energy: Elegance, Social Grace, and a Desire for Balance

As an air sign, Libra is sociable, diplomatic, and deeply concerned with the well-being of others. Known for its ability to see multiple perspectives, Libra naturally seeks to create balanced interactions, ensuring that each person feels heard and appreciated. This emphasis on equality and inclusivity is particularly relevant during the holiday season, a time when family and friends come together to celebrate, sometimes despite differing opinions or backgrounds.

Libra's aesthetic sense, inspired by its Venusian rulership, also brings a touch of elegance to holiday festivities. Libra enjoys creating visually pleasing spaces and arranging gatherings that appeal to all senses, combining style with comfort to craft an environment that feels warm and inviting. For Libra, beauty is not simply about appearance but about the overall experience, including the mood, ambiance, and the way people interact. By balancing elegance with approachability, Libra energy encourages us to celebrate Christmas in a way that feels cohesive, joyful, and inclusive.

Creating a Harmonious Atmosphere: Libra's Approach to Décor and Ambiance

Libra has a natural talent for creating beautiful, harmonious environments that instantly put guests at ease. When it comes to holiday décor, Libra prefers a balanced and refined aesthetic, often favoring soft colors, elegant textures, and thoughtfully curated pieces that contribute to a cohesive atmosphere. Libra's sense of style is subtle yet impactful, focusing on creating a space that feels both sophisticated and welcoming.

For those inspired by Libra energy, holiday décor can be an opportunity to blend classic elements with modern elegance. Soft, neutral tones like cream, blush, or gentle golds create a serene backdrop, while touches of sparkle or metallics add festive charm without overwhelming the space. Libra also appreciates symmetry and proportion, so arranging decorations in pairs or balanced groupings can enhance the sense of harmony in the room.

Lighting plays an essential role in Libra's approach to ambiance. Soft, warm lighting, whether from candles, string lights, or dimmable lamps, helps create a soothing atmosphere that encourages guests to relax and enjoy each other's company. Adding elements like plush blankets, comfortable seating, and gentle background music further enhances the sense of tranquility, making each guest feel at home. For Libra, the goal is to create a visually pleasing yet understated environment that invites people to gather, connect, and experience the holiday spirit in a peaceful, balanced setting.

Libra's Hosting Style: Diplomacy, Inclusivity, and Social Harmony

Libra is renowned for its social grace and diplomatic nature, making Libra individuals natural hosts who excel at bringing people together. During the holiday season, Libra's influence encourages us to approach gatherings with a spirit of inclusivity and fairness, ensuring that each guest feels valued and respected. Libra's knack for conversation and ability to bridge divides make them adept at managing group dynamics, smoothing over tensions, and creating an atmosphere of understanding and respect.

To host with Libra's style, start by considering the guest list carefully, balancing personalities and interests to create a dynamic yet harmonious group. For Libra, inclusivity is essential, so they often take the time to ensure that each person's preferences and needs are considered. This might mean preparing dishes that cater to dietary restrictions, seating arrangements that encourage new connections, or activities that engage everyone.

Libra's approach to hosting also involves gentle mediation, ensuring that conversations flow smoothly and any potential conflicts are handled with tact. For Libra, a successful gathering is one where every guest feels appreciated and included, and they are known for going out of their way to make each person feel welcome. Those who wish to embody Libra energy can encourage conversation, acknowledge each guest's presence, and foster an environment where everyone feels comfortable expressing themselves. By setting a tone of respect and kindness, Libra transforms holiday gatherings into experiences of genuine connection and shared joy.

The Art of Balanced Gift-Giving: Thoughtful, Tasteful, and Fair

Gift-giving under Libra's influence is marked by thoughtfulness, taste, and an emphasis on fairness. Known for their refined aesthetic and love for beauty, Libra individuals take pride in selecting gifts that are both elegant and meaningful. For Libra, the ideal gift is one that reflects the recipient's personality and interests while also aligning with their own sense of style. They are drawn to high-quality, well-designed items that carry a sense of timelessness and elegance.

Ideal gifts from a Libra might include tasteful accessories, classic fragrances, or beautifully crafted items for the home. Libra appreciates gifts that elevate everyday experiences, so items like luxurious candles, quality tea sets, or handcrafted decor can be perfect choices. Libra also values balance, so they often try to give gifts of equal value and thoughtfulness to each recipient, ensuring that no one feels overlooked or underappreciated.

When giving with Libra's influence, consider selecting gifts that encourage relaxation, beauty, or intellectual enjoyment. Items that promote self-care, such as a spa gift set or a beautifully bound book, resonate with Libra's appreciation for quality and harmony. For Libra, the presentation of the gift is also important; wrapping the gift with care, using elegant paper and a decorative touch, adds to the experience and shows thoughtfulness. By focusing on gifts that reflect both elegance and thoughtfulness, Libra reminds us that giving is an art that celebrates the beauty and individuality of each person.

Balancing Family Dynamics: Libra's Diplomatic Approach to Holiday Gatherings

Family gatherings can sometimes bring about conflicting opinions or unresolved tensions, especially during the holiday season when emotions may run high. Libra's influence encourages us to approach these situations with diplomacy and understanding, using patience and tact to create a peaceful environment where everyone feels heard. Libra's natural ability to see multiple perspectives allows them to mediate conflicts and foster harmony, making them the ideal sign for balancing family dynamics during Christmas.

Libra's approach to handling conflicts is rooted in open communication and empathy. Rather than taking sides, Libra listens to each perspective, aiming to find common ground or a compromise that honors everyone's feelings. Libra's ability to remain neutral and respectful allows them to mediate disagreements with grace, helping to defuse tension and restore balance. Those inspired by Libra's approach can foster family harmony by encouraging open dialogue, validating each person's viewpoint, and setting a tone of mutual respect.

Another aspect of Libra's influence is its emphasis on fairness, making it essential to ensure that each family member feels included and appreciated. This might involve creating a rotation for holiday traditions, so each person has a chance to share their favorite activity, or ensuring that each family member has equal time and space to participate in holiday discussions. By fostering a spirit of inclusivity, Libra's influence helps create a holiday gathering that feels balanced, respectful, and filled with genuine connection.

Self-Care and Balance: Libra's Tips for Managing Holiday Stress

Libra's love for balance extends to their personal well-being, as they recognize the importance of self-care, especially during the busy holiday season. While Libra enjoys socializing and connecting with others, they also need time to recharge and find inner balance. For Libra, self-care is about nurturing both body and mind, creating moments of peace and reflection that allow them to approach each interaction with grace and patience.

To manage holiday stress, Libra individuals can benefit from practices that promote relaxation and emotional harmony. Gentle activities like meditation, yoga, or simply spending quiet time in a beautiful space can help restore balance and prepare them for holiday gatherings. For Libra, it's also essential to set boundaries and avoid overcommitting, allowing them to enjoy the season without feeling drained. Balancing social time with personal time enables Libra to remain present and engaged, bringing their best self to each holiday interaction.

Friends and family can support Libra by acknowledging their efforts to create a harmonious environment and offering help when needed. Encouraging Libra to take breaks or providing opportunities for downtime can help them recharge, making it easier for them to maintain their natural diplomacy and positivity. By embracing self-care and prioritizing balance, Libra individuals can navigate the holiday season with their characteristic poise and charm, ensuring that each gathering is a joyful and fulfilling experience.

Final Thoughts: Celebrating Christmas with Libra's Spirit of Harmony and Balance

Libra's influence brings a sense of grace, elegance, and social harmony to the holiday season, transforming Christmas into a celebration of unity, beauty, and balance. Through their thoughtful approach to hosting, refined sense of style, and gift for diplomacy, Libra individuals remind us that the true spirit of the holidays lies in creating meaningful connections and celebrating the unique qualities of each person. By embracing Libra energy, we can enjoy a holiday experience that feels both joyful and harmonious, centered around shared moments of kindness and mutual appreciation.

This Christmas, let Libra's influence inspire you to prioritize harmony, beauty, and balance in your celebrations. Whether through carefully chosen décor, thoughtful gift-giving, or a spirit of diplomacy, Libra reminds us that the holiday season is a time to celebrate togetherness, honor each individual, and create memories that reflect the beauty of human connection. By channeling Libra's energy, we can create a Christmas experience that feels balanced, welcoming, and filled with joy—a season of true unity and festive elegance.

Chapter 8: Scorpio - Mystery and Depth in Holiday Experiences

Scorpio, the eighth sign of the zodiac, is known for its intensity, depth, and mysterious allure. Ruled by Pluto, the planet of transformation, and Mars, the planet of action, Scorpio brings a profound and introspective energy to every experience. During the holiday season, Scorpio's influence encourages us to look beyond the surface of festive celebrations, inviting us to delve into the hidden layers of meaning, tradition, and connection that Christmas holds. This chapter explores how Scorpio's energy enhances the holiday season, emphasizing the importance of meaningful interactions, personal transformation, and honoring the mysteries of life.

Scorpio's approach to Christmas is rooted in an appreciation for depth, authenticity, and intimacy. Rather than focusing on superficial festivities, Scorpio seeks to uncover the emotional and spiritual richness of the holiday, viewing it as a time for introspection, healing, and forging deeper connections. By channeling Scorpio energy, we can experience the holiday season in a way that is both profound and transformative, embracing a Christmas celebration that resonates with our innermost selves.

Scorpio Energy: Intensity, Transformation, and Emotional Depth

As a water sign, Scorpio is intuitive, emotionally complex, and highly perceptive. Known for their intensity and loyalty, Scorpio individuals have a gift for seeing beyond appearances, understanding the motivations, desires, and hidden aspects of those around them. During Christmas, Scorpio's energy encourages us to embrace the holiday season as an opportunity for introspection, genuine connection, and a deeper appreciation of the people and traditions that enrich our lives.

Scorpio's connection to Pluto, the planet of transformation, also infuses the holiday season with a sense of renewal and change. Scorpio views Christmas not just as a festive occasion but as a time for personal growth and emotional healing, allowing us to release what no longer serves us and make space for new beginnings. This transformative perspective encourages us to approach the holiday with a sense of purpose and introspection, focusing on the inner shifts that can make this season truly meaningful.

Embracing the Mysteries of the Season: Scorpio's Perspective on Holiday Traditions

Scorpio's approach to holiday traditions is marked by a fascination with the hidden meanings and histories behind them. Scorpio is naturally drawn to mystery and symbolism, appreciating holiday customs that have a sense of ritual, history, or mystique. For Scorpio, holiday traditions are not just activities—they are expressions of cultural, familial, or spiritual significance that connect us to something greater than ourselves.

Those inspired by Scorpio's energy might take the time to learn about the origins of holiday traditions, exploring their deeper meanings and historical roots. Understanding the symbolism of the Christmas tree, the Yule log, or the practice of gift-giving can add a layer of depth to the holiday experience, transforming each custom into a meaningful ritual that resonates on a soul level. Scorpio's curiosity about the unknown encourages us to honor the mystical aspects of Christmas, recognizing that these traditions carry insights and wisdom that transcend time.

Incorporating Scorpio's appreciation for mystery might also involve creating new traditions that reflect personal values and beliefs. For instance, setting aside time for quiet reflection, lighting candles to represent the return of light, or creating a ritual of gratitude can transform Christmas into a spiritual experience that speaks to the heart. By engaging with the mysteries of the season, Scorpio invites us to view Christmas as an opportunity for inner discovery and spiritual connection, making the holiday feel both profound and fulfilling.

Creating an Atmosphere of Depth and Intrigue: Scorpio-Inspired Holiday Décor

Scorpio's aesthetic is often marked by a love for dark, rich colors, luxurious textures, and dramatic lighting, creating an ambiance that feels both inviting and mysterious. During the holiday season, Scorpio-inspired décor emphasizes elegance, subtlety, and a sense of depth, creating a space where guests feel drawn in and inspired to connect on a deeper level. Scorpio's style is sophisticated and refined, with an emphasis on quality over quantity, allowing each decorative element to contribute to the overall mood.

For those inspired by Scorpio's energy, holiday décor can incorporate colors like deep burgundy, forest green, midnight blue, and black, combined with metallic accents like gold or bronze for a touch of luxury. Dim lighting, candles, and warm, ambient lights can add a sense of intimacy and intrigue, transforming the space into a sanctuary that feels both festive and introspective. Scorpio also appreciates natural elements like dark wood, stone, or crystal accents, which bring a grounding, elemental quality to the decor.

Adding personal or symbolic touches to the holiday setup can further enhance Scorpio's influence. Consider incorporating items that carry sentimental value, such as family heirlooms or unique ornaments that represent significant life events. For Scorpio, these personal touches add depth and meaning to the celebration, creating an environment where each decorative piece has a story or purpose. By creating an atmosphere that feels both mysterious and meaningful, Scorpio's energy invites us to experience the holiday season with heightened awareness and appreciation for the beauty of the unknown.

Meaningful and Intimate Gift-Giving: Scorpio's Approach to Presents

Gift-giving under Scorpio's influence is deeply personal, thoughtful, and symbolic. Scorpio individuals are known for their intuition and sensitivity, often selecting gifts that reflect their understanding of the recipient's inner desires or values. For Scorpio, a gift is more than just a physical item—it is a gesture of connection, intimacy, and insight that speaks to the depth of their relationship with the recipient.

Ideal gifts from Scorpio might include items with sentimental or symbolic value, such as a meaningful book, a handcrafted piece of jewelry, or a personal memento that holds special significance. Scorpio is drawn to items that evoke emotion or introspection, making gifts like journals, art pieces, or items that promote self-discovery particularly meaningful. Scorpio's preference for quality also means that they are likely to choose high-quality, enduring items rather than trendy or disposable gifts.

When giving with Scorpio's influence, consider selecting items that resonate with the recipient on a deeper level. A gift that reflects shared memories, a personal transformation, or an aspect of the recipient's personality can create a lasting impression, demonstrating thoughtfulness and appreciation. Scorpio also values presentation, often opting for elegant, understated wrapping that adds to the mystery and anticipation of the gift. By choosing gifts that carry personal significance and a touch of intrigue, Scorpio reminds us that the best presents are those that speak to the soul and reflect the unique bond we share with others.

Intimacy and Connection: Scorpio's Approach to Holiday Gatherings

Scorpio's approach to holiday gatherings is marked by a preference for intimate, meaningful interactions over large, bustling parties. Scorpio values depth in relationships, and they thrive in settings where they can connect with others on a profound level, creating an atmosphere where guests feel comfortable opening up and sharing personal stories. During Christmas, Scorpio's influence encourages us to prioritize quality time with loved ones, focusing on creating experiences that foster closeness and emotional connection.

For those inspired by Scorpio energy, holiday gatherings can take on a more private and reflective tone. Instead of a large party, consider hosting a smaller, more intimate gathering where guests can engage in thoughtful conversation, reflect on the past year, and express gratitude for one another. Scorpio gatherings often involve activities that encourage connection and introspection, such as storytelling, group reflections, or sharing meaningful memories.

Scorpio's sensitivity also makes them highly attuned to the emotions of others, allowing them to create a safe space where people feel heard and respected. As a host, Scorpio's role is often that of a quiet, attentive presence, gently guiding conversations and offering support when needed. By prioritizing emotional intimacy and creating an environment of trust, Scorpio transforms holiday gatherings into experiences of genuine connection, allowing guests to leave feeling understood and fulfilled.

Transformation and Reflection: Scorpio's Tips for a Meaningful Holiday Season

The holiday season often marks the end of the year, a natural time for reflection and transformation. Scorpio's influence encourages us to approach this time with a sense of purpose, using it as an opportunity for introspection, release, and renewal. For Scorpio, Christmas is more than a celebration—it is a time for emotional and spiritual growth, allowing us to let go of the past and set intentions for the future.

Scorpio individuals may find value in setting aside time for personal reflection, journaling, or meditation during the holiday season. Engaging in practices that promote self-awareness, such as listing the lessons learned over the past year or acknowledging personal growth, can enhance Scorpio's sense of purpose and fulfillment. Scorpio also benefits from rituals that facilitate emotional release, such as writing down old patterns or beliefs they wish to release and symbolically letting them go.

Friends and family can support Scorpio's need for transformation by respecting their need for quiet time or personal space during the holiday season. For Scorpio, this period of introspection is essential to maintaining balance and processing emotions, allowing them to enter the new year with clarity and intention. By embracing self-care practices that encourage emotional and spiritual growth, Scorpio individuals can fully embody their transformative energy, experiencing the holiday season as a journey of inner discovery and renewal.

Final Thoughts: Celebrating Christmas with Scorpio's Spirit of Depth and Mystery

Scorpio's influence brings a sense of mystery, depth, and emotional resonance to the holiday season, encouraging us to look beyond surface-level festivities and explore the hidden meanings within. Through their appreciation for intimate connections, symbolic gestures, and personal transformation, Scorpio individuals remind us that Christmas is not only a time for celebration but also a time for introspection, healing, and growth. By embracing Scorpio energy, we can experience the holiday season as an opportunity to connect with our innermost selves and the people who matter most.

This Christmas, let Scorpio's influence inspire you to approach the holiday with an open heart, a sense of curiosity, and a desire for meaningful connection. Whether through thoughtful gift-giving, creating a mysterious and inviting ambiance, or taking time for personal reflection, Scorpio encourages us to experience the holiday as a time of depth, renewal, and emotional discovery. By honoring the mysteries of the season and embracing

Chapter 9: Sagittarius - Adventurous Spirits and Holiday Travel

Sagittarius, the ninth sign of the zodiac, is known for its boundless energy, optimism, and love for adventure. Ruled by Jupiter, the planet of expansion and abundance, Sagittarius thrives on exploration, learning, and broadening its horizons. During the holiday season, Sagittarius's influence encourages us to embrace the spirit of adventure, whether that means traveling to new destinations, exploring different cultural traditions, or simply opening ourselves up to new experiences and perspectives. This chapter explores how Sagittarius energy can transform the holiday season, bringing a sense of wonder, freedom, and joy to our celebrations.

For Sagittarius, Christmas is not limited to tradition and routine; it's a time for discovery, exploration, and celebration of life in all its forms. Sagittarius individuals are often inspired to expand beyond their familiar surroundings, seeking new places, meeting new people, and embracing diverse customs. By channeling Sagittarius energy, we can experience the holiday season as a time of exploration and growth, blending the joy of celebration with the excitement of adventure.

Sagittarius Energy: Optimism, Curiosity, and a Love for Freedom

As a fire sign, Sagittarius is enthusiastic, open-minded, and always eager to learn. Known for their love of freedom, Sagittarius individuals value experiences over possessions, often preferring to invest in journeys, knowledge, and personal growth rather than material goods. This wanderlust-filled sign is motivated by curiosity and a desire to expand its worldview, finding fulfillment in the thrill of the unknown and the beauty of diverse cultures and perspectives.

During the holiday season, Sagittarius's influence invites us to celebrate with a sense of openness and optimism, embracing each moment as an opportunity to discover something new. Sagittarius encourages us to break free from holiday routines and seek experiences that ignite our sense of wonder. This could mean trying a new holiday tradition, visiting a place we've never been before, or meeting people from different backgrounds who enrich our understanding of the world. For Sagittarius, the holiday season is a journey, a time to collect memories and stories that become the true gifts of the season.

The Joy of Holiday Travel: Sagittarius's Adventurous Spirit on the Road

Sagittarius is the quintessential traveler of the zodiac, always ready to embark on a new journey and explore the world. During Christmas, this wanderlust can inspire us to consider travel as a way of celebrating the season. For Sagittarius, holiday travel is more than just a getaway; it's an opportunity to experience the magic of Christmas in different places, discovering new traditions, cultures, and landscapes that broaden their perspective and fill them with joy.

Those inspired by Sagittarius energy might consider planning a holiday trip that combines relaxation with exploration. This could be a winter getaway to a snowy mountain cabin, a trip to a vibrant city with unique holiday markets, or even a warm tropical destination that offers a break from the winter chill. Sagittarius loves novelty, so choosing a location with a unique cultural experience or holiday tradition can make the trip even more memorable.

For Sagittarius, travel is as much about the journey as it is about the destination. Embracing the adventure of travel—meeting new people, tasting new foods, and learning about local customs—can add excitement and richness to the holiday season. Even if a grand journey isn't possible, Sagittarius energy encourages us to take short trips, explore nearby places, or immerse ourselves in different cultures within our own communities. Whether it's a weekend road trip or a full holiday abroad, Sagittarius's adventurous spirit transforms holiday travel into an unforgettable experience of exploration and joy.

Exploring Diverse Holiday Traditions: A Sagittarius Approach to Christmas

Sagittarius's open-mindedness and curiosity make them naturally drawn to different cultural traditions and ways of celebrating the holidays. For Sagittarius, Christmas is an opportunity to explore and appreciate the diversity of holiday customs around the world, celebrating the season in ways that connect us to people and cultures beyond our own. This might mean adopting a new tradition, learning about holiday practices from other countries, or participating in multicultural holiday events.

Those inspired by Sagittarius energy might explore holiday customs from various cultures and incorporate them into their own celebrations. For example, trying traditional foods from around the world, such as Italian panettone, Mexican tamales, or Swedish glögg, can add a new flavor to the holiday feast. Participating in cultural events, such as local holiday festivals or religious services from different faiths, allows us to see the holiday season from a fresh perspective and appreciate the richness of global traditions.

For Sagittarius, these experiences are not just about adding variety—they are opportunities to learn, connect, and grow. By opening ourselves to the diverse ways in which people celebrate the season, we can gain a deeper understanding of the world and embrace the holiday spirit in its many forms. Sagittarius reminds us that Christmas is a season of unity, a time to celebrate the common values of love, kindness, and joy that connect us across cultures.

Spreading Joy and Positivity: Sagittarius's Approach to Holiday Gatherings

Sagittarius is known for its contagious positivity, infectious laughter, and love for life, making them a joyful presence at any holiday gathering. With their natural charm and enthusiasm, Sagittarius individuals bring a light-hearted, upbeat energy to celebrations, lifting spirits and encouraging everyone to relax and enjoy the moment. During Christmas, Sagittarius's influence encourages us to prioritize joy, humor, and meaningful connections, creating gatherings that are lively, warm, and inclusive.

Hosting with Sagittarius energy means focusing on creating an open, welcoming environment where everyone feels free to express themselves and have fun. Sagittarius gatherings are often casual and spontaneous, with a focus on activities that bring people together and inspire laughter. Games, storytelling, and group activities that encourage social interaction can add a touch of adventure and excitement to the gathering, ensuring that each guest feels engaged and included.

For Sagittarius, the true gift of the holiday season is the joy of sharing experiences with others. They enjoy exchanging stories, learning about people's adventures, and encouraging others to share their dreams and aspirations. Embracing Sagittarius energy in holiday gatherings means creating an atmosphere of positivity, curiosity, and support, where each person feels uplifted and inspired by the shared sense of adventure and optimism.

Meaningful and Experiential Gift-Giving: Sagittarius's Unique Approach to Presents

Sagittarius values experiences over material possessions, and their approach to gift-giving reflects this preference. Rather than focusing on traditional presents, Sagittarius individuals often choose gifts that inspire learning, exploration, or personal growth. For them, the ideal gift is one that adds value to the recipient's life by offering a new experience, expanding their horizons, or helping them pursue a passion.

Ideal gifts from Sagittarius might include travel-related items, such as a guidebook to a future travel destination, a set of luggage, or a gift card for an adventure experience like a hiking tour or a cooking class. Sagittarius also appreciates gifts that encourage intellectual curiosity, such as books on diverse cultures, philosophy, or personal development. For friends and family with a love for the outdoors, items like camping gear, a star map for stargazing, or a weekend retreat could make perfect gifts.

When giving with Sagittarius energy, consider choosing experiential gifts that create memories rather than simply providing a physical item. A weekend getaway, a workshop on a topic of interest, or tickets to a concert or cultural event are all gifts that align with Sagittarius's love for adventure and discovery. By focusing on gifts that offer the recipient a new experience or broaden their perspective, Sagittarius reminds us that the true value of a gift lies in the joy and growth it brings to the recipient.

Embracing Freedom and Flexibility: Sagittarius's Tips for Managing Holiday Stress

While the holiday season is a joyful time, it can also be filled with obligations and schedules that feel restrictive to free-spirited Sagittarius. For Sagittarius, the key to enjoying the season lies in maintaining a sense of freedom and flexibility, allowing them to experience the holiday in a way that feels authentic and unencumbered. To manage holiday stress, Sagittarius benefits from a relaxed approach, focusing on the experiences that bring them joy rather than adhering strictly to routines or expectations.

For Sagittarius, self-care during the holidays often involves taking time to reconnect with their sense of adventure, whether that means exploring nature, engaging in a favorite hobby, or planning a small getaway. Even a simple walk in a new park or trying a new activity can help Sagittarius feel invigorated and recharged. Embracing spontaneity and leaving room for last-minute plans allows Sagittarius to feel free and adaptable, enjoying the holiday season in a way that aligns with their natural flow.

Friends and family can support Sagittarius by being understanding of their need for flexibility and freedom, encouraging them to express their adventurous side and explore new experiences. By approaching the season with a spirit of openness, Sagittarius can fully embrace the holiday's joy, making each moment feel like an exciting chapter in the larger journey of life. Sagittarius's positivity and curiosity remind us that the holiday season doesn't have to be perfect—it just needs to be filled with moments that make us feel alive and connected to the world around us.

Final Thoughts: Celebrating Christmas with Sagittarius's Adventurous Spirit

Sagittarius's influence brings a sense of wonder, excitement, and boundless joy to the holiday season, transforming Christmas into an opportunity for exploration, connection, and personal growth. Through their love for travel, curiosity about different cultures, and focus on meaningful experiences, Sagittarius individuals remind us that the true essence of the season lies in embracing the unknown, celebrating diversity, and approaching each moment with a sense of openness and adventure. By channeling Sagittarius energy, we can experience the holiday season as a journey of discovery, filled with unforgettable moments and joyful connections.

This Christmas, let Sagittarius's influence inspire you to break free from routine, explore new places and traditions, and prioritize experiences that bring meaning and joy. Whether through holiday travel, trying diverse customs, or simply connecting with loved ones in new ways, Sagittarius encourages us to make the most of the holiday season by expanding our horizons and celebrating the adventure of life. By embracing Sagittarius's spirit, we can create a holiday experience that feels exciting, transformative, and deeply fulfilling—a season of true exploration and boundless joy.

Chapter 10: Capricorn - Tradition, Discipline, and Festivity

Capricorn, the tenth sign of the zodiac, is known for its steadfastness, practicality, and dedication to tradition. Ruled by Saturn, the planet of discipline and structure, Capricorn brings a sense of purpose, reverence for heritage, and an ability to create lasting, meaningful experiences. During the holiday season, Capricorn's influence encourages us to honor the rituals that bring us together, embrace the beauty of tradition, and balance celebration with a mindful approach to planning and preparation. This chapter explores how Capricorn's energy shapes the holiday season, turning it into a time of stability, reflection, and heartfelt festivity.

For Capricorn, Christmas is about more than festivities—it is a season to reinforce values, connect with loved ones, and celebrate in a way that honors both the past and the future. With their love for tradition and disciplined approach, Capricorn individuals are often the foundation of holiday gatherings, bringing organization, elegance, and authenticity to each aspect of the celebration. By channeling Capricorn's energy, we can experience a holiday season that is both festive and grounded, blending joy with purpose and tradition with mindful planning.

Capricorn Energy: Stability, Responsibility, and Respect for Tradition

As an earth sign, Capricorn is practical, patient, and highly focused, often driven by long-term goals and a desire for stability. Known for their work ethic and commitment to quality, Capricorn individuals bring a sense of discipline and purpose to all they do, including holiday celebrations. For Capricorn, Christmas is not just about festivities but about creating meaningful connections and upholding traditions that bring a sense of continuity and security to family and friends.

Capricorn's connection to Saturn, the planet of discipline and structure, inspires them to approach the holiday season with care, attention to detail, and a sense of responsibility. Capricorn energy is also deeply rooted in values and legacy, making it especially relevant during a season that often involves family, heritage, and the passing down of customs from one generation to the next. With Capricorn's influence, we are encouraged to view Christmas as a time to honor both our personal and cultural traditions, reinforcing the bonds that make the holiday season truly meaningful.

Honoring Family Traditions: Capricorn's Approach to Holiday Rituals

For Capricorn, traditions are a way of grounding ourselves in our heritage and connecting with the values that define us. Capricorn is naturally drawn to rituals and customs, viewing them as sacred practices that bring depth and continuity to holiday celebrations. Whether it's decorating the tree in a certain way, cooking family recipes, or sharing stories around the table, Capricorn cherishes these customs, understanding that they hold the memories and lessons of the past.

To embrace Capricorn energy, consider reviving or reinforcing family traditions during the holiday season. This might mean preparing a special meal that has been passed down through generations, incorporating heirloom decorations into the décor, or creating a family photo album that tells the story of Christmases past. Capricorn encourages us to honor these traditions with intention, viewing them not just as routines but as expressions of love, connection, and shared history.

For those wishing to start new traditions, Capricorn reminds us to approach this thoughtfully, creating rituals that are meaningful and have the potential to be passed down through the years.

This could be a family holiday letter, a shared activity like tree decorating or baking, or a reflective tradition, such as sharing goals and dreams for the coming year. By focusing on traditions that align with our values, Capricorn energy allows us to celebrate the holiday season in a way that feels rooted, purposeful, and deeply fulfilling.

Balancing Discipline with Festivity: Capricorn's Methodical Approach to Holiday Planning

Capricorn's disciplined nature makes them skilled at organizing and preparing for holiday festivities, ensuring that each detail is thoughtfully planned and executed. Capricorn's approach to holiday preparations is systematic and meticulous, often starting early and setting realistic goals to avoid last-minute stress. By applying their methodical mindset, Capricorn is able to create a holiday experience that feels smooth, organized, and enjoyable for everyone involved.

To channel Capricorn's planning prowess, begin by creating a holiday checklist or schedule that outlines tasks such as gift shopping, meal preparation, and event planning. Capricorn appreciates structure and efficiency, so breaking tasks into manageable steps can prevent overwhelm and allow for a balanced approach to holiday preparations. Capricorn is also known for their budgeting skills, often setting a holiday budget that keeps spending in check without sacrificing quality. This practical approach ensures that resources are used wisely, allowing for a holiday season that feels abundant without unnecessary extravagance.

Capricorn's disciplined approach also extends to time management, helping them strike a balance between social obligations, family gatherings, and moments of personal relaxation. Those inspired by Capricorn's energy can benefit from setting boundaries and making intentional choices about how they spend their time during the holiday season, ensuring that each moment feels meaningful. By blending discipline with celebration, Capricorn creates a holiday season that is as enjoyable as it is purposeful, allowing them to fully appreciate the fruits of their labor.

Timeless Elegance in Décor: Capricorn's Classic Approach to Holiday Aesthetics

Capricorn's refined taste and love for quality are reflected in their approach to holiday décor, which often emphasizes timeless elegance, natural materials, and understated beauty. Rather than following fleeting trends, Capricorn prefers décor that feels classic and enduring, using elements that will stand the test of time. For Capricorn, holiday decorations are an investment in creating a warm, welcoming atmosphere that feels both sophisticated and deeply comforting.

To decorate with Capricorn energy, focus on natural elements and neutral tones, such as evergreen branches, pinecones, and candles, which create a grounding and calming ambiance. Capricorn appreciates earthy colors, such as deep greens, rich browns, and subtle golds, which convey warmth without overwhelming the space. Quality is key for Capricorn, so choosing durable, well-crafted decorations—like handmade ornaments, real greenery, or vintage items—adds an element of authenticity and lasting value to the décor.

Adding heirlooms or personal touches is another way to infuse Capricorn's sense of legacy into holiday decorating. Using family ornaments, vintage glassware, or even framed holiday photos can create a space that feels both elegant and meaningful. Capricorn's love for tradition extends to the visual aspects of Christmas, reminding us that holiday décor can be more than just beautiful—it can be a reflection of the values, memories, and connections that make the season special.

Thoughtful and Practical Gift-Giving: Capricorn's Approach to Presents

Capricorn's approach to gift-giving is practical, thoughtful, and value-driven, often choosing items that reflect their understanding of the recipient's needs and preferences. Known for their love of quality and durability, Capricorn individuals are likely to select gifts that are useful, well-made, and aligned with the recipient's interests. For Capricorn, a gift is an investment in the relationship, demonstrating their appreciation and respect for the person's unique qualities and aspirations.

Ideal gifts from Capricorn might include high-quality items that promote comfort, productivity, or personal growth, such as a durable leather journal, a classic watch, or a luxurious cashmere blanket. Capricorn also values practicality, so gifts that have functional value—like a beautiful cookbook, an elegant planner, or premium skincare products—are thoughtful choices that the recipient can use and appreciate over time.

When giving with Capricorn's influence, consider focusing on gifts that have a lasting impact, whether by supporting the recipient's goals, enhancing their well-being, or adding to their home in a meaningful way. Capricorn also values the thought behind the gift, often taking the time to add a handwritten note or a personal touch that makes the gift feel sincere. By prioritizing quality and thoughtfulness, Capricorn reminds us that the best gifts are those that show genuine care and contribute to the recipient's life in a meaningful way.

Creating a Festive Atmosphere of Connection and Reflection

Capricorn's approach to holiday gatherings is grounded in a desire for meaningful connection and shared reflection. For Capricorn, Christmas gatherings are an opportunity to strengthen bonds, celebrate accomplishments, and set intentions for the coming year. Capricorn's thoughtful nature makes them skilled at fostering an atmosphere that encourages deep conversation, mutual appreciation, and a sense of belonging.

To host with Capricorn energy, consider organizing a gathering that blends festivity with purpose, focusing on activities that foster connection and reflection. This could mean hosting a holiday dinner where each guest shares a personal highlight from the year, organizing a family storytelling session, or creating a gratitude ritual where loved ones express their appreciation for one another. Capricorn gatherings are often intimate, focusing on quality time with loved ones rather than grand parties or elaborate events.

Capricorn's influence also encourages us to celebrate achievements and honor the milestones of the past year. Whether through a toast to shared successes, a reflective activity like writing down intentions, or a meaningful discussion about personal growth, Capricorn invites us to approach the holiday season with gratitude and purpose. By blending celebration with reflection, Capricorn transforms holiday gatherings into experiences that feel both joyful and deeply fulfilling, fostering connections that endure beyond the season.

Discipline and Self-Care: Capricorn's Tips for Managing Holiday Stress

While Capricorn is known for their resilience and ability to handle responsibilities, the holiday season can be demanding, especially for those who take on the role of planner or organizer. To manage holiday stress, Capricorn benefits from setting clear priorities, practicing self-discipline, and taking time for self-care. For Capricorn, self-care is about creating balance, ensuring that they have time to rest and recharge while still fulfilling their commitments.

Capricorn can benefit from setting boundaries and delegating tasks where possible, allowing them to focus on the aspects of the holiday season that bring them the most joy. Taking time for relaxation, such as enjoying a quiet evening by the fire, journaling, or engaging in a favorite hobby, can help Capricorn feel grounded and maintain their energy. As Capricorn is goal-oriented, setting specific, realistic goals for the season—whether it's budgeting, planning, or organizing gatherings—can help them stay on track and avoid overwhelm.

Friends and family can support Capricorn by acknowledging their efforts, offering assistance, and respecting their need for structure. By balancing responsibility with moments of rest, Capricorn can approach the holiday season with their usual grace and determination, ensuring that each aspect of Christmas reflects their love and dedication. Capricorn's disciplined approach reminds us that the holiday season is as much about personal well-being as it is about celebrating with others, making time for both festivity and self-care.

Final Thoughts: Celebrating Christmas with Capricorn's Spirit of Tradition and Purpose

Capricorn's influence brings a sense of stability, tradition, and purpose to the holiday season, transforming Christmas into a celebration of legacy, connection, and meaningful experience. Through their appreciation for quality, dedication to planning, and respect for tradition, Capricorn individuals remind us that the true spirit of the holiday lies not in fleeting pleasures but in the values and connections that endure. By channeling Capricorn energy, we can experience Christmas as a time of reflection, celebration, and gratitude, honoring the traditions and relationships that make this season so special.

This Christmas, let Capricorn's influence inspire you to approach the holiday with intention, discipline, and a love for meaningful connection. Whether through carefully planned gatherings, thoughtful gift-giving, or the creation of lasting traditions, Capricorn encourages us to celebrate with a sense of purpose and to invest in the experiences that bring depth and fulfillment to our lives. By embracing Capricorn's spirit, we can create a holiday season that feels both joyful and deeply resonant—a true celebration of tradition, family, and enduring values.

Chapter 11: Aquarius - Innovative Celebrations and Unique Gifts

Aquarius, the eleventh sign of the zodiac, is known for its originality, forward-thinking, and humanitarian spirit. Ruled by Uranus, the planet of innovation and change, Aquarius brings a fresh, unconventional energy to everything it touches. During the holiday season, Aquarius encourages us to step outside of traditional customs, explore new ways of celebrating, and embrace diversity in our gatherings and gift-giving. This chapter explores how Aquarius's influence can transform the holiday season, inspiring us to celebrate with creativity, inclusivity, and an eye toward the future.

For Aquarius, Christmas is an opportunity to connect with others in meaningful, unexpected ways. Aquarius individuals are often drawn to celebrations that emphasize shared experiences, social impact, and personal expression, and they bring a sense of open-mindedness and curiosity to the holiday. By channeling Aquarius's energy, we can celebrate the season in a way that feels unique, memorable, and reflective of who we truly are, creating a holiday experience that is as innovative as it is heartfelt.

Aquarius Energy: Individuality, Innovation, and a Love for Community

As an air sign, Aquarius is intellectual, idealistic, and highly adaptable, valuing freedom, originality, and social connections. Known for their progressive thinking and desire to make a positive impact, Aquarius individuals are often motivated by a sense of purpose and a desire to improve the world around them. During the holiday season, Aquarius's influence encourages us to think beyond tradition and embrace the possibilities of celebrating in new, inclusive, and meaningful ways.

Aquarius's connection to Uranus, the planet of revolution and innovation, gives this sign a knack for thinking outside the box. Whether through unique gatherings, unconventional gifts, or socially conscious choices, Aquarius approaches Christmas as an opportunity for creativity and exploration. Aquarius energy invites us to view the holiday season not only as a time for tradition but as a time to celebrate the diversity and originality within each of us, creating celebrations that reflect our individuality while connecting us with others.

Rethinking Holiday Gatherings: Aquarius's Innovative Approach to Celebration

Aquarius's approach to holiday gatherings is anything but conventional. Rather than following a set formula, Aquarius enjoys reimagining what a holiday celebration can be, adding unexpected elements that encourage guests to connect, learn, and engage in new experiences. For Aquarius, a perfect holiday gathering might blend socializing with creativity, intellectual stimulation, or a shared cause, creating an environment that feels inclusive and thought-provoking.

One way to incorporate Aquarius energy is by hosting a themed holiday gathering that reflects a shared interest or value. For example, a "Global Christmas" theme could allow guests to bring foods, decorations, or stories from various cultures, celebrating diversity while adding a global perspective to the holiday. Alternatively, an "Eco-Friendly Christmas" theme could encourage guests to participate in sustainable practices, such as recycling gift wrap, bringing reusable decorations, or opting for plant-based holiday dishes.

Interactive elements are also key to Aquarius gatherings. Activities like collaborative games, group storytelling, or crafting sessions allow guests to actively participate in the celebration, creating shared memories and connections. Aquarius also values inclusivity, so finding ways to make everyone feel welcomed and appreciated—such as by providing vegan or allergen-friendly foods, hosting virtual options for those who cannot attend in person, or creating a quiet space for introspective guests—can create an atmosphere where everyone feels at home.

Aquarius gatherings are ultimately about creating a sense of community and shared purpose. For Aquarius, holiday celebrations are more than just social events; they are opportunities to bring people together in a meaningful way, creating experiences that challenge traditional norms while embracing a spirit of inclusivity, learning, and creativity.

Unique and Personal Décor: Aquarius's Unconventional Holiday Aesthetic

Aquarius has an eclectic, avant-garde aesthetic, often favoring décor that is colorful, unexpected, or symbolic. Rather than following traditional holiday decorating schemes, Aquarius enjoys creating a unique atmosphere that reflects their individuality and love for experimentation. For Aquarius, holiday décor is a form of self-expression, and they are drawn to items that have personal significance, reflect diverse cultures, or incorporate unusual designs.

To decorate with Aquarius energy, consider exploring a nontraditional color palette, such as turquoise, silver, and lavender, or adding quirky accents like vintage ornaments, abstract art pieces, or DIY decorations. Aquarius loves mixing styles, blending modern and retro, vibrant and neutral, or eclectic and minimalistic elements to create a space that feels both unique and welcoming. Incorporating metallic or reflective surfaces, like mirrors or glass, can also add a futuristic touch that aligns with Aquarius's love for innovation.

Aquarius also appreciates décor that tells a story or serves a purpose. Incorporating handmade items, symbolic decorations, or pieces that support a cause can make the holiday setup feel meaningful and aligned with Aquarius's humanitarian values. For example, choosing ornaments crafted by local artisans, using fair-trade holiday decorations, or incorporating elements from global cultures can create a festive space that feels both stylish and ethically mindful.

Creating an inclusive and accessible atmosphere is another hallmark of Aquarius's approach to décor. Providing cozy, adaptable seating, incorporating sensory-friendly lighting, or creating designated spaces for conversation or quiet reflection can ensure that each guest feels comfortable and included. By blending style with purpose, Aquarius's unique holiday décor transforms the festive setting into a place where individuality is celebrated, and diversity is embraced.

Socially Conscious and Thoughtful Gift-Giving: Aquarius's Approach to Presents

Gift-giving under Aquarius's influence is characterized by thoughtfulness, innovation, and social awareness. Aquarius individuals are known for their idealism and generosity, often choosing gifts that reflect their values or support causes they care about. For Aquarius, a gift is not just a token of appreciation but an opportunity to create a positive impact, express individuality, or foster learning and growth.

Ideal gifts from Aquarius might include experiences, educational tools, or items that promote creativity or well-being. Aquarius is likely to give gifts such as a subscription to a learning platform, a ticket to an art exhibit, or a donation to a charity in the recipient's name. For friends and family with a passion for sustainability, eco-friendly gifts, like reusable kitchenware, organic skincare, or a zero-waste starter kit, can align with Aquarius's values and inspire others to adopt mindful practices.

Aquarius is also drawn to gifts that reflect diversity and inclusivity. For example, choosing items from minority-owned businesses, fair-trade goods, or culturally significant pieces can add depth and meaning to the exchange. Aquarius appreciates gifts that spark conversation or broaden perspectives, so books on social justice, multicultural cookbooks, or films from around the world are thoughtful choices that align with Aquarius's global outlook.

When giving with Aquarius energy, consider choosing items that inspire the recipient to think, create, or make a difference. Personalized gifts that reflect shared memories or support the recipient's passions can create a lasting impression. Aquarius also enjoys the element of surprise, so presenting the gift in an unconventional way—such as a scavenger hunt or a creative wrapping method—can add an extra layer of joy and excitement to the experience. By focusing on gifts that are meaningful, socially conscious, and aligned with the recipient's values, Aquarius reminds us that the true gift lies in the thought and purpose behind each present.

Embracing Inclusivity and Diversity in Holiday Celebrations

Aquarius is naturally inclusive, valuing diversity and seeking to connect with people from all walks of life. During the holiday season, Aquarius encourages us to celebrate in a way that honors and respects the uniqueness of each individual, creating an environment where everyone feels welcome and valued. For Aquarius, Christmas is an opportunity to bridge divides, bring people together, and celebrate the common values that unite us all.

Those inspired by Aquarius energy can incorporate inclusive practices into their holiday gatherings by being mindful of dietary preferences, cultural differences, and accessibility needs. For example, offering a variety of food options, accommodating various faith-based holiday customs, and providing materials for guests to learn about different traditions can make the celebration feel more inclusive. Hosting a "holiday around the world" event, where each guest shares a unique cultural tradition or dish, can add diversity to the celebration while fostering understanding and appreciation.

Creating an atmosphere of inclusivity also involves encouraging open-mindedness and conversation. Aquarius gatherings often prioritize meaningful discussions, group activities, or collaborative projects that allow guests to connect on a deeper level. Incorporating group reflections, gratitude rituals, or story-sharing sessions can create an environment where each person feels seen and valued. By embracing a spirit of inclusivity and empathy, Aquarius transforms holiday gatherings into spaces where everyone can celebrate their individuality while connecting with others.

Managing Holiday Stress with Aquarius's Love for Freedom and Flexibility

While the holiday season is often filled with obligations and traditions, Aquarius values freedom and flexibility, often preferring celebrations that feel relaxed and spontaneous. To manage holiday stress, Aquarius benefits from creating a balance between social gatherings and personal time, allowing them to enjoy the season without feeling restricted or overwhelmed.

For Aquarius, self-care during the holidays often involves stepping back from rigid schedules, embracing open-ended plans, and giving themselves the freedom to celebrate in their own unique way. This might mean incorporating solo activities, like reading, journaling, or exploring a new creative hobby, as part of their holiday routine. Embracing flexibility also allows Aquarius to adapt to unexpected changes, keeping their holiday experience light-hearted and free-spirited.

Friends and family can support Aquarius by respecting their need for independence and encouraging them to bring their unique ideas into the celebration. By allowing Aquarius the freedom to express themselves and create moments of personal joy, they can fully engage with the holiday season in a way that feels authentic and aligned with their values. Aquarius's innovative approach reminds us that there is no single "right" way to celebrate, encouraging us to explore diverse paths to holiday happiness.

Final Thoughts: Celebrating Christmas with Aquarius's Spirit of Innovation and Inclusivity

Aquarius's influence brings a sense of creativity, inclusivity, and open-mindedness to the holiday season, transforming Christmas into a celebration of diversity, individuality, and social connection. Through their unique approach to gatherings, thoughtful gift-giving, and commitment to inclusivity, Aquarius individuals remind us that the true magic of the holidays lies in embracing the qualities that make us unique and connecting with others in meaningful ways. By channeling Aquarius energy, we can create a holiday season that is as innovative as it is heartfelt, celebrating the joy of togetherness while honoring our differences.

This Christmas, let Aquarius's influence inspire you to step outside the ordinary, try something new, and celebrate the season in a way that feels authentic and inspired. Whether through unique holiday gatherings, socially conscious gift choices, or the creation of an inclusive atmosphere, Aquarius encourages us to make the holiday season a time of discovery, compassion, and shared humanity. By embracing Aquarius's spirit, we can create a holiday experience that is both memorable and transformative—a celebration that honors our individuality while bringing us closer together.

Chapter 12: Pisces - Spiritual Reflection and Holiday Dreams

Pisces, the twelfth sign of the zodiac, is known for its deep compassion, intuitive insight, and spiritual sensitivity. Ruled by Neptune, the planet of dreams and mysticism, Pisces brings a soulful, imaginative quality to everything it encounters. During the holiday season, Pisces energy invites us to step away from the hustle and bustle, seeking moments of quiet reflection, emotional connection, and spiritual exploration. This chapter explores how Pisces's influence enhances the holiday season, transforming it into a time of deep introspection, empathy, and a celebration of the intangible beauty that makes this season truly special.

For Pisces, Christmas is more than a festive gathering—it's a sacred time for emotional connection, reflection on the year, and connecting with the divine. Pisces individuals are naturally drawn to the mystical and unseen, embracing Christmas as an opportunity to honor both their inner world and their compassion for others. By channeling Pisces energy, we can approach the holiday season as a time for spiritual renewal, quiet gratitude, and dreams for the future, experiencing Christmas in a way that feels both magical and meaningful.

Pisces Energy: Compassion, Intuition, and Spiritual Sensitivity

As a water sign, Pisces is highly sensitive, empathetic, and intuitive, deeply attuned to the emotions and energies around them. Known for their compassion and understanding, Pisces individuals feel a strong connection to others and often experience a profound sense of unity with the world. During the holiday season, Pisces's influence encourages us to prioritize kindness, mindfulness, and self-reflection, approaching Christmas with a spirit of love, forgiveness, and a desire for inner peace.

Pisces's connection to Neptune, the planet of dreams and spirituality, enhances their intuitive abilities, inspiring a deeper awareness of the mystical aspects of life. This influence invites us to honor the unseen dimensions of the holiday season, viewing it as a time for healing, gratitude, and connecting with our higher selves. By embracing Pisces energy, we can create a holiday experience that goes beyond material celebrations, focusing instead on the spiritual and emotional gifts that bring lasting fulfillment.

Spiritual Reflection: Pisces's Approach to Holiday Contemplation

For Pisces, the holiday season is a time for spiritual reflection, inviting moments of introspection and connection with the divine. Rather than focusing solely on external festivities, Pisces views Christmas as an opportunity to turn inward, exploring the lessons, growth, and blessings of the past year. This practice of reflection allows Pisces to approach the holiday season with a deep sense of gratitude and an awareness of the spiritual journey they've undertaken.

To channel Pisces energy, consider setting aside time for quiet contemplation during the holiday season. This might involve journaling about the highs and lows of the past year, meditating on personal growth, or expressing gratitude for the people and experiences that have enriched your life. Pisces finds meaning in the simple act of reflection, seeing it as a way to honor their journey and prepare for the year ahead with renewed purpose and clarity.

Pisces also has a natural affinity for ritual, finding comfort in practices that foster spiritual connection. Creating a holiday ritual that involves lighting candles, saying prayers, or practicing mindfulness can add a layer of depth to the celebration. These practices don't have to be religious; they can simply be moments of peace and introspection that bring a sense of calm and focus. By embracing Pisces's reflective nature, we can transform the holiday season into a sacred time of healing, growth, and connection with our inner selves.

Embracing the Mystical and Symbolic: Pisces's Approach to Holiday Traditions

Pisces is drawn to the mystical, often finding meaning in symbolism and metaphor. For Pisces, holiday traditions are not just routines but sacred rituals that carry deeper spiritual significance. Whether it's decorating the Christmas tree, lighting candles, or exchanging gifts, Pisces approaches each custom with a sense of reverence, viewing it as an opportunity to connect with the mystery and beauty of the season.

To honor Pisces's love for symbolism, consider exploring the deeper meanings behind holiday traditions. Understanding the origins of holiday customs, such as the symbolism of evergreen trees, the use of lights to represent hope, or the act of giving as a symbol of love and gratitude, can add a layer of depth to the celebration. For Pisces, these symbols are reminders of the spiritual truths that underlie the holiday, turning each tradition into a meaningful ritual.

Creating new symbolic traditions that reflect personal values or beliefs can also enhance the holiday experience. For example, writing a letter of gratitude to loved ones, creating a vision board for the coming year, or lighting a candle for each family member can serve as meaningful ways to honor the spirit of the season. By focusing on the mystical and symbolic, Pisces energy transforms Christmas into an experience of connection, wonder, and spiritual renewal.

Dreamy and Ethereal Décor: Pisces's Unique Holiday Aesthetic

Pisces has a dreamy, ethereal aesthetic, often favoring colors, textures, and elements that evoke a sense of calm, beauty, and imagination. Rather than following a specific holiday theme, Pisces décor often reflects a blend of nature, softness, and spiritual symbolism, creating an environment that feels both comforting and otherworldly. For Pisces, holiday décor is an expression of their inner world, bringing a touch of magic and serenity to the space.

To decorate with Pisces energy, consider using soft, tranquil colors like lavender, pale blue, seafoam green, and silver, which create a soothing, mystical ambiance. Incorporating gentle lighting, such as fairy lights, candles, or salt lamps, can add warmth and softness to the space, creating an inviting atmosphere where guests feel at ease. Pisces also appreciates natural elements, such as crystals, seashells, or greenery, which bring a grounding, organic quality to the décor.

Personal touches and symbolic items are essential for Pisces-inspired holiday décor. Adding decorations that hold sentimental value, like family heirlooms, handmade ornaments, or symbols of hope and healing, can make the space feel uniquely personal. Pisces also enjoys incorporating elements that inspire reflection or introspection, such as angel figurines, dreamcatchers, or symbolic artwork. By blending beauty with meaning, Pisces's holiday décor transforms the festive environment into a sanctuary of peace and inspiration.

Thoughtful and Heartfelt Gift-Giving: Pisces's Approach to Presents

Gift-giving under Pisces's influence is characterized by empathy, intuition, and a desire to create emotional connections. Pisces individuals are known for their compassionate nature and often choose gifts that reflect their understanding of the recipient's emotional needs or desires. For Pisces, a gift is not just a physical item—it's an expression of love, care, and spiritual connection, chosen with the intention of bringing comfort, joy, or healing to the recipient.

Ideal gifts from Pisces might include items that promote relaxation, creativity, or personal growth, such as a journal, a mindfulness book, or a set of essential oils. Pisces also appreciates gifts that encourage self-reflection, such as a beautiful tarot or oracle deck, a guided meditation app, or a meaningful piece of artwork. For friends and family members who enjoy nurturing their inner worlds, a cozy blanket, a candle, or a handmade piece of jewelry can be perfect choices that reflect Pisces's sensitivity and thoughtfulness.

When giving with Pisces energy, consider choosing gifts that feel personal, spiritual, or comforting. Handmade items, sentimental mementos, or experiences like a spa day, a nature retreat, or a creative workshop can create lasting memories and reflect the care that went into selecting the gift. Pisces also values presentation, often wrapping gifts with a touch of whimsy or elegance, such as with ribbon, lavender sprigs, or personalized tags. By focusing on gifts that nurture the soul and create moments of peace, Pisces reminds us that the best presents are those that come from the heart and touch the spirit.

Creating a Tranquil and Supportive Atmosphere: Pisces's Approach to Holiday Gatherings

Pisces's approach to holiday gatherings is rooted in compassion, empathy, and a desire for authentic connection. Rather than focusing on grand events or elaborate parties, Pisces values intimate, meaningful gatherings where guests feel comfortable sharing their thoughts, feelings, and dreams. During Christmas, Pisces's influence encourages us to create a tranquil, supportive environment where people can relax, reflect, and connect on a deeper level.

For those inspired by Pisces energy, holiday gatherings can take on a peaceful and reflective tone, incorporating gentle music, soft lighting, and comfortable seating that allows guests to unwind. Pisces also appreciates interactive elements that encourage emotional connection, such as group gratitude practices, story-sharing sessions, or collaborative art projects. These activities create an atmosphere of acceptance and understanding, allowing each guest to feel seen and valued.

Pisces's compassionate nature makes them highly attuned to the needs of others, allowing them to create a safe space for guests to express themselves freely. By fostering an environment of empathy and support, Pisces transforms holiday gatherings into experiences of true connection, providing a sanctuary where guests can leave behind the stress of the season and embrace the joy of simply being together. For Pisces, the holiday season is about honoring each person's unique journey and finding beauty in the shared human experience.

Embracing Rest and Spiritual Self-Care: Pisces's Tips for Managing Holiday Stress

The holiday season can be emotionally overwhelming, especially for Pisces, who is highly sensitive to the energies around them. To manage holiday stress, Pisces benefits from prioritizing rest, self-care, and spiritual practices that allow them to recharge and find inner peace. For Pisces, self-care during the holidays is about nurturing their emotional and spiritual well-being, ensuring they can fully embrace the beauty and meaning of the season.

For Pisces, relaxation practices such as meditation, gentle yoga, or listening to calming music can create moments of serenity and reflection. Taking time for personal rituals, like lighting a candle, practicing gratitude, or journaling, can help Pisces stay grounded and centered. Pisces also benefits from creating boundaries around social gatherings, allowing them to balance time with loved ones and moments of solitude.

Friends and family can support Pisces by acknowledging their need for quiet time, offering understanding, and respecting their sensitivity. By allowing Pisces to rest, reflect, and engage in self-care, loved ones can help them experience the holiday season with renewed energy and a sense of spiritual connection. Pisces's gentle approach to the holiday season reminds us that true joy comes from within, and that taking time for ourselves allows us to give more fully to others.

Final Thoughts: Celebrating Christmas with Pisces's Spirit of Reflection and Compassion

Pisces's influence brings a sense of depth, spirituality, and heartfelt compassion to the holiday season, transforming Christmas into a celebration of connection, healing, and inner peace. Through their emphasis on spiritual reflection, meaningful gifts, and authentic gatherings, Pisces individuals remind us that the holiday season is an opportunity to honor our inner worlds, connect with loved ones, and nurture our souls. By channeling Pisces energy, we can experience Christmas as a time of dreams, compassion, and gratitude, creating a holiday that feels both magical and profoundly fulfilling.

This Christmas, let Pisces's influence inspire you to embrace the holiday season with an open heart, a spirit of reflection, and a desire for connection. Whether through thoughtful gift-giving, quiet moments of contemplation, or creating an atmosphere of warmth and empathy, Pisces encourages us to celebrate the season in a way that honors both our spiritual and emotional selves. By embodying Pisces's spirit, we can create a holiday experience that resonates with peace, compassion, and a sense of wonder—a true celebration of the dreams and love that unite us all.

Part 2: **Solar Eclipses & Christmas**

Chapter 13: Solar Eclipse Mysteries During December

Solar eclipses, one of the most awe-inspiring phenomena in the night sky, have captivated humanity's imagination for millennia. Occurring when the Moon passes directly between the Earth and the Sun, a solar eclipse temporarily obscures the Sun's light, casting a shadow over parts of the Earth. In December, solar eclipses are rare but hold special significance, adding an element of mystery and transformation to the holiday season. This chapter explores the mysteries of solar eclipses in December, examining their astronomical mechanics, historical symbolism, and astrological meaning, along with ways to harness their powerful energy for personal reflection and growth during the holiday season.

For many cultures, a solar eclipse has represented both awe and foreboding, a time when the world pauses to witness the extraordinary alignment of celestial bodies. The energy of a solar eclipse is unique, bringing themes of transformation, revelation, and new beginnings. When it falls during December, near the end of the year, a solar eclipse becomes a potent moment for closure, reflection, and intention-setting for the year ahead. By understanding the mysteries of solar eclipses in December, we can approach the holiday season with a heightened sense of awareness, allowing this celestial event to inspire change, growth, and insight.

The Astronomy of Solar Eclipses: Understanding the December Phenomenon

A solar eclipse occurs when the Moon moves between the Earth and the Sun, casting a shadow on Earth's surface and temporarily blocking sunlight. There are several types of solar eclipses, each with its own visual and astronomical characteristics:

1. **Total Solar Eclipse**: The Moon completely covers the Sun, casting a shadow that turns day into night for a few brief moments. This type of eclipse is the most dramatic, allowing observers in the path of totality to see the Sun's corona, or outer atmosphere, glowing around the Moon's edges.
2. **Annular Solar Eclipse**: The Moon passes in front of the Sun but does not completely cover it, resulting in a "ring of fire" effect. This occurs when the Moon is at a point in its orbit farther from Earth, making it appear smaller relative to the Sun.
3. **Partial Solar Eclipse**: The Moon partially obscures the Sun, creating a crescent shape as the Moon's shadow moves across the Sun's surface.

In December, solar eclipses are relatively uncommon but occur periodically due to the alignment of the Earth, Moon, and Sun in their respective orbits. The month of December is significant because it marks the winter solstice in the Northern Hemisphere, a time when daylight is at its shortest and introspection is naturally encouraged. The occurrence of a solar eclipse near the solstice adds a layer of cosmic mystery, amplifying the themes of reflection, renewal, and transformation associated with the year's end.

Cultural and Historical Symbolism of Solar Eclipses

Throughout history, solar eclipses have been revered and feared across cultures, often viewed as mystical events that signal change, transformation, or divine intervention. Ancient civilizations regarded solar eclipses as messages from the heavens, interpreting them through myth, religion, and astrology.

- **Mesopotamia and Babylon**: Ancient Mesopotamians interpreted solar eclipses as warnings from the gods, often seen as omens that could foretell changes in leadership or natural calamities. Babylonian astrologers carefully observed eclipse patterns to predict significant events.
- **China**: In ancient China, eclipses were thought to represent the devouring of the Sun by a celestial dragon. To ward off this dark energy, people would make noise by banging drums or shooting arrows into the sky, attempting to scare away the dragon and restore the Sun.
- **Mesoamerica**: The Maya and Aztec cultures observed eclipses with a sense of awe, incorporating them into their complex astronomical and calendrical systems. Eclipses were seen as part of cosmic cycles, with implications for both earthly events and the spiritual world.
- **Europe**: In medieval Europe, eclipses were often associated with portents of change, sometimes feared as omens of war, plague, or the death of a ruler. However, as understanding of astronomy grew, eclipses came to be seen more as natural events than divine interventions.

In December, near the time of the winter solstice, a solar eclipse takes on an added layer of symbolism. As a period of darkness and transformation, the winter solstice represents the return of light and the promise of new beginnings. A solar eclipse amplifies this energy, becoming a powerful reminder of the cyclical nature of life and the ever-present opportunity for rebirth and renewal.

The Astrological Influence of a December Solar Eclipse

Astrologically, a solar eclipse is a time of powerful new beginnings, where the energy of the New Moon combines with the intensity of the Sun's temporary obscuration. Solar eclipses are often seen as cosmic resets, encouraging us to reflect on our lives, let go of outdated beliefs or patterns, and set intentions for growth and transformation. When a solar eclipse occurs in December, it carries the additional symbolism of the end of the calendar year, a time when many people naturally reflect on their past and look toward the future.

In astrology, the sign in which a solar eclipse occurs is significant, as it highlights the themes and lessons associated with that sign. For example:

- **Sagittarius Solar Eclipse**: If a solar eclipse occurs in Sagittarius, it emphasizes themes of expansion, truth-seeking, and adventure. Sagittarius energy encourages us to explore new perspectives, embrace learning, and seek out personal freedom and purpose. During a December eclipse in Sagittarius, there may be a focus on redefining beliefs or setting goals that expand our horizons in the coming year.
- **Capricorn Solar Eclipse**: A solar eclipse in Capricorn is rooted in themes of responsibility, discipline, and ambition. Capricorn energy urges us to set practical goals, focus on long-term

achievements, and honor our commitments. A December eclipse in Capricorn may prompt us to consider our career paths, family responsibilities, and ways we can build lasting foundations for the future.

The energy of a solar eclipse, especially in December, offers a unique window for personal transformation and intention-setting. Unlike a typical New Moon, which also encourages new beginnings, a solar eclipse acts as a powerful catalyst for change, often revealing hidden insights, prompting unexpected shifts, or encouraging us to face unresolved issues. This cosmic event provides a rare opportunity to end the year with clarity, renewed purpose, and a commitment to personal growth.

Harnessing the Energy of a December Solar Eclipse for Personal Reflection

The energy of a solar eclipse is potent and transformative, and there are several ways to harness its influence for personal reflection and growth during December. By using this time mindfully, we can align with the themes of closure, new beginnings, and spiritual awakening that a solar eclipse brings to the holiday season.

1. **Set Clear Intentions for the New Year**: A December solar eclipse is an ideal time to set intentions for the year ahead, focusing on areas of life that require growth, healing, or transformation. Reflect on the past year, consider what you'd like to release, and set intentions for the changes you wish to create in the coming months. Writing these intentions down or speaking them aloud can amplify their power.
2. **Reflect on Past Challenges and Lessons Learned**: A solar eclipse encourages us to look within and examine the lessons from our experiences. Take time to reflect on the challenges you've faced throughout the year, acknowledging the growth and wisdom they've brought. Embrace any pain or mistakes as part of your journey, allowing yourself to release lingering negativity and welcome a fresh start.
3. **Meditate on the Darkness and Light**: The symbolism of the Sun being obscured by the Moon during a solar eclipse can be a powerful metaphor for self-reflection. Consider meditating during the eclipse, focusing on the themes of light and darkness within yourself. Acknowledge any "shadows" or unexamined areas of your life, inviting them into the light of awareness for healing and growth.
4. **Create a Ritual for Releasing and Renewal**: Engage in a personal ritual that marks the end of the year and the eclipse as a turning point. This could involve lighting a candle for each intention, writing down what you'd like to release and then safely burning the paper, or visualizing yourself stepping into a new chapter. Rituals help anchor our intentions and provide a tangible sense of closure and renewal.
5. **Explore Dreams and Intuition**: Solar eclipses heighten our sensitivity to intuition, making them a powerful time for dream work or intuitive practices. Pay attention to any dreams or insights that arise around the eclipse, as they may offer guidance or inspiration for the path ahead. Journaling about your dreams, feelings, or thoughts during this time can help you process and understand the messages your subconscious may be trying to communicate.

Embracing the Mystery and Magic of a December Solar Eclipse

A December solar eclipse is a profound event, one that reminds us of the vast mysteries of the universe and our own lives. This rare alignment encourages us to embrace change, trust in the unknown, and remain open to life's transformations. As the Sun's light is temporarily obscured, we are reminded of the cyclical nature of darkness and light, endings and beginnings, loss and renewal.

The holiday season, often associated with reflection and gratitude, is an ideal time to align with the energy of a solar eclipse. By approaching this cosmic event with openness and reverence, we can experience it as a time of deep spiritual connection, self-awareness, and growth. Whether through quiet reflection, ritual, or intention-setting, the mysteries of a December solar eclipse can guide us into the new year with purpose, insight, and a renewed commitment to personal evolution.

Final Thoughts: The Gift of a Solar Eclipse in December

A solar eclipse during December offers a powerful and transformative experience, adding a layer of mystery, magic, and cosmic significance to the holiday season. Through its themes of closure, new beginnings, and spiritual illumination, a December eclipse provides a rare opportunity to reflect, renew, and embrace the possibilities of the future. By attuning to the energy of this celestial event, we can deepen our understanding of ourselves and the world, allowing the mysteries of the universe to guide us into the new year with hope, strength, and vision.

This Christmas, let the energy of the solar eclipse inspire you to look beyond the surface, seek out hidden truths, and embrace the path of transformation. Whether through self-reflection, ritual, or personal intention-setting, allow this rare alignment of the Sun, Moon, and Earth to awaken your spirit, guiding you toward a brighter, more meaningful future. The mysteries of the solar eclipse are a reminder that we are part of a larger cosmic dance, one that continually invites us to grow, evolve, and dream anew.

Chapter 14: Eclipse Cycles and Their Christmas Influence

Eclipses have fascinated humanity for centuries, their patterns and cycles influencing various aspects of life and spirituality. Solar and lunar eclipses occur in a rhythmic cycle, known as the Saros cycle, creating repeating patterns of cosmic alignment over centuries. Eclipses near Christmas are especially potent, as they bring both the energy of celestial transformation and the reflective atmosphere of the holiday season. This chapter explores the significance of eclipse cycles, how they shape the themes of our lives, and the unique influence these cycles have when they occur around Christmas.

In astrology, eclipses are seen as powerful agents of change, marking pivotal moments in both individual and collective journeys. When they align with Christmas, a season traditionally associated with reflection, gratitude, and new beginnings, these cosmic events enhance the depth of the holiday experience. By understanding the cycles of eclipses and their influence on our lives, we can appreciate their role as markers of growth and transformation, especially during the spiritually significant Christmas season.

Understanding Eclipse Cycles: The Saros Cycle and Its Repeating Patterns

Eclipses follow a predictable pattern known as the **Saros cycle**, a period of approximately 18 years, 11 days, and 8 hours. The Saros cycle occurs due to the intricate alignments of the Sun, Earth, and Moon, resulting in a series of eclipses that repeat almost identically every 18 years. Each cycle contains a sequence of solar and lunar eclipses, and each eclipse within the cycle progressively shifts in position, creating a rhythm of cosmic alignment that has been observed and documented by ancient civilizations and modern astronomers alike.

1. **Solar Eclipses in the Saros Cycle**: Within the Saros cycle, solar eclipses often alternate between total and annular types, with each eclipse occurring slightly north or south of the previous one. This progression creates an "eclipse family" within the Saros cycle, with each eclipse in the series bringing a similar theme of transformation but manifesting in different geographic locations.

2. **Lunar Eclipses in the Saros Cycle**: Lunar eclipses within a Saros cycle mirror the pattern of solar eclipses, following the same rhythmic cycle. Lunar eclipses are associated with emotional shifts, closures, and revelations, providing complementary energy to the new beginnings prompted by solar eclipses.

3. **The Nodal Cycle**: Another key factor in understanding eclipses is the nodal cycle, which is the path where the Moon's orbit intersects with the Earth's orbit around the Sun. Known as the North and South Nodes, these points move backward through the zodiac over an 18.6-year cycle, with each eclipse season occurring when the Sun is near one of these nodes. This backward movement of the nodes creates patterns and themes that repeat in our lives, helping us navigate lessons, growth, and purpose over time.

Every 18 years, as a particular Saros cycle repeats, the themes, energies, and transformations associated with that cycle return, offering us a new opportunity to reflect on and build upon past lessons. During Christmas, these cycles can amplify the already reflective energy of the holiday season, encouraging us to examine patterns in our lives, honor the growth we've experienced, and set intentions for future transformation.

The Influence of Eclipse Cycles on Holiday Themes

When an eclipse falls near Christmas, it amplifies the themes of the holiday season, infusing it with a profound sense of mystery, introspection, and spiritual growth. Eclipses during Christmas tend to resonate with the holiday's emphasis on gratitude, forgiveness, and rebirth, creating a unique alignment that deepens our experience of the season. Some of the ways eclipse cycles influence holiday themes include:

1. **Reflection and Renewal**: Christmas is often a time for looking back on the year, reflecting on accomplishments, relationships, and growth. An eclipse near Christmas encourages deeper reflection, bringing hidden patterns, insights, and subconscious motivations to the surface. Solar eclipses, associated with new beginnings, invite us to start anew, while lunar eclipses, which symbolize closure, encourage us to release old habits or beliefs that no longer serve us.

2. **Spiritual Transformation**: The holiday season is traditionally a time for spiritual connection and introspection. Eclipses, as celestial events that temporarily obscure the Sun or Moon, symbolize journeys into the unknown and the transformative power of darkness. During Christmas, this energy enhances our spiritual practices, inviting us to explore deeper questions about life, purpose, and our connection to the divine.

3. **Family and Ancestral Healing**: Christmas is often celebrated with family, and an eclipse during this season can bring attention to ancestral patterns and family dynamics. Eclipses connected to the lunar nodes, especially, are thought to influence our karmic paths, highlighting unresolved patterns or relationships within family lineages. This influence can serve as an opportunity to address these patterns, heal old wounds, and create a more harmonious family environment.

4. **Collective Shifts and Social Change**: Eclipses are not only personal but also collective events that influence global consciousness. When an eclipse occurs near Christmas, it resonates with themes of peace, goodwill, and unity, encouraging a broader reflection on societal values and our collective aspirations. Solar eclipses may signal the beginning of social shifts or transformations, while lunar eclipses can bring issues to light, prompting us to reconsider our roles as members of a larger community.

By recognizing these influences, we can harness the unique energy of an eclipse cycle during Christmas, making the holiday season a time for personal and collective growth. Each eclipse brings an opportunity for profound change, and when it aligns with Christmas, it offers a cosmic invitation to embrace transformation and deepen our understanding of the interconnectedness of life.

Harnessing the Energy of Eclipse Cycles During Christmas

Understanding the cyclical nature of eclipses allows us to approach the holiday season with greater awareness, aligning our personal growth with the larger cosmic rhythms. There are several ways to harness the energy of eclipse cycles during Christmas, making the most of their transformative influence:

1. **Reflect on Patterns from Past Cycles**: As eclipses repeat every 18 years, reflecting on past cycles can reveal themes, patterns, or life lessons that are resurfacing for further growth. Think back to the past 18-year intervals to identify any similarities in challenges, achievements, or personal changes. Journaling about these insights can help clarify the purpose of current events and provide direction for future choices.

2. **Set Intentions Aligned with the Eclipse Energy**: Eclipses are powerful times for setting intentions, especially when they coincide with New or Full Moons. During a Christmas eclipse, consider setting intentions that reflect both your personal and spiritual aspirations. Ask yourself what you wish to release, transform, or bring into your life, focusing on how these changes align with the holiday themes of love, forgiveness, and renewal.

3. **Engage in Ancestral or Family Rituals**: Since eclipses often highlight family patterns, this is an ideal time to honor your ancestors or engage in family healing. Reflect on traditions passed down through generations, or perform a ritual that acknowledges family members who have influenced you. You might light a candle for a loved one, share stories, or create a family tree to honor your lineage and connect with the wisdom of your ancestors.

4. **Practice Meditation and Self-Reflection**: Eclipses are times of internal focus, and the holiday season is already a period of quiet introspection. Consider meditating on your life path, visualizing the upcoming year, or exploring deeper questions about your spiritual journey. Meditation practices focused on the chakras, particularly the heart and third eye, can help enhance your intuition and connect you to the spiritual insights of the eclipse cycle.

5. **Engage in Collective Acts of Service**: The Christmas season emphasizes goodwill, compassion, and generosity. When an eclipse occurs during this time, it amplifies the desire to contribute to the greater good. Consider participating in acts of service, supporting causes you believe in, or engaging in community events that promote unity and peace. By aligning with the collective energy of the eclipse, you can help create positive social change and contribute to the upliftment of those around you.

Astrological Signs and Eclipse Cycles: Their Influence on Christmas Energy
Each eclipse season occurs within a particular zodiac sign, which shapes the themes and energies that the eclipse brings. When an eclipse falls near Christmas, the astrological sign it occurs in provides insight into the specific lessons and transformations that are emphasized during the holiday season:

- **Aries**: An eclipse in Aries brings themes of courage, independence, and new beginnings. During Christmas, this energy encourages us to take bold steps toward personal goals, assert our individuality, and embrace change with enthusiasm.
- **Taurus**: Eclipses in Taurus focus on stability, abundance, and material well-being. When occurring during Christmas, this influence invites us to reflect on our values, cherish the beauty of simplicity, and cultivate gratitude for life's basic pleasures.
- **Gemini**: An eclipse in Gemini highlights communication, learning, and adaptability. A Christmas eclipse in Gemini encourages meaningful conversations, the sharing of ideas, and a curiosity about different perspectives, making it an ideal time for connection and understanding.
- **Cancer**: Eclipses in Cancer emphasize family, home, and emotional security. During Christmas, this energy deepens our connection to loved ones, bringing opportunities for emotional healing and the creation of nurturing, harmonious family dynamics.
- **Leo**: Eclipses in Leo bring themes of creativity, self-expression, and joy. During Christmas, a Leo eclipse encourages celebration, the appreciation of beauty, and the courage to embrace one's unique gifts.
- **Virgo**: An eclipse in Virgo emphasizes health, service, and organization. A Christmas eclipse in Virgo is a time to consider how we can be of service to others, improve our routines, and focus on well-being and gratitude.
- **Libra**: Eclipses in Libra focus on balance, relationships, and harmony. When a Libra eclipse occurs near Christmas, it highlights the importance of unity, fairness, and creating balanced connections within family and community.
- **Scorpio**: An eclipse in Scorpio brings transformation, depth, and renewal. During Christmas, Scorpio energy encourages emotional release, introspection, and the courage to confront hidden truths for inner growth.
- **Sagittarius**: Eclipses in Sagittarius emphasize exploration, belief systems, and personal freedom. A Sagittarius eclipse near Christmas invites us to expand our worldview, connect with our spiritual beliefs, and embrace adventure.
- **Capricorn**: An eclipse in Capricorn brings themes of discipline, responsibility, and tradition. During Christmas, a Capricorn eclipse invites us to honor our commitments, set goals for the future, and find stability within ourselves and our families.

- **Aquarius**: Eclipses in Aquarius highlight innovation, community, and social change. A Christmas eclipse in Aquarius encourages collective action, creativity, and the celebration of individuality within community.
- **Pisces**: Eclipses in Pisces focus on compassion, spirituality, and intuition. A Pisces eclipse near Christmas enhances our connection to the divine, inviting us to reflect on our dreams and embrace empathy, forgiveness, and peace.

Final Thoughts: The Gift of Eclipse Cycles During Christmas

Eclipse cycles bring a powerful, transformative influence to the holiday season, deepening our experience of Christmas and enhancing our journey of self-discovery, healing, and growth. By aligning our intentions and actions with the energy of the eclipse cycle, we can embrace the mysteries of life, honor our personal and family legacies, and create a holiday season that is rich with meaning, insight, and compassion.

This Christmas, let the cycles of eclipses inspire you to explore the rhythms and patterns of your own life, reflecting on the past and setting intentions for the future. Through personal reflection, family healing, and acts of kindness, you can harness the cosmic energy of the eclipse cycle to make this holiday season a time of profound transformation and joyful renewal.

Chapter 15: Historical Eclipses During the Holiday Season

Throughout history, solar and lunar eclipses occurring near the holiday season have fascinated and influenced humanity in profound ways. Seen as divine messages, omens of change, or celestial spectacles, eclipses during Christmas time have been documented, celebrated, and sometimes feared across cultures. This chapter delves into significant historical eclipses that occurred around Christmas, exploring how they influenced religious beliefs, political events, cultural interpretations, and the collective consciousness. By understanding the impact of these historical eclipses, we gain insight into the lasting power of celestial phenomena and their unique resonance during the holiday season.

Eclipses that align with Christmas amplify the introspective and transformative energy of the holiday, marking them as moments of reflection, spiritual awakening, and even social change. For many civilizations, an eclipse near this time of year held profound symbolic meaning, representing the themes of rebirth, revelation, and the thin veil between the physical and spiritual worlds. By examining these notable historical eclipses, we can appreciate the ways they have shaped humanity's understanding of the cosmos, the divine, and the meaning of Christmas.

Early Interpretations of Eclipses Near Christmas

Ancient cultures paid close attention to eclipses, often interpreting them as messages from the gods or signs of impending change. In societies where the Sun and Moon were worshiped as deities, an eclipse was seen as a disturbance in the divine order, leading people to believe that the heavens were communicating directly with them. Early civilizations like the Babylonians, Egyptians, Chinese, and Maya developed complex astronomical systems to predict eclipses, attempting to understand the cosmic patterns behind these mysterious occurrences.

During the holiday season, eclipses took on even greater significance. The winter solstice, marking the return of light as days grow longer, was a symbol of hope and renewal for many ancient cultures. An eclipse during this period would enhance these themes, often seen as a celestial marker of the cycles of darkness and light, death and rebirth. This connection to the holiday season made eclipses even more potent symbols, aligning with religious celebrations and moments of communal reflection.

Notable Historical Eclipses Near Christmas

Several significant eclipses have occurred around the holiday season, each with its own cultural, political, or religious impact. The following historical eclipses highlight how these celestial events have been perceived and interpreted, reflecting the diverse ways societies have responded to the mysteries of the cosmos.

1. The Solar Eclipse of December 24, 968 AD

In the year 968 AD, a total solar eclipse occurred on Christmas Eve, darkening parts of Europe, the Middle East, and Asia. This eclipse took place during the Middle Ages, a time when eclipses were often viewed with fear and superstition. In Europe, the eclipse was seen as a dark omen, and its proximity to Christmas intensified its impact, sparking widespread fear and speculation among religious communities.

The eclipse also coincided with a time of significant political tension in the Byzantine Empire. For many, the sudden darkening of the Sun was interpreted as a sign of divine judgment, potentially forewarning political instability or moral decline. Some historical records from the period suggest that the eclipse influenced the decisions of leaders, who took the event as a call to examine their rule and prepare for possible unrest. Though rooted in fear, the eclipse's impact on leaders and communities demonstrated the powerful influence celestial events had on medieval societies, particularly during sacred times like Christmas.

2. The Solar Eclipse of December 25, 1033 AD

A solar eclipse on Christmas Day in 1033 AD became an iconic celestial event, occurring exactly 1,000 years after the birth of Jesus Christ, as traditionally dated by early Christian historians. This rare alignment amplified the symbolism of Christmas and carried deep significance for the Christian world, which saw it as an omen or even a miraculous sign.

In Europe, religious leaders and scholars interpreted the eclipse as a cosmic reminder of the birth, death, and resurrection of Christ, viewing the obscuration of the Sun as a metaphor for the darkness that Christ's light had come to dispel. This eclipse led to an increase in religious fervor and was regarded as a message of renewal and divine intervention. The solar eclipse of 1033 AD served as a powerful reminder of faith for the Christian world and was later recorded in religious texts, leaving a legacy of mysticism and reverence.

3. The Solar Eclipse of December 22, 1870

The solar eclipse on December 22, 1870, visible across Europe and North America, occurred just a few days before Christmas, captivating people and scientists alike. This eclipse took place during a period when astronomy had advanced significantly, and the event was widely documented and observed by scientists who were eager to study the Sun's corona.

In England, the eclipse was observed by astronomers who gathered data that contributed to the understanding of solar prominences and the Sun's magnetic field. The eclipse became an opportunity for public education and brought people together in awe of the natural world, aligning the scientific curiosity of the era with the wonder of the holiday season. This eclipse demonstrated the shift from mystical interpretations of eclipses to scientific exploration, but it still retained a sense of spiritual mystery, as it reminded people of the vastness of the universe and humanity's place within it.

4. The Solar Eclipse of December 25, 1935

The solar eclipse of December 25, 1935, was an annular eclipse, forming a "ring of fire" effect around the Moon and visible over parts of Southeast Asia, the Pacific, and North America. Occurring on Christmas Day, this eclipse was viewed as a symbol of hope and resilience during a difficult time, as much of the world was still feeling the effects of the Great Depression.

In the United States, the eclipse was widely covered in newspapers and became a subject of fascination, drawing people outdoors on Christmas morning to witness the celestial event. The eclipse served as a reminder of the cycles of hardship and renewal, inspiring people to find strength in the face of adversity. Its alignment with Christmas provided a hopeful message, suggesting that even in times of darkness, there is a "ring of light" that can guide people forward.

5. The Solar Eclipse of December 4, 2002

The solar eclipse of December 4, 2002, occurred near the beginning of December, close enough to the holiday season to carry spiritual significance. This eclipse was visible over parts of Africa and Australia, with a partial view in parts of Asia and the Southern Hemisphere. Astrologically, the eclipse fell in the sign of Sagittarius, emphasizing themes of exploration, truth, and new perspectives.

In the early 2000s, there was a growing interest in spiritual practices and alternative perspectives, and this eclipse was seen by some as a sign of expanded consciousness and self-discovery. With its proximity to the holiday season, the 2002 eclipse inspired reflection on the journeys, both physical and spiritual, that shape our lives. Astrologers suggested that this eclipse was an invitation to seek knowledge, explore new paths, and set intentions for the future. For many, the eclipse added a layer of introspective energy to the holiday season, aligning with the Christmas themes of rebirth and spiritual awakening.

How Historical Eclipses Have Shaped the Holiday Season

Historical eclipses occurring near Christmas have influenced not only how people celebrate but also how they perceive the spiritual and mystical dimensions of the holiday season. These eclipses have encouraged introspection, a deeper appreciation for the mysteries of life, and a reminder of humanity's connection to the cosmos. Some key influences of historical eclipses on the holiday season include:

1. **Symbolism of Darkness and Light**: Eclipses amplify the symbolism of darkness and light, a theme central to Christmas. For ancient and modern cultures alike, a solar eclipse during Christmas has served as a cosmic reminder of the triumph of light over darkness, aligning with the spiritual message of hope, salvation, and renewal.
2. **Divine Signs and Religious Reflection**: Eclipses near Christmas have often been interpreted as divine signs, prompting people to reflect on their faith, spiritual beliefs, and connection to the divine. Historical records show that religious leaders and communities have seen these eclipses as messages of change, urging people to realign with their values or deepen their spiritual commitments.
3. **Political and Social Influence**: In certain periods, Christmas eclipses have impacted politics and social dynamics, as leaders interpreted these events as omens, sometimes influencing political decisions, treaties, or royal decrees. Eclipses near the holiday season have occasionally marked pivotal historical shifts, seen as catalysts for change in governance or public sentiment.
4. **Advancement of Scientific Understanding**: As knowledge of astronomy grew, eclipses near Christmas inspired scientific curiosity and public engagement. From ancient astrologers to modern astronomers, people have used these eclipses to deepen their understanding of the Sun, Moon, and celestial mechanics, linking scientific discovery with seasonal wonder.
5. **Personal and Collective Reflection**: Eclipses near Christmas encourage collective reflection, aligning with the holiday's themes of gratitude, introspection, and renewal. Historical eclipses during the holiday season have inspired people to reflect on the past year, consider their life's purpose, and set intentions for the future.

Final Thoughts: The Enduring Power of Christmas Eclipses

Historical eclipses near Christmas have left a lasting mark on human culture, inspiring awe, reverence, and reflection. From divine omens to scientific milestones, these eclipses have shaped our understanding of the holiday season as a time of transformation, unity, and cosmic wonder. Each eclipse offers a reminder of the interconnectedness of all things, encouraging us to honor both the cycles of the heavens and the rhythms of our lives.

This Christmas, let the legacy of historical eclipses inspire you to embrace the mysteries of the season with an open heart and a reflective spirit. Whether through personal introspection, spiritual connection, or simply appreciating the beauty of the cosmos, a Christmas eclipse is an invitation to journey inward, honor the past, and welcome the light of a new beginning.

Part 3: **Moon Phases in December**

Chapter 16: New Moon - Setting Christmas Intentions

The New Moon, a powerful phase of the lunar cycle, represents new beginnings, fresh starts, and the planting of seeds for the future. Occurring when the Moon is positioned between the Earth and the Sun, the New Moon marks a time of darkness in the night sky, symbolizing the potential for growth and transformation. When a New Moon aligns with the Christmas season, it amplifies the energy of renewal, making it an ideal moment for setting intentions, reflecting on personal goals, and manifesting a vision for the year ahead. This chapter explores the spiritual and practical aspects of setting Christmas intentions with the New Moon, helping us embrace this cosmic opportunity to align with our dreams and create lasting positive change.

For many, Christmas is a time of reflection, gratitude, and anticipation for the coming year. The alignment of a New Moon with this holiday season offers a powerful moment to harness both lunar energy and the themes of the holiday, inviting us to release the past, focus on the present, and plant the seeds for future growth. By understanding the meaning and potential of the New Moon during Christmas, we can create a meaningful ritual of intention-setting that honors our inner desires and aligns with our higher purpose.

Understanding the Power of the New Moon

In astrology and spirituality, the New Moon is regarded as a phase of beginnings, when the Moon's light is not yet visible, symbolizing a clean slate and the potential for creation. This darkness encourages introspection, allowing us to look within, assess our lives, and set goals that resonate with our true selves. During the New Moon, the energy is quieter and more reflective, making it a time for deep contemplation and vision-setting rather than outward action.

The New Moon's energy is subtle yet potent, often compared to the planting of seeds that will sprout in the coming weeks and months. Just as a gardener prepares the soil and plants seeds with care, setting intentions during the New Moon allows us to lay the groundwork for the future, focusing on what we want to bring into our lives. Each lunar cycle lasts approximately 29.5 days, so the intentions we set during the New Moon will naturally grow and evolve as the Moon progresses through its phases, culminating in the Full Moon, when manifestations reach their peak.

During Christmas, a New Moon brings an added dimension of spiritual depth, aligning with the themes of rebirth, gratitude, and joy. As we reflect on the year that has passed and look forward to the one ahead, the New Moon offers a perfect opportunity to pause, connect with our inner selves, and set meaningful intentions for personal and spiritual growth.

The Significance of a New Moon During Christmas

When a New Moon falls near Christmas, its influence magnifies the introspective and transformative energy of the holiday season. Christmas, a time traditionally associated with celebration, reflection, and giving, becomes even more significant as the New Moon encourages us to turn inward and explore our deepest desires. The convergence of these energies supports a practice of setting intentions that are not only personal but also aligned with the spirit of the season.

The New Moon during Christmas also resonates with themes of peace, renewal, and hope. Just as the holiday season marks the end of the calendar year, a New Moon marks the beginning of a new lunar cycle, creating a powerful alignment that emphasizes closure and the potential for fresh starts. This timing encourages us to reflect on what we are ready to release, who we wish to become, and how we can embrace a life that brings us closer to joy, purpose, and fulfillment.

Preparing to Set Christmas Intentions with the New Moon

Setting intentions during the New Moon requires a mindful approach, creating a quiet space for introspection, clarity, and focus. During the holiday season, with its festivities and social gatherings, it can be challenging to find time for personal reflection. However, taking even a few moments to center yourself and prepare your intentions can create a powerful ritual that aligns with the magic of both Christmas and the New Moon.

To prepare for setting Christmas intentions with the New Moon, consider the following steps:

1. **Create a Sacred Space**: Find a quiet, comfortable space where you can relax and connect with yourself. You might want to light a candle, burn incense, or play calming music to create an atmosphere that feels peaceful and inviting. This space can be a special corner in your home, a cozy spot by the Christmas tree, or even a place outdoors where you feel connected to nature.

2. **Reflect on the Past Year**: Before setting intentions, take time to reflect on the past year. Think about the challenges you faced, the lessons you learned, and the achievements that made you proud. Acknowledge any lingering emotions and consider what you are ready to release as you move forward. This process of reflection creates space for new intentions to flourish.

3. **Identify Your Core Desires**: Ask yourself what truly matters to you. Consider what brings you joy, what fulfills you, and what you wish to manifest in your life. During the Christmas season, think about how your intentions can reflect the holiday's themes of love, kindness, and unity. Write down your core desires and focus on the areas of life where you wish to grow or create change.

4. **Set an Intention with Clarity**: Once you have reflected on your desires, choose one or more specific intentions for the New Moon. An intention should be clear, positive, and stated in the present tense, as though it is already happening. For example, instead of saying, "I want to be more peaceful," say, "I am filled with peace and calm in my daily life." This language helps align your subconscious with your goals, making them more powerful.

Crafting a Christmas New Moon Ritual

Creating a ritual for setting intentions during the New Moon and Christmas allows you to connect more deeply with your goals and honor the transformative energy of this special alignment. Rituals help solidify our intentions, creating a sense of purpose and commitment that supports our personal growth.

Here are some ideas for a Christmas New Moon ritual:

1. **Write Down Your Intentions**: Begin by writing your intentions on a piece of paper. Be as specific as possible, focusing on your goals in areas such as relationships, career, health, spirituality, or personal growth. Writing solidifies your thoughts and helps bring clarity to your desires. You may also want to include intentions related to giving, compassion, or community, aligning with the holiday spirit.

2. **Light a Candle for Each Intention**: If you have multiple intentions, consider lighting a candle for each one, symbolizing the light you are bringing into your life. As you light each candle, visualize your intention coming to fruition, imagining yourself embodying the qualities you wish to cultivate. The candlelight represents the warmth and hope of Christmas, as well as the energy of the New Moon.

3. **Create a Vision Board or Sacred Collage**: A vision board or collage is a visual representation of your intentions, filled with images, words, and symbols that align with your goals. Use magazines, photographs, or drawings to create a representation of what you wish to manifest in the coming year. This creative process can be a meditative practice, helping you clarify your desires while celebrating the possibilities ahead.

4. **Perform a Gratitude Practice**: The holiday season is an ideal time to express gratitude, and a New Moon ritual offers the perfect opportunity to reflect on all that you are thankful for. Take a few moments to appreciate the blessings in your life, acknowledging the people, experiences, and growth that have shaped your journey. Gratitude is a powerful force that aligns with abundance, helping your intentions manifest with greater ease.

5. **Seal Your Intentions with a Symbolic Gesture**: Choose a symbolic gesture to mark the completion of your ritual. This could be as simple as folding your intention paper and placing it under a crystal, burning it in a fireproof bowl to release it to the universe, or keeping it on your altar as a reminder of your goals. This act seals your intentions and signifies your commitment to manifesting them.

Following Through: Manifesting Intentions Beyond the New Moon

Setting intentions is only the first step; manifesting them requires focus, dedication, and trust. As the New Moon energy begins to wane and the Moon progresses through its phases, use the following practices to keep your intentions alive and support your journey of transformation:

1. **Stay Aligned with Your Intentions**: Keep your written intentions or vision board somewhere visible as a reminder of your goals. Reflect on them regularly, staying mindful of your commitment to personal growth and positive change. This practice helps reinforce your intentions and encourages you to make choices that align with your desired outcomes.
2. **Take Inspired Action**: The New Moon is a time for setting intentions, but it's important to take practical steps toward achieving your goals as well. Break down your intentions into manageable actions and create a plan for moving forward. Small steps, taken consistently, help transform intentions into tangible realities.
3. **Celebrate Progress, No Matter How Small**: Every step forward is worth celebrating. Take time to acknowledge your progress, appreciating the growth and changes you've achieved, no matter how small. This attitude of gratitude and celebration keeps you motivated and aligned with the positive energy of your intentions.
4. **Trust in Divine Timing**: Intentions do not always manifest immediately; some may take time to come to fruition. Trust that your desires will unfold at the right moment, staying patient and open to the journey. The holiday season reminds us of the beauty of faith, encouraging us to hold hope for the future even if results aren't immediate.
5. **Reflect During the Full Moon**: The Full Moon is the culmination of the lunar cycle, a time for celebrating what has come to fruition and releasing anything that no longer serves us. When the Full Moon arrives, take a moment to reflect on the intentions you set during the New Moon, celebrating any progress you've made and adjusting your goals as needed.

The Spiritual Gift of Christmas Intentions with the New Moon

Setting Christmas intentions with the New Moon is a powerful practice that honors both the energy of the holiday season and the potential for transformation offered by the lunar cycle. This alignment of celestial and seasonal energy reminds us that we have the power to create positive change, bringing our dreams closer to reality through mindfulness, dedication, and faith.

As we journey into the New Year, the intentions set during this sacred time act as guiding lights, helping us navigate the challenges and opportunities that lie ahead. By aligning with the New Moon's energy, we deepen our connection to the universe, enhancing our ability to manifest a life that resonates with our true purpose.

Final Thoughts: A Christmas Gift of Renewal and Transformation

The New Moon during Christmas is a cosmic gift, inviting us to celebrate not only the holiday season but also the potential within each of us to grow, change, and create. By setting intentions during this powerful lunar phase, we honor the spirit of Christmas as a time for reflection, gratitude, and rebirth. Embrace this opportunity to set meaningful intentions, allowing the magic of the New Moon and the joy of Christmas to guide you into a New Year filled with purpose, peace, and infinite possibility.

Chapter 17: Waxing Crescent - Building Holiday Momentum

The Waxing Crescent Moon, the phase that follows the New Moon, is a time of growth, action, and focused intention. As the Moon's light begins to reappear in the sky, this phase symbolizes the transition from planning to implementation, encouraging us to take the first steps toward manifesting our goals. During the holiday season, the Waxing Crescent phase aligns beautifully with the energy of building momentum, excitement, and joy, making it an ideal time to actively bring our Christmas intentions to life.

In the context of the lunar cycle, the Waxing Crescent is a period of gentle yet determined growth, urging us to nurture the seeds we planted during the New Moon. With its influence, we are encouraged to stay committed to our intentions, take inspired action, and overcome any initial doubts or obstacles that may arise. During the holiday season, the Waxing Crescent Moon helps us embrace the joy of giving, the anticipation of celebration, and the importance of turning intentions into tangible reality. By harnessing this energy, we can deepen our holiday experience, fostering connections, gratitude, and positivity that resonate well beyond the season.

The Meaning of the Waxing Crescent Moon

The Waxing Crescent Moon appears as a slim, curved sliver of light in the night sky, growing brighter each evening. This phase symbolizes the gradual unfolding of our intentions and the initial stages of bringing our desires into reality. In the broader context of the lunar cycle, the Waxing Crescent is the time for setting a foundation, embracing the momentum of growth, and committing to the actions needed to realize our goals.

While the New Moon represents introspection and setting intentions, the Waxing Crescent is about moving from thought to action. This is when we take those first steps, however small, to bring our dreams to life. It is a phase that calls for patience, persistence, and courage, as it often brings to light the challenges or hesitations we must overcome to reach our goals. During this phase, it is essential to trust in the journey, knowing that each action we take is contributing to the bigger picture.

In the holiday season, the Waxing Crescent invites us to bring the spirit of our intentions into our celebrations and interactions. Whether our goals relate to personal growth, family connection, or holiday traditions, this phase reminds us to take tangible steps to make this season meaningful and aligned with our true desires.

Building Holiday Momentum: Turning Christmas Intentions into Action

The Waxing Crescent Moon during Christmas is a powerful time to build momentum toward a joyful, meaningful holiday experience. As we move from intention to action, this phase encourages us to create plans, take initiative, and stay focused on the holiday spirit we wish to cultivate. The following steps can help us use the Waxing Crescent energy to actively shape our holiday season:

1. **Refine Your Intentions**: Revisit the intentions you set during the New Moon. With the energy of the Waxing Crescent, consider how you can make these intentions actionable. If your goal is to foster family connection, consider planning specific activities or outings that bring loved ones together. If your intention is self-care, identify small rituals or practices that you can incorporate into your holiday routine.

2. **Create a Holiday Plan**: The Waxing Crescent is a great time for planning. Develop a clear outline for your holiday activities, gifts, gatherings, and self-care. Make a to-do list that includes both small and large tasks, ensuring that each step aligns with your holiday intentions. By organizing your time and energy, you can prevent holiday stress and focus on what truly matters.

3. **Focus on Relationships**: The holiday season is often centered around relationships, and the Waxing Crescent encourages us to take proactive steps to strengthen connections. Reach out to friends and family, plan a gathering, or send a thoughtful message to someone you appreciate. Building momentum in relationships can deepen the sense of togetherness that makes the holiday season special.

4. **Bring Joy to Others**: As we transition from intention to action, the Waxing Crescent phase reminds us to share the joy of the holiday season with those around us. Engage in acts of kindness, volunteer for a cause you care about, or surprise someone with a thoughtful gesture. Each small act of giving or compassion adds to the momentum of joy and generosity that defines the spirit of Christmas.

5. **Embrace Holiday Creativity**: Whether it's decorating, cooking, gift-making, or crafting, allow the Waxing Crescent to inspire your creativity. Creating holiday decor, making homemade gifts, or trying out new recipes can add excitement and personal expression to your celebrations. Creative activities also help to bring the intentions you've set to life, making them tangible and present in your holiday experience.

Overcoming Initial Challenges and Staying Committed

During the Waxing Crescent phase, it's common to encounter initial obstacles or self-doubt. This is the time when resistance may arise, testing our commitment to our intentions. In the holiday season, this could appear as stress, feelings of overwhelm, or even questioning the relevance of certain traditions or responsibilities. However, overcoming these challenges is part of building momentum and growth.

1. **Acknowledge Any Doubts or Fears**: It's natural to feel apprehensive when turning intentions into action, especially when holiday expectations can add pressure. Take a moment to acknowledge any doubts or fears that may arise. Recognize them without judgment and remind yourself of the purpose and joy behind your holiday intentions.

2. **Break Down Tasks into Manageable Steps**: Large goals or holiday plans can feel overwhelming if viewed as a whole. Break down your goals into small, achievable steps, focusing on one task at a time. This approach helps you stay present, reducing stress and allowing you to fully enjoy each part of the holiday process.

3. **Stay Focused on Your Purpose**: When challenges arise, reconnect with the "why" behind your holiday intentions. Remind yourself why these intentions matter, whether it's fostering family connection, nurturing self-care, or creating a memorable holiday experience. This reminder can re-energize your efforts and provide clarity on what is most important.

4. **Celebrate Small Wins**: Recognize each step forward as an accomplishment. The Waxing Crescent phase is about gradual growth, so take time to celebrate small victories, whether it's completing a holiday task, achieving a personal goal, or simply feeling more connected to loved ones. Each small win adds to the momentum, making the holiday season feel joyful and fulfilling.

Rituals and Practices for the Waxing Crescent Holiday Season

To harness the energy of the Waxing Crescent Moon during Christmas, consider incorporating rituals and practices that support growth, joy, and connection. These practices can help you stay aligned with your intentions and bring momentum to your holiday experience.

1. **Create a Vision Board for the Holiday Season**: Vision boards are visual representations of your goals and intentions. Use holiday-themed images, quotes, and symbols that align with the intentions you set during the New Moon. Include pictures of family gatherings, acts of kindness, self-care symbols, or anything that represents the energy you wish to bring to Christmas. Display it in a visible place as a reminder of your goals.
2. **Affirmations for Holiday Momentum**: Affirmations are positive statements that help keep your mind focused on your goals. During the Waxing Crescent, choose affirmations that align with growth, joy, and holiday connection. Examples include: "I am creating a joyful and meaningful holiday season," "My actions bring love and warmth to those around me," or "Each step I take brings me closer to a fulfilling holiday experience."
3. **Light a Candle to Build Energy**: Lighting a candle can symbolize the growing light of the Waxing Crescent Moon and the holiday season. As you light the candle, focus on your intentions and visualize the energy of growth and joy expanding with each day. This ritual can be a daily practice, allowing you to check in with your intentions and keep building momentum.
4. **Make a Holiday Gratitude Jar**: The holiday season is a time for gratitude, and creating a holiday gratitude jar can be a powerful way to stay connected to this energy. Each day, write down something you're grateful for, a small victory, or a positive memory from the day and place it in the jar. By Christmas, you'll have a collection of beautiful moments to reflect on, celebrating the joy you built throughout the season.
5. **Practice Self-Compassion**: Building momentum during the holidays can be challenging, especially if emotions or family dynamics bring stress. Practicing self-compassion helps you stay centered and kind to yourself. Each day, take a moment to check in with your emotional state, offering yourself patience, kindness, and understanding. Remember that the journey toward fulfilling intentions is as valuable as the destination.

Aligning with the Waxing Crescent's Energy for a Joyful Holiday Season

The Waxing Crescent Moon during Christmas is a time to bring excitement, creativity, and action to our holiday experience. By aligning with its energy, we can deepen our connection to our intentions, building momentum in a way that feels joyful, purposeful, and true to ourselves. This phase encourages us to embrace the joy of each small step, celebrating the journey of growth as much as the outcome.

1. **Stay Present and Enjoy the Process**: The Waxing Crescent phase is about building step-by-step, allowing each action to contribute to the larger goal. Stay present with each holiday task, whether it's wrapping gifts, decorating, or preparing meals, savoring the experience and enjoying each moment of the journey.

2. **Balance Action with Rest**: Building momentum doesn't mean pushing yourself to exhaustion. Embrace moments of rest and recharge to maintain a balanced approach to the holiday season. Take breaks to meditate, practice mindfulness, or simply enjoy a peaceful moment with family, allowing yourself to recharge as you move forward.

3. **Incorporate Holiday Traditions with Intention**: Use the Waxing Crescent energy to reconnect with meaningful traditions, adapting or creating new ones that align with your current values and goals. Whether it's baking with family, sharing stories, or creating handmade gifts, let each tradition reflect the spirit of the holiday season.

4. **Stay Open to Adaptations**: The Waxing Crescent is a phase of gradual growth, reminding us that flexibility can be a key part of building momentum. If plans change or challenges arise, stay open to adapting, finding new ways to honor your intentions and enjoy the holiday season.

Final Thoughts: Embracing Growth and Joy with the Waxing Crescent

The Waxing Crescent Moon during Christmas is a reminder that every intention, action, and step forward builds the holiday season into a time of joy, connection, and fulfillment. By aligning with the energy of growth, taking inspired actions, and nurturing our intentions, we can create a holiday experience that feels authentic and vibrant.

As you move through the Waxing Crescent phase, remember that the journey is as valuable as the destination. Each day, each effort, and each small step contributes to the bigger picture, transforming the holiday season into a meaningful celebration of love, gratitude, and growth. This Christmas, let the Waxing Crescent guide you in building holiday momentum that will echo into the New Year, reminding you of the beauty of creating joy, one step at a time.

Chapter 18: First Quarter - Taking Action for the Festivities

The First Quarter Moon, halfway between the New Moon and the Full Moon, is a time of decisive action, forward momentum, and overcoming obstacles. As the Moon reaches its half-lit phase, it symbolizes a moment of clarity and determination, encouraging us to actively pursue our goals. During the holiday season, the First Quarter phase represents a period of energetic engagement, when we transform our holiday intentions and preparations into concrete action. This chapter explores how to harness the energy of the First Quarter Moon to take meaningful steps toward creating a joyful, fulfilling, and festive Christmas experience.

In the First Quarter phase, the Moon's light increases, signaling growth and resilience. This phase often brings challenges or moments of resistance, testing our commitment to our goals and providing us with an opportunity to demonstrate our dedication. During Christmas, these moments of action and perseverance align with the holiday spirit of generosity, preparation, and celebration, encouraging us to embrace the season fully. By channeling the First Quarter's energy, we can approach our holiday plans with enthusiasm, focus, and a willingness to bring joy into our lives and the lives of others.

The Meaning of the First Quarter Moon

The First Quarter Moon represents a critical turning point in the lunar cycle. As the Moon's light grows, so does the need for active participation in manifesting our intentions. Unlike the introspective phases of the New Moon and Waxing Crescent, the First Quarter is about tangible action and progress. It's a time when obstacles may arise, prompting us to make decisions, overcome challenges, and remain committed to our goals.

In the context of the lunar cycle, the First Quarter is like the "action phase" of a project, where initial ideas and plans are tested in real time. This phase often brings up hidden issues or resistance, offering an opportunity to confront and resolve them. It's a time to take risks, make adjustments, and move forward with confidence, trusting in the process and the momentum we've built. By taking action now, we ensure that our efforts will lead to greater fulfillment as we approach the culmination of the Full Moon.

During the holiday season, the First Quarter Moon aligns with the bustling preparations, excitement, and social interactions that are often part of Christmas. Whether it's finalizing holiday plans, organizing gatherings, or making meaningful purchases, the First Quarter encourages us to put our intentions into action and fully engage with the festivities.

Taking Bold Steps for a Memorable Holiday Season

The First Quarter Moon is a time to turn holiday ideas into reality. As the phase of dynamic action, it encourages us to commit to our holiday plans, overcome any lingering hesitations, and move forward with enthusiasm. Here are ways to take bold, intentional steps toward creating a holiday season filled with joy and purpose:

1. **Finalize Your Holiday Plans**: Now is the time to put the finishing touches on holiday plans. Whether it's deciding on a holiday menu, scheduling gatherings, or planning gift exchanges, make your decisions with clarity and confidence. Avoid overthinking; instead, commit to a direction and follow through. The energy of the First Quarter supports decisive action, helping you move forward with ease.

2. **Tackle Major Holiday Preparations**: The First Quarter is a perfect time for hands-on tasks and projects. Start decorating, wrap gifts, prepare festive meals, or engage in holiday crafts. These activities bring your holiday vision to life and help set the festive atmosphere. This is the time to take pride in your preparations, knowing that each action contributes to the joy of the holiday season.

3. **Overcome Challenges with Flexibility**: In the First Quarter phase, challenges are natural, as they test our commitment and resilience. If plans don't go as expected or obstacles arise, stay flexible and find creative solutions. Embrace any changes as part of the process, adapting as needed to ensure a joyful holiday experience. Remember that overcoming these small challenges adds to the holiday's meaning and helps you stay focused on what truly matters.

4. **Involve Family and Friends**: The holiday season is about connection, and the First Quarter Moon's energy encourages collaborative efforts. Invite loved ones to help with preparations, whether it's decorating, cooking, or organizing events. Working together creates shared memories, strengthens bonds, and ensures that the holiday season is a collective celebration. If certain tasks feel overwhelming, asking for help can be both practical and heartwarming.

5. **Engage in Holiday Acts of Kindness**: The First Quarter is about taking positive action, making it an ideal time to spread joy through small acts of kindness. Consider giving back to the community, volunteering, or performing a random act of kindness for someone in need. This can range from donating to a charity, preparing care packages, or simply offering a kind gesture to a stranger. These actions embody the spirit of Christmas and align with the First Quarter's theme of outward-focused, purposeful activity.

Staying Focused and Overcoming Holiday Challenges

The First Quarter phase often brings challenges that test our commitment. During the holiday season, this can manifest as seasonal stress, last-minute changes, or feelings of overwhelm as we juggle responsibilities. However, by staying focused and grounded, we can navigate these challenges with grace, transforming potential stressors into opportunities for growth and connection.

1. **Prioritize What Truly Matters**: During the holidays, it's easy to feel pressured by expectations or caught up in the busyness of the season. Take a step back and consider what truly matters to you. Focus on activities, relationships, and traditions that bring joy and meaning to your life. Let go of tasks or obligations that feel burdensome or do not align with your holiday intentions.

2. **Practice Mindfulness and Gratitude**: Staying mindful during the holiday season can help you remain present and connected to the joy of each moment. Take a few minutes each day to pause, breathe deeply, and reflect on what you're grateful for. This simple practice can keep you centered, allowing you to approach holiday activities with a calm and open heart.

3. **Set Boundaries with Holiday Commitments**: While the First Quarter Moon encourages action, it's essential to balance productivity with self-care. Set boundaries around commitments that may lead to burnout. Allow yourself to say "no" when necessary, protecting your energy so you can focus on what truly matters. The holiday season is about enjoyment and connection, so honor your own needs as you engage with the festivities.

4. **Maintain a Flexible Attitude**: Holiday plans can sometimes change unexpectedly, and this phase may bring adjustments or last-minute decisions. Embrace flexibility, understanding that shifts in plans are natural. Maintaining a lighthearted and adaptable attitude can help you navigate these changes, ensuring that you remain open to the beauty of the season.

5. **Remember to Have Fun**: The First Quarter Moon is not just about tasks; it's about joy and taking bold steps toward what makes you happy. Engage in activities that make you feel connected to the holiday spirit, whether that's listening to Christmas music, watching holiday movies, or spending time with loved ones. The energy of action includes celebration, so allow yourself to have fun as you build holiday momentum.

Rituals and Practices for the First Quarter Holiday Season

Incorporating rituals and practices during the First Quarter Moon can help you stay aligned with the holiday season's spirit, supporting your intentions with purposeful action. These practices can bring mindfulness and meaning to your holiday preparations, creating a season that is as fulfilling as it is festive.

1. **Create a Holiday Action Plan**: Write down specific holiday tasks and goals, including deadlines and priorities. Breaking down each goal into manageable steps can make it easier to focus and avoid feeling overwhelmed. Keep your action plan visible as a reminder of your intentions and progress, celebrating each task you complete.

2. **Hold a Family or Friend Gathering Ceremony**: During the First Quarter Moon, bring together friends or family members to set collective intentions for the holiday season. Share your goals, reflect on favorite traditions, and discuss how you can support each other's holiday plans. This ceremony can deepen connections and create a sense of unity and shared purpose.

3. **Perform a Candle-Lighting Ritual**: The First Quarter Moon is a time of illumination and growth. Light a candle to symbolize your holiday intentions, visualizing each flame as a representation of the joy, love, and warmth you wish to bring into your holiday experience. Consider lighting a candle for each intention or goal, creating a small altar of light and positivity.

4. **Write Down Holiday Affirmations**: Affirmations are powerful tools for staying focused and grounded. Write down affirmations that resonate with your holiday intentions, such as "I am creating a joyful and meaningful holiday season" or "I am present and grateful for each moment." Recite these affirmations daily to reinforce your mindset and stay connected to your holiday goals.

5. **Create a Gratitude Garland or Tree**: Set up a holiday garland or tree where family members can add notes of gratitude. Each day or week, write down something you're thankful for and hang it on the garland or place it on the tree. By the end of the season, you'll have a beautiful display of gratitude that reflects the spirit of Christmas and the growth of the First Quarter Moon.

Aligning with the First Quarter's Energy for a Joyful Holiday Season

The First Quarter Moon during Christmas invites us to take purposeful, inspired action, building momentum and excitement for the holiday season. By actively engaging in holiday preparations and embracing the spirit of giving and joy, we can create a season that feels vibrant, meaningful, and aligned with our intentions.

1. **Embrace Boldness in Holiday Plans**: The First Quarter is a time for courage and confidence. Approach your holiday plans with an open mind, ready to try new activities, connect with others, and explore fresh traditions. Embracing boldness can add a sense of adventure to the season, enriching your experience and creating lasting memories.
2. **Celebrate Progress**: Each action you take, whether big or small, is a step toward realizing your holiday vision. Take time to celebrate your progress, appreciating the joy that each accomplishment brings. Recognize that each effort, no matter how small, contributes to a meaningful holiday season.
3. **Stay Connected to the Spirit of Giving**: The First Quarter Moon encourages outward-focused energy, making it an ideal time to practice generosity and kindness. Reach out to friends, family, or your community, finding ways to share the holiday spirit through acts of kindness. Giving back during the holiday season is a powerful way to connect with the values of Christmas and make a positive impact on others.
4. **Balance Action with Rest**: While the First Quarter phase is about action, balance is key. Make time for relaxation and self-care, ensuring that your holiday preparations don't become overwhelming. When you feel energized and rested, you'll approach the holiday season with more joy and presence.

Final Thoughts: Creating a Festive, Action-Packed Holiday Season

The First Quarter Moon during Christmas is a time of excitement, determination, and joyful action. By aligning with its energy, we can turn holiday intentions into real, tangible experiences, embracing the season with focus, love, and purpose. Each step we take contributes to a memorable, fulfilling holiday season that reflects our deepest desires and intentions.

As you move through this phase, remember that the true beauty of the holidays lies in the connections you create, the joy you share, and the memories you make. With each action, the festive energy of the First Quarter Moon builds, transforming your intentions into a holiday season that is truly magical. Embrace this moment of growth, take bold steps forward, and let the First Quarter guide you into a Christmas filled with warmth, celebration, and boundless joy.

Chapter 19: Full Moon - Peak Energy and Holiday Cheer

The Full Moon, a time of culmination, illumination, and heightened emotions, represents the peak of the lunar cycle's energy. As the Moon reaches its brightest, it casts a powerful light that reveals both accomplishments and insights, encouraging celebration, connection, and gratitude. When a Full Moon aligns with the holiday season, it amplifies the spirit of Christmas, creating a cosmic invitation to celebrate, reflect, and share joy. This chapter explores how to harness the Full Moon's energy for a vibrant, fulfilling, and heart-centered holiday season, embracing both the festive cheer and the opportunity for deep connection and gratitude.

The Full Moon is a moment of fruition, when the intentions set during the New Moon and the efforts made during the Waxing phases come to life. It's a time to appreciate all that has been achieved, while also releasing what no longer serves us. During Christmas, this energy encourages us to immerse ourselves in the festivities, embrace moments of togetherness, and revel in the warmth and love that the season brings. The Full Moon offers us a powerful reminder to appreciate the blessings in our lives and to share our joy with those around us.

The Meaning of the Full Moon

The Full Moon is a phase of illumination, representing a peak in the lunar cycle where the Moon is fully visible and at its most radiant. This phase brings clarity, revelation, and heightened emotions, acting as a mirror that reflects back our progress, intentions, and relationships. In astrology, the Full Moon is often seen as a time of balance, as the Sun and Moon stand in opposition, creating a harmony between our inner and outer worlds. It's a time for celebration and expression, as well as introspection and release.

The Full Moon also has a profound spiritual significance, symbolizing the completion of a cycle and the fulfillment of intentions. This is the time to acknowledge our achievements, honor our growth, and release any lingering negativity. The energy of the Full Moon encourages us to celebrate life, find joy in connection, and honor our journey. During Christmas, these themes align beautifully with the spirit of the holiday, as we gather with loved ones, reflect on the year, and embrace the blessings of togetherness.

\Celebrating the Holidays with Full Moon Energy

The Full Moon during Christmas is an invitation to embrace the holiday season in all its fullness, encouraging us to dive into the celebrations with open hearts and open minds. It's a time for expressing gratitude, spreading joy, and appreciating the connections we have with others. Here are some ways to celebrate the holiday season with the peak energy of the Full Moon:

1. **Host a Full Moon Gathering**: The Full Moon's energy is ideal for socializing and connecting with others. Consider hosting a holiday gathering with friends or family under the light of the Full Moon. Whether it's an evening of storytelling, sharing a festive meal, or singing holiday songs, a Full Moon gathering is a chance to celebrate joy and connection with loved ones. Include activities like expressing gratitude, sharing memories from the year, or setting intentions for the coming one.

2. **Express Gratitude for the Year's Blessings**: The Full Moon is a time for gratitude, a moment to appreciate what has come to fruition. During Christmas, take a moment to reflect on the blessings, accomplishments, and experiences that have enriched your year. Write down what you're grateful for, and if you're with loved ones, consider sharing your gratitude out loud. Expressing gratitude helps deepen the holiday's meaning, reinforcing a sense of connection and appreciation.

3. **Embrace the Festive Spirit Fully**: The Full Moon is a phase of abundance, a time to celebrate without holding back. During Christmas, let yourself immerse fully in the holiday spirit. Decorate your home, wear festive clothing, play holiday music, and engage in traditions that bring you joy. This is the time to celebrate life's beauty and share your joy with others. By embracing the festive spirit, you align with the Full Moon's energy of fullness, radiance, and connection.

4. **Exchange Heartfelt Gifts**: The Full Moon encourages generosity and giving from the heart. During the holiday season, choose gifts that hold meaning, whether handmade or thoughtfully chosen, and exchange them with loved ones in a spirit of gratitude and joy. Let each gift be a symbol of your appreciation and connection, reinforcing the bonds you share with those around you. When you give from the heart, you align with the Full Moon's energy of abundance and love.

5. **Practice Self-Compassion and Self-Care**: The Full Moon often heightens emotions, making it essential to practice self-compassion and self-care. During the holiday season, honor your needs and take time for yourself amid the celebrations. Engage in a relaxing activity, such as taking a walk, meditating, or enjoying a warm bath, to center yourself and maintain inner balance. By nurturing yourself, you can fully embrace the joy and connections of the holiday season with an open heart.

Embracing Holiday Reflection and Release with the Full Moon
While the Full Moon is a time of celebration, it's also a moment for release, as it illuminates aspects of our lives that may no longer serve us. During the holiday season, this process of release can be especially meaningful, helping us let go of any lingering emotions, stresses, or patterns as we prepare for a new year. Embracing both reflection and release during this phase allows us to move forward with clarity and an open heart.

1. **Reflect on Personal Growth**: The Full Moon is a time to honor our journey, celebrating the growth and lessons we've gained throughout the year. Take a moment to reflect on how you've grown, what you've learned, and the challenges you've overcome. Acknowledge your progress with kindness, appreciating your resilience and the strength you've developed. Reflecting on personal growth adds depth to the holiday season, grounding it in the appreciation of your own journey.

2. **Release Lingering Tensions**: The Full Moon's energy encourages us to release negativity and make peace with the past. During the holiday season, this can involve forgiving any misunderstandings or tensions that may have arisen during the year, whether with family, friends, or within yourself. Use this moment to let go of any stress or negative emotions, allowing yourself to move forward with a clear and open heart.

3. **Perform a Full Moon Release Ritual**: To mark the completion of the lunar cycle, consider performing a release ritual. Write down any thoughts, beliefs, or habits you wish to release, then safely burn or bury the paper as a symbolic act of letting go. As you do so, visualize yourself releasing these energies, making space for peace, joy, and positivity. This ritual aligns with the Full Moon's theme of release, creating space for new beginnings and growth.

4. **Focus on Intuitive Insights**: The Full Moon is a time of heightened intuition, providing clarity and insight. Listen to any intuitive feelings or thoughts that arise, trusting your inner wisdom as you navigate the holiday season. You might find that certain realizations come to light, offering guidance for the new year or helping you see relationships or experiences in a new light. These insights can help shape your holiday season, bringing depth and meaning to your celebrations.

Rituals and Practices for a Full Moon Holiday Celebration

Incorporating Full Moon rituals into your holiday season can help you stay aligned with the energy of abundance, joy, and gratitude, enhancing your connection to the season's spirit. Here are some rituals and practices to embrace during a Full Moon Christmas:

1. **Create a Full Moon Gratitude Circle**: Gather friends or family members in a circle to share what they're grateful for from the past year. Each person can take turns expressing gratitude, creating a shared space of appreciation. This practice deepens the connections within the group and amplifies the energy of gratitude, aligning beautifully with both the Full Moon and Christmas.

2. **Prepare a Festive Full Moon Feast**: The Full Moon is a time of abundance, and sharing a special meal can embody the spirit of celebration. Prepare a festive meal with loved ones, using seasonal ingredients and traditional holiday dishes. As you gather around the table, take a moment to offer gratitude for the food, the hands that prepared it, and the joy of sharing a meal with others. This feast becomes a symbol of love, abundance, and the beauty of togetherness.

3. **Charge Crystals or Personal Objects**: The Full Moon's energy is ideal for charging crystals or meaningful objects, such as jewelry, keepsakes, or holiday ornaments. Place these items in the moonlight overnight, allowing them to absorb the Full Moon's energy. These charged items can serve as reminders of your intentions and the joyful energy of the season, carrying the Full Moon's radiance into the new year.

4. **Write a Holiday Reflection Letter**: Write a letter to yourself reflecting on the year, expressing gratitude for your growth, experiences, and any challenges you've faced. Include words of encouragement and love, acknowledging the strength and wisdom you've gained. Seal the letter and set it aside to revisit next year, creating a tradition of self-reflection and appreciation.

5. **Create a Moonlit Holiday Altar**: An altar dedicated to the Full Moon and the holiday season can serve as a focal point for your intentions and celebrations. Include items that represent abundance, joy, and gratitude, such as candles, crystals, holiday ornaments, and photos of loved ones. This altar becomes a sacred space where you can reflect, set intentions, and connect with the season's spirit.

Aligning with the Full Moon's Energy for a Joyful Holiday Season

The Full Moon during Christmas is a potent reminder of life's beauty, inviting us to celebrate with open hearts, deepen connections, and honor our journey. By embracing the Full Moon's energy, we can enhance our holiday experience, creating memories and bonds that resonate deeply.

1. **Celebrate Your Achievements**: Acknowledge the progress you've made over the year, celebrating your accomplishments and growth. Each step you've taken, whether big or small, has led you to this moment. Recognizing your achievements aligns with the Full Moon's energy of abundance, helping you approach the new year with confidence and pride.
2. **Foster Deeper Connections**: The Full Moon is a time for open-hearted connections, making it ideal for deepening relationships with loved ones. Spend quality time with family and friends, engaging in meaningful conversations, sharing memories, and expressing love. By focusing on the people who matter most, you enrich the holiday season with warmth and compassion.
3. **Embrace the Magic of the Moment**: The Full Moon and Christmas are both times of wonder and magic. Allow yourself to be fully present in each moment, savoring the beauty and joy of the holiday season. Whether you're watching holiday lights, enjoying a festive meal, or sharing a laugh with loved ones, let each experience fill your heart with happiness.
4. **Set Intentions for the Coming Year**: As the Full Moon marks the culmination of the lunar cycle, it's also a time for setting intentions for the future. Reflect on your dreams and goals for the new year, considering how you can carry forward the joy, love, and gratitude of the holiday season. Setting these intentions under the Full Moon adds an extra layer of energy, helping you manifest a fulfilling and purposeful year ahead.

Final Thoughts: A Full Moon Christmas of Joy, Love, and Illumination

The Full Moon during Christmas is a gift of light, joy, and deep connection, inviting us to celebrate life in all its fullness. By aligning with its energy, we embrace the holiday season as a time of abundance, reflection, and gratitude, creating a Christmas filled with meaning and wonder.

As you celebrate under the Full Moon's light, let yourself be fully present, honoring the journey that has led you here. With each gathering, each act of giving, and each moment of joy, you create a season that reflects the beauty of life itself. Embrace this moment of peak energy and holiday cheer, letting the Full Moon guide you into a Christmas season that shines with love, fulfillment, and boundless gratitude.

Chapter 20: Waning Moon - Reflection and Post-Holiday Calm

The Waning Moon, the phase that follows the Full Moon, represents a period of introspection, release, and winding down. As the Moon's light gradually fades, it encourages us to slow down, reflect on recent experiences, and prepare to let go of what no longer serves us. In the days following the holiday season, this phase aligns perfectly with the natural desire to rest, unwind, and gain perspective on the festivities. This chapter explores the energy of the Waning Moon and how we can harness it for post-holiday reflection, self-care, and renewal, honoring both the joyful memories and the lessons we've gathered.

The Waning Moon's gentle energy supports us in transitioning from the peak excitement of the holidays to a quieter, more contemplative space. During this phase, we are encouraged to reflect on the experiences, connections, and insights of the season, allowing ourselves to embrace both gratitude and closure. As we ease into the new year, the Waning Moon offers a valuable opportunity to release any lingering holiday stress or expectations, finding balance and calm after a season of celebration.

The Meaning of the Waning Moon

The Waning Moon marks the second half of the lunar cycle, moving from the illumination of the Full Moon to the darkness of the New Moon. This phase symbolizes a time of reflection, closure, and release, when we are called to let go of what no longer aligns with our goals or well-being. In astrology and spirituality, the Waning Moon is seen as a period for healing and introspection, inviting us to slow down, conserve our energy, and focus inward.

As the Moon's light wanes, it encourages us to gently withdraw from the outer world, seeking peace and renewal within. This is an ideal time for self-care, contemplation, and finishing any lingering tasks from the previous cycle. In the days following the holiday season, the Waning Moon helps us transition from the excitement of celebration to a more grounded, reflective state. By embracing its energy, we can honor our holiday experiences, release any residual stress, and prepare ourselves for the new beginnings to come.

Reflecting on the Holiday Season with the Waning Moon

The Waning Moon is an ideal time to look back on the holiday season, appreciating its joys and learning from its challenges. Reflection during this phase allows us to fully integrate the experiences of the holidays, recognizing what brought us happiness, connection, and fulfillment. By taking a moment to reflect, we can preserve the positive memories of the season while letting go of any stress or unmet expectations.

1. **Review Holiday Memories**: Look back on the holiday season with gratitude, recalling the special moments, gatherings, and acts of kindness that brought you joy. Whether it was a family tradition, a meaningful gift exchange, or a quiet evening of connection, cherish the experiences that made the season memorable. Consider keeping a holiday journal where you write down highlights, favorite memories, and anything that brought you happiness.

2. **Acknowledge Personal Growth**: The holiday season often brings insights and growth, as we navigate relationships, manage responsibilities, and set intentions. Reflect on any lessons you learned, whether they were related to patience, generosity, resilience, or communication. Acknowledge the ways in which you grew or overcame challenges, appreciating your progress as part of your journey.

3. **Practice Gratitude for Connections**: The holidays are a time for connection, and the Waning Moon encourages us to honor and appreciate the relationships in our lives. Reflect on the moments of connection you shared with loved ones, whether through conversations, shared meals, or acts of giving. Take a moment to express gratitude for these connections, recognizing the love and support that enriches your life.

4. **Identify Areas for Change or Growth**: While reflecting on the season, consider any areas that may need adjustment in the future. Perhaps there were moments of stress or expectations that felt overwhelming, or maybe certain traditions no longer align with your values. The Waning Moon encourages gentle introspection, allowing you to identify ways to create a more balanced, joyful holiday experience in the future.

Embracing Post-Holiday Calm and Release

As the Waning Moon encourages us to wind down, it's an ideal time to let go of any residual holiday stress, unmet expectations, or lingering pressures. The holiday season can be demanding, and this phase provides a space for release, allowing us to create peace and closure as we transition into the new year.

1. **Release Holiday Expectations**: The holidays often come with expectations, whether related to family dynamics, gift-giving, or personal goals. Use the Waning Moon's energy to release any lingering expectations, letting go of any guilt, disappointment, or perfectionism. Remind yourself that the holidays are about connection and joy, and embrace a sense of peace with what was.

2. **Declutter and Organize**: The Waning Moon is a time for clearing out, making it an excellent opportunity to tidy up after the holidays. Consider decluttering your home, putting away holiday decorations, or donating items that no longer serve a purpose. This physical clearing aligns with the Waning Moon's theme of release, helping you create a sense of order and calm in your environment.

3. **Engage in a Gentle Release Ritual**: A simple release ritual can help you let go of any lingering stress or emotions. Write down anything you wish to release from the holiday season, whether it's stress, disappointment, or any specific tension. Then, burn the paper in a fireproof bowl or tear it into small pieces, visualizing yourself letting go of these energies. This ritual creates a symbolic closure, helping you move forward with clarity and lightness.

4. **Practice Restorative Self-Care**: The Waning Moon is a time for self-care and relaxation. Embrace activities that restore your energy, such as meditation, gentle yoga, a warm bath, or simply spending quiet time in nature. Focus on self-care practices that help you feel grounded and centered, honoring your body's need to recharge after the holidays.

5. **Reflect on Intentions for the New Year**: While the Waning Moon is more about release than setting intentions, it's still an ideal time to think about your hopes for the coming year. Reflect on what you wish to bring into your life, considering ways to integrate the lessons and joys of the holiday season. As the New Moon approaches, you can prepare yourself to set fresh intentions with a clear mind and an open heart.

Cultivating Inner Peace and Balance After the Festivities

After the excitement of the holiday season, the Waning Moon encourages us to find balance and cultivate inner peace. This phase offers an invitation to slow down, reconnect with ourselves, and embrace a quieter, more centered state. Embracing the calm of the Waning Moon allows us to create a sense of grounding and contentment as we transition into the new year.

1. **Practice Mindful Breathing**: A simple but effective way to cultivate inner peace is through mindful breathing. Take a few minutes each day to sit quietly, close your eyes, and focus on your breath. With each exhale, imagine releasing any remaining holiday stress, allowing yourself to feel lighter and more grounded. Mindful breathing can bring a sense of calm and clarity, especially during the reflective Waning Moon.

2. **Journal for Emotional Release**: Journaling is a powerful tool for reflection and release. Take some time to write freely about your holiday experience, acknowledging any emotions that arise. Whether it's joy, gratitude, or stress, allowing yourself to express these feelings on paper can help you process and release them. Use this journaling practice to clarify your thoughts, gain insights, and embrace emotional clarity.

3. **Spend Time in Nature**: Nature has a grounding effect, helping us reconnect with the earth's rhythms and find peace within ourselves. During the Waning Moon, take a walk in a natural setting, such as a park, forest, or beach, allowing yourself to unwind in the beauty of your surroundings. Nature provides a soothing backdrop for reflection, helping you let go of tension and find harmony after the holiday season.

4. **Reconnect with Daily Routines**: The holiday season often brings changes in routines, and the Waning Moon is an ideal time to return to a sense of regularity. Reestablishing simple daily routines, such as morning meditation, exercise, or meal preparation, can help you feel more grounded and balanced. These routines provide stability, allowing you to move forward with a sense of calm and order.

5. **Practice Gratitude Meditation**: Gratitude helps us appreciate the beauty of life, even in moments of rest and reflection. Consider incorporating a gratitude meditation into your routine, where you focus on the blessings of the holiday season and the people who bring joy to your life. This meditation can be as simple as closing your eyes, taking a few deep breaths, and mentally listing things you're grateful for. Gratitude aligns perfectly with the Waning Moon's gentle energy, creating a peaceful space for reflection.

Rituals and Practices for Waning Moon Reflection

Rituals during the Waning Moon can help you align with its energy of release, calm, and introspection. These practices encourage reflection, closure, and the embracing of inner peace as the holiday season comes to a close.

1. **Create a Post-Holiday Reflection Journal**: Set aside a journal dedicated to post-holiday reflection. Write down highlights, lessons learned, and any insights gained during the season. This journal can serve as a source of inspiration and wisdom, reminding you of the joys and growth experienced during the holidays. Use it as a tool to release any lingering emotions and gain perspective on your journey.

2. **Hold a Letting-Go Ceremony**: Gather loved ones for a simple letting-go ceremony, where each person has the opportunity to reflect on the holiday season and release any lingering stress or tension. You can light a candle, meditate together, or share intentions for the new year. This ceremony provides a gentle space for closure and collective reflection, honoring the season's journey.

3. **Practice Yin Yoga for Release**: Yin yoga, a slow and meditative form of yoga, is ideal for the Waning Moon's energy of release. This practice involves holding poses for an extended period, encouraging deep relaxation and letting go. Yin yoga helps release physical tension and emotional stress, aligning perfectly with the Waning Moon's call for introspection and rest.

4. **Use Crystals for Calm and Reflection**: Certain crystals, such as amethyst, rose quartz, and clear quartz, promote calm, peace, and clarity. Meditate with these crystals or place them in your environment during the Waning Moon phase. Their soothing energy can support your reflection, helping you process your holiday experiences and embrace a sense of calm and closure.

5. **Create a Restorative Space in Your Home**: Dedicate a small space in your home to rest and relaxation, perhaps by setting up a cozy chair, a few soft blankets, and calming elements like candles or essential oils. This restorative space becomes a sanctuary where you can retreat during the Waning Moon phase, providing a peaceful environment for unwinding and reflecting after the holidays.

Embracing the Waning Moon's Energy for Post-Holiday Renewal

The Waning Moon during the post-holiday period is a reminder to slow down, find peace, and honor the journey of the season. By aligning with its energy, we create space for inner balance, clarity, and renewal, ensuring that we carry forward the season's positive energy without lingering stress or expectations.

1. **Create a Sense of Inner Balance**: As the Waning Moon guides us inward, embrace practices that promote balance in mind, body, and spirit. Engage in calming activities that help you stay grounded, whether through meditation, gentle movement, or creative expression. Inner balance fosters peace, allowing you to move forward with renewed clarity and strength.

2. **Carry Forward the Season's Lessons**: The lessons and joys of the holiday season do not have to end with the festivities. Reflect on what you learned, how you grew, and what brought you happiness. Consider ways to carry these experiences forward into the new year, integrating them into your daily life as sources of inspiration and guidance.

3. **Embrace a Spirit of Letting Go**: The Waning Moon encourages us to release with grace, accepting that not every holiday expectation or plan may have come to fruition. Embrace a spirit of letting go, knowing that each experience holds meaning and that peace comes from acceptance. This release allows you to approach the new year with a sense of freedom and openness.

4. **Prepare for New Beginnings**: As the Waning Moon approaches the New Moon, it signals the end of one cycle and the beginning of another. Embrace this moment as a chance to rest, renew, and prepare for fresh intentions. Reflect on what you hope to manifest in the coming year, setting the stage for new growth and opportunities.

Final Thoughts: A Peaceful Transition with the Waning Moon

The Waning Moon after the holiday season offers a gentle space for reflection, release, and calm. By honoring this phase, we create a meaningful transition from the excitement of the holidays to a more introspective, grounded state, carrying forward both the joys and the lessons of the season.

As you embrace the post-holiday calm, let the Waning Moon's energy guide you in finding peace, balance, and clarity. This time of gentle release allows you to close the year with a grateful heart, making room for the new beginnings that await. Let this phase remind you that rest is an essential part of the journey, bringing both closure and renewal as you move into the next cycle with a peaceful spirit and an open heart.

Part 4: **Celestial Events and Their Festive Influence**

Chapter 21: Christmas Star - Myths and Astrology

The Christmas Star, also known as the Star of Bethlehem, is a symbol steeped in mystery, myth, and celestial wonder. Traditionally associated with the birth of Jesus, the Christmas Star has inspired countless interpretations, from religious and historical accounts to astrological theories and cosmic events. This chapter delves into the origins, myths, and meanings of the Christmas Star, exploring how ancient civilizations interpreted this phenomenon and examining its significance in astrology and modern astronomy. By understanding the Christmas Star through both mythological and astrological lenses, we can gain insight into its enduring allure and its symbolic role as a guiding light during the holiday season.

The idea of a bright star guiding travelers, bringing hope, and illuminating the night sky is central to the Christmas story and speaks to universal themes of wonder, spiritual revelation, and guidance. For astrologers, the Christmas Star represents cosmic alignment, divine timing, and a powerful reminder of humanity's connection to the heavens. By unraveling the legends and potential celestial explanations behind the Christmas Star, we can appreciate its significance as both a historical and symbolic event, one that continues to inspire awe and reflection during the holiday season.

Origins and Myths of the Christmas Star

The Christmas Star originates from the Biblical account of the Nativity, specifically in the Gospel of Matthew. According to Christian tradition, the Star of Bethlehem appeared in the sky, guiding the Magi, or Wise Men, from the East to the birthplace of Jesus. The star was described as unusually bright, capturing the Magi's attention and prompting their journey to honor the new-born king. This celestial event was interpreted as a sign from the heavens, signaling the arrival of a divine being and fulfilling ancient prophecies.

For centuries, theologians, historians, and scientists have debated the nature of the Christmas Star. While some consider it a miraculous sign, others have sought to identify a natural astronomical event that could explain the bright light described in the Nativity story. Ancient civilizations, known for their reverence for the stars, also recognized the appearance of unusual celestial events as symbols of great change or divine intervention, linking them to significant historical moments.

The Christmas Star, regardless of its specific origin, has inspired numerous myths, folklore, and symbolic interpretations across cultures:

1. **Symbol of Divine Guidance**: The Christmas Star is seen as a symbol of divine guidance, believed to be a heavenly sign leading the Wise Men to their destination. This theme of guidance and revelation has since become associated with the star, representing the light that directs us toward truth, purpose, and spiritual awakening.

2. **Fulfillment of Prophecy**: For early Christians, the Christmas Star represented the fulfillment of Old Testament prophecies regarding the birth of a Messiah. The star was viewed as a cosmic confirmation of Jesus's divine nature, providing reassurance that celestial forces aligned to mark the arrival of a savior.

3. **Illumination of Darkness**: Stars have long symbolized hope and illumination, especially during dark times. The Christmas Star's appearance over Bethlehem is seen as a metaphor for light entering the world, a message of peace, love, and new beginnings in the face of hardship or despair.

4. **Symbol of Cosmic Harmony**: For ancient astronomers, the alignment of celestial bodies signified cosmic harmony. The Christmas Star, whether a unique alignment or a rare astronomical event, is seen as a moment when the heavens and Earth aligned, representing balance, unity, and the interconnectedness of all life.

Astrological Perspectives on the Christmas Star

From an astrological perspective, the Christmas Star holds significant meaning, as astrologers have long believed that celestial events influence both individual and collective consciousness. The study of the Christmas Star offers insight into how cosmic alignments shape spiritual narratives, providing an astrological interpretation of the star's symbolism and impact.

1. **Jupiter and Saturn Conjunctions**: One of the most popular astrological theories about the Christmas Star is that it was a rare conjunction of Jupiter and Saturn. When these two powerful planets align closely in the sky, they create a bright "double star" effect, as was observed in December 2020. Jupiter, representing expansion, wisdom, and divine favor, combined with Saturn, symbolizing structure, discipline, and karma, signifies a blending of spiritual and material energy. In ancient astrology, the conjunction of Jupiter and Saturn was often seen as a harbinger of significant social change or the arrival of a great leader. This interpretation aligns with the idea that the Christmas Star symbolized the birth of a figure who would bring profound transformation.

2. **Jupiter and Venus Conjunctions**: Another theory suggests that the Christmas Star may have been a conjunction of Jupiter and Venus, two of the brightest planets in the sky. Venus represents love, beauty, and harmony, while Jupiter amplifies these qualities, creating a powerful celestial display associated with peace, abundance, and unity. A conjunction of these two planets could have appeared as an extraordinarily bright "star," embodying the qualities of love and divine favor. Astrologically, this conjunction would be interpreted as a blessing and a sign of goodwill, aligning well with the Christmas message of peace and joy.

3. **The Role of Regulus**: Some astrologers theorize that the Christmas Star involved Regulus, the brightest star in the constellation Leo, known as the "Heart of the Lion." In astrology, Regulus is associated with royalty, leadership, and courage. A conjunction between Jupiter and Regulus in Leo, combined with a close alignment with other planets, would symbolize the birth of a powerful leader or divine king. This interpretation aligns with the narrative of the Wise Men seeking the "King of the Jews," as Leo is a sign traditionally linked to kingship and divine right.

4. **The Influence of a Comet or Supernova**: Another potential explanation for the Christmas Star is a comet or supernova. While not strictly astrological, these celestial phenomena have significant symbolism. Comets were historically seen as harbingers of change, transformation,

or divine intervention, while supernovas represented the death and rebirth of stars. Both events would have been interpreted as powerful cosmic symbols, seen by ancient astrologers as signs that great shifts were underway on Earth.

5. **The Spiritual Significance of the Star**: Beyond specific planetary alignments, the Christmas Star represents the broader theme of divine timing and cosmic alignment. In astrology, the arrival of significant celestial events is often viewed as divinely timed, meant to bring guidance or facilitate transformation. The Christmas Star, therefore, symbolizes the idea that certain events and individuals are destined to have a profound impact on the world, aligning with the energy and purpose of the cosmos.

Christmas Star in Mythology and Symbolism Across Cultures

The idea of a guiding star or celestial light is a recurring motif in many cultures and mythologies, symbolizing hope, guidance, and the journey toward enlightenment. The Christmas Star, though primarily associated with Christian tradition, resonates with universal themes that appear in other cultural stories and legends.

1. **The North Star (Polaris)**: In many cultures, the North Star, or Polaris, has symbolized guidance and constancy, as it remains fixed in the night sky, guiding travelers and sailors for centuries. The North Star is often seen as a beacon of hope, providing direction for those who feel lost. Its symbolism aligns with the Christmas Star, representing a celestial light that guides us toward a greater purpose.

2. **The Egyptian Star of Isis**: In ancient Egypt, the star Sirius, known as the "Star of Isis," was revered as a symbol of rebirth and renewal. Its annual appearance marked the flooding of the Nile, a time of fertility and prosperity. This "savior star" bears symbolic similarities to the Christmas Star, representing the return of life, hope, and new beginnings.

3. **The Star of the Zoroastrians**: In Zoroastrianism, the birth of a savior figure is foretold by the appearance of a bright star, aligning with the Magi's journey in the Nativity story. The Zoroastrian tradition associates stars with divine messages and guidance, viewing them as symbols of cosmic harmony and prophetic vision. The Zoroastrian star myths likely influenced early Christian interpretations of the Christmas Star.

4. **The Wishing Star in Folklore**: Many cultures have stories of wishing upon a star, believing that the stars grant dreams, blessings, and guidance to those who seek them. The Christmas Star can be seen as a symbol of hope and the fulfillment of dreams, representing the power of faith and intention to bring our desires to life.

5. **Native American Star Symbolism**: For some Native American tribes, stars were seen as ancestors or spiritual guides. The appearance of a bright star was interpreted as a message or a blessing, a sign that the spirits were watching over the people. This connection between stars and guidance aligns with the idea of the Christmas Star as a protective light, guiding humanity toward a higher purpose.

Modern Interpretations and Legacy of the Christmas Star

The Christmas Star's legacy endures as a symbol of faith, hope, and divine guidance. In modern astrology and spirituality, it continues to be celebrated as a reminder of cosmic alignment and spiritual transformation, inspiring those who seek meaning and purpose. Each year, as people gather to celebrate Christmas, the image of the Christmas Star invokes a sense of wonder and encourages reflection on themes of love, unity, and divine purpose.

1. **Guiding Light in Challenging Times**: In times of hardship or uncertainty, the Christmas Star serves as a reminder of hope and resilience. Its symbolism encourages us to look beyond the immediate struggles and seek higher meaning, trusting that guidance and peace are available to those who look within and beyond.

2. **Symbol of Divine Timing**: For astrologers, the Christmas Star represents divine timing, a cosmic alignment that signals the arrival of transformative energies. It reminds us that certain events and encounters are destined, aligning with the greater flow of the universe. This perspective inspires faith in life's timing, trusting that each moment unfolds as it is meant to.

3. **Inspiration for Personal Transformation**: The Christmas Star invites us to embark on our own journey of self-discovery and spiritual growth. Just as the Wise Men followed the star in search of truth, we, too, are encouraged to seek wisdom, connect with our inner guidance, and pursue our highest potential. The Christmas Star's message of seeking light and truth resonates with our own paths of self-discovery.

4. **Celebration of Unity and Connection**: The Christmas Star represents unity, connecting the heavens and Earth, the divine and the human. Its light reminds us of our connection to each other and to the cosmos, inspiring us to find common ground and celebrate the shared humanity that unites us during the holiday season.

Final Thoughts: The Christmas Star as a Symbol of Hope and Cosmic Connection

The Christmas Star, with its rich tapestry of myths, astrology, and spiritual symbolism, stands as a beacon of hope, guiding us through the mysteries of life and the holiday season. Whether seen as a miraculous event, an astronomical phenomenon, or a symbol of divine guidance, the Christmas Star embodies the universal themes of love, unity, and spiritual awakening.

This Christmas, let the message of the Christmas Star inspire you to embrace hope, seek your own path to truth, and trust in the journey. As a symbol of cosmic alignment and divine purpose, the Christmas Star reminds us that we are all connected to a greater whole, bound by light, wonder, and the eternal quest for meaning. Embrace its light as you celebrate the season, finding joy and guidance in the celestial mystery that continues to inspire hearts across the ages.

Chapter 22: Winter Solstice - The Turning of Seasons

The Winter Solstice, the shortest day and longest night of the year, is a moment of profound transition, marking the official start of winter and the gradual return of light. Occurring around December 21st in the Northern Hemisphere, the solstice holds deep cultural, spiritual, and astrological significance, symbolizing rebirth, renewal, and the cyclical nature of life. Celebrated across cultures as a time of reflection, gratitude, and hope, the Winter Solstice invites us to embrace the beauty of darkness while welcoming the promise of light's return. This chapter explores the myths, customs, and astrological insights of the Winter Solstice, examining how this celestial event influences our understanding of transformation, resilience, and the turning of the seasons.

In many traditions, the Winter Solstice is celebrated as a sacred occasion, a time to pause, reflect, and reconnect with nature's cycles. As the day when the Sun appears to stand still before beginning its ascent, the solstice symbolizes a "pause" in the cosmic dance, a time for us to contemplate life's mysteries, honor the past, and set intentions for the future. By understanding the Winter Solstice's rich cultural and astrological meanings, we can deepen our appreciation for its role in the holiday season and its invitation to align with the rhythms of the Earth.

The Meaning of the Winter Solstice

The term "solstice" derives from the Latin words *sol* (sun) and *sistere* (to stand still), referring to the Sun's apparent halt in its southward journey before reversing direction. The Winter Solstice occurs when the Sun reaches its lowest point in the sky, resulting in the shortest day and longest night of the year. This celestial event happens because of Earth's axial tilt, which causes one hemisphere to receive less sunlight during winter, while the opposite hemisphere experiences summer.

Astronomically, the Winter Solstice marks a turning point in the solar cycle. After the solstice, the days gradually grow longer as the Sun begins its journey back toward the equator. This shift from darkness to light has made the solstice a powerful symbol of renewal, hope, and transformation in cultures worldwide. The solstice embodies the idea of rebirth, as life begins to reawaken in the depths of winter, foreshadowing the warmth and abundance of spring.

Spiritually, the Winter Solstice is often associated with the concepts of introspection, inner strength, and resilience. The longest night represents a journey inward, encouraging us to reflect on the past year, release what no longer serves us, and find strength within ourselves. The gradual return of light serves as a reminder of life's cyclical nature, inspiring us to embrace change and renew our faith in the future.

Winter Solstice Myths and Traditions Across Cultures

The Winter Solstice has been celebrated for millennia, with ancient civilizations marking it as a sacred time for rituals, feasts, and festivals. Many of these traditions honor the Sun's return, embodying themes of rebirth, unity, and the triumph of light over darkness. Here are some of the most prominent Winter Solstice myths and customs from cultures around the world:

1. **Yule (Nordic and Celtic)**: Yule, celebrated by ancient Germanic and Celtic tribes, is one of the oldest solstice festivals. During Yule, people gathered to honor the rebirth of the Sun god, symbolized by the lighting of the Yule log, which was burned to bring warmth and dispel darkness. Decorated with holly, ivy, and mistletoe, the Yule log represented protection,

renewal, and the promise of new life. This festival also included feasting, gift-giving, and the use of evergreen trees to symbolize eternal life—a tradition that eventually evolved into the modern Christmas tree.

2. **Dongzhi Festival (China)**: The Dongzhi Festival, celebrated in China, marks the Winter Solstice as a time for family gatherings, honoring ancestors, and enjoying warming foods. Rooted in Taoist and Confucian beliefs, the festival celebrates the balance of yin and yang, with the solstice marking the moment when darkness (yin) reaches its peak before giving way to the light (yang). The festival encourages gratitude, unity, and harmony, as families come together to feast on dishes like tangyuan (rice dumplings), symbolizing reunion and renewal.

3. **Inti Raymi (Inca)**: The Inca civilization celebrated the Winter Solstice with Inti Raymi, the Festival of the Sun, which took place in June (during the Southern Hemisphere's winter). Dedicated to Inti, the Incan Sun god, the festival involved music, dancing, and offerings to honor the Sun's life-giving power. Though Inti Raymi is held during the Southern Hemisphere's solstice, it shares similar themes of reverence for the Sun, renewal, and the restoration of balance.

4. **Shab-e Yalda (Persia)**: Shab-e Yalda, or Yalda Night, is an Iranian festival celebrated on the longest night of the year. This ancient Persian tradition involves gathering with family, sharing stories, and reading poetry, particularly the works of Hafez. Yalda, which means "birth," honors the triumph of light over darkness as people wait for the dawn, symbolizing the rebirth of the Sun and the victory of good over evil. Pomegranates, nuts, and watermelon are commonly enjoyed, representing prosperity, protection, and life.

5. **Saturnalia (Rome)**: Saturnalia, an ancient Roman festival, was held in honor of Saturn, the god of agriculture. During Saturnalia, social norms were relaxed, and roles were reversed, with masters serving their slaves and people exchanging gifts. The festival, which lasted for several days around the Winter Solstice, was a time of feasting, merriment, and generosity, embodying themes of renewal, abundance, and equality. Saturnalia's customs of gift-giving and celebration influenced modern Christmas traditions.

6. **Amaterasu and the Cave (Japan)**: In Japanese mythology, the goddess Amaterasu, the deity of the Sun, retreats into a cave after a quarrel, plunging the world into darkness. The gods attempt to coax her out, and eventually, Amaterasu is lured by laughter and merriment, emerging from the cave to restore light to the world. This myth, though not a direct Winter Solstice celebration, parallels the solstice theme of darkness giving way to light and the return of joy and warmth.

Astrological Significance of the Winter Solstice

In astrology, the Winter Solstice occurs when the Sun enters Capricorn, a sign associated with discipline, structure, and resilience. Capricorn, ruled by Saturn, embodies the energy of endurance and groundedness, qualities essential for navigating winter's challenges and preparing for the future. The Sun's journey into Capricorn marks the start of a new astrological season, encouraging us to set practical goals, assess our achievements, and cultivate inner strength.

The Winter Solstice is also a time when the Sun is at its farthest point from the celestial equator, symbolizing the duality between light and dark, life and death. This cosmic alignment encourages us to examine our own lives, honoring both our shadows and our light. Astrologically, the solstice represents a point of introspection and self-discovery, a time to evaluate our paths, release the past, and prepare for a new cycle of growth.

Celebrating the Winter Solstice: Rituals and Reflections

Celebrating the Winter Solstice offers an opportunity to honor nature's cycles, embrace stillness, and set intentions for the year ahead. The following rituals and practices can help us align with the solstice energy, bringing a sense of peace, renewal, and inner clarity.

1. **Reflect on the Past Year**: The Winter Solstice is a time to pause and reflect on the journey of the past year. Take a moment to consider the experiences, lessons, and achievements that have shaped you. Journal about your growth, challenges, and moments of joy, acknowledging both the light and darkness within your journey. This reflection creates a foundation of gratitude and understanding as you prepare to move forward.

2. **Set Intentions for the New Year**: As the Sun begins its journey back toward longer days, the solstice is an ideal time to set intentions. Write down your goals for the coming year, focusing on what you wish to bring into your life. Consider intentions that align with Capricorn's energy of discipline and resilience, such as cultivating healthy habits, committing to personal growth, or working toward long-term goals. These intentions help you plant seeds for the year ahead.

3. **Light Candles or a Yule Log**: Lighting candles or a Yule log is a traditional way to honor the return of the Sun. As you light the candles or log, reflect on the light's symbolism, representing hope, renewal, and warmth. Let this light fill you with a sense of optimism and purpose, illuminating your path as you move into the new year.

4. **Meditate on Balance and Renewal**: Meditation is a powerful way to connect with the Winter Solstice's energy of balance and introspection. Consider a meditation focused on the themes of balance, imagining yourself finding harmony between light and dark, action and rest, giving and receiving. Visualize yourself releasing old energies and welcoming a sense of renewal, allowing the solstice's energy to bring peace and clarity.

5. **Create a Nature Altar**: The Winter Solstice is a time to reconnect with nature, so consider creating an altar with natural elements like pinecones, evergreen branches, stones, and winter fruits. Each item on your altar can represent an aspect of the season—strength, resilience, growth, or beauty. Spend time at this altar as a reminder of your connection to the Earth and its cycles, honoring the wisdom and beauty of winter.

6. **Gather for a Solstice Feast**: Sharing a meal with loved ones is a traditional way to celebrate the solstice. Prepare a meal with seasonal ingredients like root vegetables, grains, and winter fruits, and share it in a spirit of gratitude. During the meal, take turns expressing what you're grateful for or your hopes for the coming year. This gathering celebrates the bonds of community, warmth, and abundance even in the heart of winter.

7. **Release Ceremony for Letting Go**: The solstice is an ideal time for letting go of the past. Write down any habits, beliefs, or memories you wish to release, then perform a release ceremony by safely burning or burying the paper. As you release these old energies, imagine making space for new growth and experiences in your life, aligning with the solstice theme of renewal.

Embracing the Spiritual Lessons of the Winter Solstice

The Winter Solstice is more than an astronomical event; it holds profound spiritual lessons that encourage us to honor the cycles of life, embrace stillness, and find strength within. By attuning to these lessons, we can deepen our understanding of the season's beauty and its influence on our personal growth.

1. **The Power of Darkness and Inner Reflection**: The longest night of the year reminds us of the value of darkness, both external and internal. Just as plants grow roots in the dark soil, we, too, develop resilience, wisdom, and self-awareness in times of introspection. The Winter Solstice teaches us to embrace the stillness of winter as a time for inner growth and self-discovery.

2. **Rebirth and Renewal**: The Sun's return symbolizes rebirth, showing us that every cycle of darkness is followed by light. This lesson of renewal encourages us to trust life's rhythms, knowing that difficult times will give way to new beginnings. The solstice invites us to let go of what no longer serves us and to welcome change with an open heart.

3. **Finding Balance in Nature's Cycles**: The solstice embodies the balance of light and dark, reminding us to seek harmony within ourselves and our lives. This balance encourages us to honor both activity and rest, giving and receiving, strength and vulnerability. By embracing balance, we align with the wisdom of nature, finding peace and resilience in life's natural rhythms.

4. **Gratitude for Life's Abundance**: The Winter Solstice, a time of scarcity and simplicity, teaches us to appreciate the abundance we do have. In the darkness of winter, we are reminded to cherish the warmth of loved ones, the beauty of nature, and the small blessings of daily life. This gratitude deepens our connection to the world, helping us approach the new year with a grateful and open heart.

Final Thoughts: The Winter Solstice as a Beacon of Hope and Renewal

The Winter Solstice, with its themes of darkness, light, and rebirth, offers a moment of quiet beauty and profound reflection. By aligning with its energy, we embrace the lessons of resilience, gratitude, and renewal, allowing this turning point in the seasons to inspire us as we enter the new year.

As you celebrate the Winter Solstice, let it be a reminder of the beauty of stillness, the strength found in inner reflection, and the promise of light's return. This solstice, honor the darkness and welcome the dawn, finding peace in the cycles that shape our lives and strength in the journey that lies ahead.

Chapter 23: Constellations Visible During the Holidays

The winter night sky offers some of the most stunning and recognizable constellations, as the cold, clear air allows the stars to shine brightly against the dark backdrop. For centuries, people have looked to these constellations for navigation, storytelling, and inspiration, finding guidance and wonder in their celestial patterns. During the holiday season, constellations like Orion, Taurus, Gemini, and Perseus dominate the sky, each with its own rich mythology and symbolic meaning. In this chapter, we'll explore the constellations visible during the holidays, their legends, and their significance, providing insights into the mysteries and magic of the winter night sky.

Winter constellations not only offer a spectacular visual display but also serve as symbols of resilience, strength, and adventure—qualities that align beautifully with the themes of the holiday season. By understanding the stories and science behind these constellations, we can deepen our appreciation of the winter sky and the timeless wonder of the stars that have inspired countless generations.

1. Orion the Hunter

Orion, one of the most recognizable and beloved constellations, dominates the winter sky with its iconic "belt" of three stars. Located near the celestial equator, Orion is visible from almost every part of the world, making it a prominent feature of the holiday night sky. According to Greek mythology, Orion was a great hunter, and his constellation tells stories of adventure, strength, and pursuit.

- **Mythology**: Orion was a mighty hunter, famed for his strength and skill. Different myths surround his death—some say he was killed by a scorpion sent by the goddess Artemis, while others suggest he was slain by the Earth goddess Gaia. After his death, Orion was placed in the sky as a constellation, forever pursuing his prey, represented by the nearby constellations Taurus the Bull and Lepus the Hare.
- **Key Stars**: Orion's most notable stars include **Betelgeuse**, a red supergiant that forms his shoulder, and **Rigel**, a bright blue-white supergiant marking his foot. **Bellatrix**, another star in Orion's shoulder, and the three stars of Orion's Belt—**Alnitak, Alnilam,** and **Mintaka**—are also prominent features that make this constellation easy to identify.
- **Notable Objects**: Orion contains one of the most famous deep-sky objects, the **Orion Nebula** (M42), a vast stellar nursery where new stars are born. This nebula is visible to the naked eye and appears as a faint, misty patch below Orion's Belt, making it a highlight for stargazers during the holiday season.
- **Symbolism**: Orion's resilience, strength, and quest for adventure reflect the spirit of winter, a season of perseverance and wonder. His story of endless pursuit and bravery offers inspiration, reminding us of the beauty in exploration, curiosity, and facing challenges head-on.

2. Taurus the Bull

Taurus, a zodiac constellation, is visible just above Orion and can be identified by its bright star, Aldebaran. Representing the Bull, Taurus is associated with themes of strength, fertility, and stability, and it has been revered in cultures around the world as a symbol of power and endurance.

- **Mythology**: In Greek mythology, Taurus is linked to the story of Zeus, who transformed himself into a bull to carry off Europa, a Phoenician princess. Taurus has also been seen as representing the Cretan Bull, a powerful creature captured by the hero Heracles in one of his twelve labors. Taurus was an important constellation for many ancient cultures, including the Egyptians and Mesopotamians, symbolizing the power and life-giving force of the bull.
- **Key Stars**: **Aldebaran**, a red giant, is the brightest star in Taurus and marks the bull's "eye." Near Aldebaran is the **Hyades** star cluster, which forms a V-shape representing the bull's face. Another notable feature in Taurus is the **Pleiades** star cluster, also known as the Seven Sisters, located above the bull's back. The Pleiades are easily visible to the naked eye and have been admired across cultures for their beauty.
- **Notable Objects**: The **Crab Nebula** (M1) is a famous supernova remnant located in Taurus. It is the remains of a massive star that exploded in 1054 AD, a sight documented by astronomers from China, Japan, and the Arab world. Though not visible without a telescope, the Crab Nebula holds significance as a marker of celestial events.
- **Symbolism**: Taurus represents strength, resilience, and the nurturing qualities of nature. During winter, Taurus reminds us of the steadfast power within each of us and encourages us to hold onto hope as we endure the darker months, with the promise of spring and renewal just around the corner.

3. Gemini the Twins

Gemini, another zodiac constellation, is visible above Orion and features two bright stars, Castor and Pollux, which represent the heads of the mythological twins. As the season of Christmas brings people together, Gemini embodies the themes of companionship, loyalty, and connection.

- **Mythology**: In Greek mythology, Castor and Pollux were the sons of Zeus and mortal women. Known for their close bond, the twins were inseparable and fought alongside each other in many adventures. When Castor was killed in battle, Pollux asked Zeus to allow them to remain together forever. In response, Zeus placed them in the sky as the constellation Gemini.
- **Key Stars**: **Castor** and **Pollux** are the brightest stars in Gemini, representing the heads of the twins. Castor is a multiple-star system, while Pollux is an orange giant and the brighter of the two. These stars create a unique pattern in the sky, making Gemini easy to identify.
- **Notable Objects**: Gemini contains the **Eskimo Nebula** (NGC 2392), a planetary nebula visible through a telescope. This nebula resembles a face surrounded by a fur hood, giving it its unique name. Another interesting object is the **Gemini Cluster** (NGC 2158), an open cluster located near the star M35.
- **Symbolism**: Gemini represents unity, loyalty, and the beauty of connection, making it a fitting constellation for the holiday season. The story of Castor and Pollux reminds us of the strength found in relationships and the bonds that sustain us, especially during times of celebration and togetherness.

4. Perseus the Hero

Perseus, a hero from Greek mythology, is a prominent winter constellation located to the north of Taurus. Known for his bravery and adventure, Perseus represents courage, protection, and the power to overcome obstacles.

- **Mythology**: Perseus is celebrated in mythology for slaying the Gorgon Medusa and saving the princess Andromeda from a sea monster. Perseus's adventures made him a celebrated figure in Greek mythology, symbolizing heroism and resilience. After his death, he was honored by the gods and placed among the stars as a constellation.
- **Key Stars**: The brightest star in Perseus is **Mirfak**, a yellow-white supergiant located at the heart of the constellation. Another notable star is **Algol**, also known as the Demon Star, a variable star that represents the eye of Medusa. Algol's changing brightness, caused by an eclipsing binary system, makes it an intriguing feature for stargazers.
- **Notable Objects**: The **Double Cluster** (NGC 869 and NGC 884), located between Perseus and Cassiopeia, is a stunning pair of open star clusters visible to the naked eye. These clusters, filled with young, bright stars, are a popular target for winter stargazing and represent Perseus's beauty and strength.

- **Symbolism**: Perseus's story of courage and resilience is fitting for the holiday season, reminding us to face challenges with bravery. His constellation inspires us to find inner strength and embrace the journey, even when faced with difficulties, as we look forward to new beginnings.

5. Auriga the Charioteer

Auriga, known as the Charioteer, is a bright winter constellation that sits near Taurus. Recognized by its brightest star, Capella, Auriga is associated with themes of guidance, protection, and skill.

- **Mythology**: In Greek mythology, Auriga is often depicted as a charioteer holding a goat. The story varies, with some sources identifying Auriga as Erichthonius, a king of Athens who invented the chariot. Another interpretation associates Auriga with the goat Amalthea, who nursed Zeus as a child, representing protection and nurturing.
- **Key Stars**: **Capella**, the sixth-brightest star in the night sky, is the most notable star in Auriga. Capella is a yellow giant star system that is easily identifiable and represents the goat Amalthea in the myth. The constellation also includes stars such as **Menkalinan** and **El Nath**, adding to its distinctive pentagonal shape.
- **Notable Objects**: Auriga contains three beautiful open star clusters—**M36**, **M37**, and **M38**—which are visible through binoculars or small telescopes. These clusters are young and vibrant, adding to the constellation's appeal for winter stargazing.
- **Symbolism**: Auriga's association with charioteers and protectors makes it a symbol of guidance and strength. The constellation encourages us to embrace our role as caretakers and leaders, protecting and guiding others through life's journey, especially during the holiday season when unity and care are central.

6. Cassiopeia the Queen

Cassiopeia, easily recognizable by its W or M shape, is a constellation associated with royalty, beauty, and resilience. Located near Perseus, Cassiopeia shines brightly in the winter sky, offering a unique visual pattern that is easy to identify.

- **Mythology**: In Greek mythology, Cassiopeia was the queen of Ethiopia, known for her beauty and vanity. She boasted that she was more beautiful than the sea nymphs, angering Poseidon, who sent a sea monster to her kingdom. As punishment, she was placed in the sky in a position that causes her to hang upside down at certain times of the year.
- **Key Stars**: **Schedar**, the brightest star in Cassiopeia, marks the heart of the queen, while other notable stars like **Caph**, **Ruchbah**, and **Navi** form the constellation's W shape.
- **Notable Objects**: Cassiopeia is home to the **Heart and Soul Nebulae** (IC 1805 and IC 1848), a pair of emission nebulae located near the constellation's outer edges. Another notable object is the **Pac-Man Nebula** (NGC 281), named for its resemblance to the classic arcade character.

- **Symbolism**: Cassiopeia's story represents the themes of beauty, humility, and resilience. Her placement in the sky reminds us of the importance of balance and humility, even as we celebrate and appreciate beauty during the holiday season.

Embracing the Holiday Constellations: Stargazing and Reflection

Winter constellations offer both beauty and inspiration, encouraging us to take time for stargazing, reflection, and wonder during the holiday season. Each constellation tells a story of strength, love, protection, and adventure, reminding us of the enduring themes that connect humanity with the cosmos.

1. **Bundle Up for Stargazing**: Winter nights can be cold, but bundling up and stepping outside to observe the night sky is well worth it. Look for clear, moonless nights when stars are most visible. Bring a star chart, binoculars, or a telescope if possible, and enjoy the splendor of the winter constellations.
2. **Reflect on the Myths and Meanings**: As you gaze at each constellation, consider its story and symbolism. Reflect on the qualities of strength, resilience, and unity, and how these values align with the spirit of the holiday season. Stargazing can be a meditative experience, helping us connect with something greater than ourselves.
3. **Share the Experience**: Stargazing is a wonderful activity to share with family and friends. Take a moment to point out the constellations, tell their stories, and appreciate the beauty of the night sky together. Sharing this experience deepens the bonds of connection, creating lasting memories.
4. **Use Constellations for Intention-Setting**: The myths of the constellations can inspire personal intentions. For example, Orion may inspire courage, Gemini can remind you of the importance of connection, and Cassiopeia encourages humility. Let these symbols guide your reflections and intentions for the coming year.

Final Thoughts: The Magic of Holiday Constellations

The constellations visible during the holidays offer more than just a stunning visual display; they are windows into ancient stories, universal values, and the beauty of the cosmos. As you look up at the winter sky, let these constellations remind you of the resilience, strength, and wonder that lie within each of us.

This holiday season, embrace the magic of the night sky, allowing the stars to inspire you with their timeless tales and enduring brilliance. Through stargazing, storytelling, and reflection, the holiday constellations become more than celestial patterns—they become companions on our journey, lighting our way with wonder and wisdom.

Chapter 24: The Meaning of Yule and Its Celestial Influence

Yule, an ancient festival celebrating the winter solstice and the return of light, is one of the oldest known winter celebrations. Rooted in Nordic, Celtic, and Germanic traditions, Yule represents a time of rebirth, introspection, and celebration as the longest night of the year gives way to gradually lengthening days. Though often associated with Christmas in modern times, Yule has its own unique customs, symbols, and significance. This chapter explores the meaning of Yule, its celestial connections, and how it reflects humanity's deep relationship with the cycles of nature and the cosmos.

Yule's celebration of the Sun's return has profound celestial implications. It marks the point when the Sun, at its lowest point in the sky, begins its ascent, symbolizing rebirth and renewal. This celestial shift has inspired rituals, myths, and cultural practices across history. By understanding the traditions and celestial influences of Yule, we can appreciate how this ancient holiday continues to resonate as a time of hope, warmth, and connection with nature and the cosmos.

The Origins and Meaning of Yule

The word *Yule* originates from the Old Norse word *jól* and the Old English *geōl*, referring to the winter festival celebrated by Germanic, Norse, and Celtic peoples. Yule was traditionally held in late December, aligning with the winter solstice, which marked the shortest day and longest night of the year. Celebrated as a turning point in the cycle of the Sun, Yule embodies themes of rebirth, warmth, and the triumph of light over darkness.

Ancient cultures saw Yule as a time to honor the cyclical nature of life, recognizing that the period of cold and darkness was necessary before the Sun's return could bring growth, abundance, and renewal. Yule was a reminder of the importance of patience, resilience, and trust in nature's rhythms, encouraging communities to gather, feast, and share warmth during the coldest time of the year.

In Norse mythology, Yule was associated with Odin, the god of wisdom, magic, and transformation. Odin was believed to ride through the skies during this time, leading a mystical procession known as the Wild Hunt. Other mythological figures associated with Yule include the Norse god Freyr, a symbol of fertility and sunlight, and the Celtic Green Man, a spirit of the forest and rebirth. These deities represented the life-giving forces of nature, ensuring the return of warmth, growth, and abundance.

Yule's Celestial Influence: The Winter Solstice and Sun's Return

Yule's timing aligns with the winter solstice, the day when the Earth's axial tilt is such that one hemisphere receives the least sunlight, creating the longest night of the year. From a celestial perspective, the winter solstice is a time of pause and transition. The Sun reaches its lowest arc in the sky, appearing to "stand still" for a few days before gradually rising higher each day. This return of the Sun is central to Yule's symbolism, as it signifies the rebirth of light and the promise of warmer, longer days ahead.

1. **Celestial Significance of the Winter Solstice**: The winter solstice is a point of profound cosmic balance, marking a turning point in the Sun's journey. From an astronomical standpoint, the solstice represents a shift in energy, a "cosmic reset" as Earth realigns with the Sun's light. Ancient cultures saw this event as a moment of renewal, believing that the rebirth of the Sun was a divine act, restoring balance and life to the world.

2. **The Sun's Journey and Yule's Themes of Renewal**: In the ancient Yule festival, the rebirth of the Sun symbolized the endurance of life. People celebrated the Sun's slow but steady ascent, interpreting it as a reminder that all endings are followed by new beginnings. Just as the Sun must descend to rise again, Yule teaches that periods of darkness or hardship are temporary and give way to growth and renewal.

3. **Astrological Significance of the Solstice**: Astrologically, the winter solstice occurs when the Sun enters Capricorn, a zodiac sign associated with structure, resilience, and mastery over adversity. Capricorn's influence during Yule aligns with the themes of endurance, responsibility, and strength, encouraging us to ground ourselves, reflect on the past year, and prepare for the future. This cosmic alignment underscores Yule's message of stability and renewal, as Capricorn energy helps us find the strength to endure and build foundations for the year ahead.

Yule Traditions and Rituals

Yule is celebrated with customs that reflect its themes of warmth, community, and the return of light. Many of these traditions, such as the Yule log, the use of evergreens, and feasting, have influenced modern Christmas practices, preserving Yule's spirit of celebration and hope. Here are some of the most enduring Yule traditions and their meanings:

1. **The Yule Log**: One of the most iconic symbols of Yule is the Yule log, a large log burned on the hearth throughout the holiday. Traditionally, a piece of the previous year's Yule log was saved to light the new one, symbolizing continuity and protection. The Yule log was adorned with holly, ivy, and pine, which were thought to ward off evil spirits and bring good fortune. The burning of the Yule log represents warmth, light, and the hope that spring will soon return.

2. **Evergreens**: Evergreen plants such as holly, mistletoe, and ivy are central to Yule, symbolizing life's endurance through winter's cold. These plants, which remain green year-round, represent resilience, protection, and the promise of renewal. Mistletoe, in particular, was sacred to the Druids, symbolizing fertility, protection, and the joining of heaven and Earth. Evergreens continue to be used in modern holiday decor as reminders of Yule's themes of life and resilience.

3. **The Winter Feast**: Yule was a time for gathering and sharing food, with communities coming together for feasts that celebrated the bounty of the previous harvest. These feasts were filled with seasonal foods like root vegetables, nuts, and preserved meats, symbolizing the community's ability to endure and thrive despite winter's scarcity. The feast represented abundance, gratitude, and the joy of companionship, qualities that are still celebrated in modern holiday meals.

4. **Decorating with Lights**: Candles and lanterns were used during Yule to symbolically invite the Sun's return, illuminating homes and warding off winter's darkness. This tradition evolved into the custom of decorating with holiday lights, bringing warmth and brightness to the dark nights of winter. Lighting candles during Yule represents hope, welcoming the Sun's light back into the world and creating an atmosphere of peace and joy.

5. **The Wild Hunt and Honoring Ancestors**: The Norse belief in the Wild Hunt—a spectral procession led by Odin across the winter sky—was a key part of Yule mythology. Many believed that the spirits of the dead joined the Hunt, and so Yule was seen as a time to honor ancestors and offer protection to wandering spirits. Setting out food and drinks as offerings to ancestors and the spirits of nature was common, representing gratitude and reverence for those who came before.

6. **Gift Giving and Generosity**: Yule was a time of generosity and gift-giving, rooted in the communal spirit of the season. Families and neighbors exchanged small gifts, often handmade, as tokens of goodwill and affection. This tradition evolved into the modern practice of giving holiday gifts, emphasizing the importance of community, sharing, and appreciation during the winter months.

Yule's Spiritual Lessons and Symbolism

Yule is more than a seasonal celebration; it is a deeply symbolic ritual that teaches us about life's cyclical nature, the strength within ourselves, and our connection to the Earth and cosmos. The following lessons and symbols capture Yule's enduring wisdom and its invitation to align with nature's rhythms:

1. **Embracing Darkness as Part of the Journey**: Yule teaches us that darkness is a natural and necessary part of life's cycle. Just as the longest night of the year is followed by the return of light, Yule reminds us that periods of challenge or introspection ultimately lead to growth and renewal. This lesson encourages acceptance, resilience, and trust in life's ebb and flow.

2. **Celebrating Community and Connection**: Yule is a celebration of warmth, unity, and togetherness, reinforcing the importance of community during winter's most difficult days. The holiday reminds us that we are stronger together, inspiring us to nurture our connections with family, friends, and community. The feasts, gift-giving, and gatherings of Yule reflect the power of love and support.

3. **Rebirth and Renewal**: The return of the Sun after the winter solstice symbolizes rebirth and transformation. Yule teaches us to embrace the potential for new beginnings, encouraging us to release what no longer serves us and to welcome opportunities for growth. As we look toward the New Year, Yule invites us to set intentions and move forward with renewed hope and purpose.

4. **Honoring Nature's Cycles**: Yule's focus on the Sun's journey and the changing seasons reflects humanity's deep connection to nature. This holiday encourages us to honor the Earth, recognize the importance of balance, and appreciate the cycles that sustain life. Yule reminds us of our place in the universe, fostering a sense of humility, gratitude, and reverence for nature's beauty.

5. **Inviting Light into Our Lives**: The act of lighting candles and decorating with evergreens symbolizes the renewal of hope and the desire for inner light. Yule invites us to kindle our inner flame, cultivate positivity, and share warmth with others. This symbolism encourages us to look within, finding light even in the darkest times and spreading that light to those around us.

Modern Yule Celebrations and Practices

Today, Yule is celebrated by many who wish to honor its themes of nature, spirituality, and seasonal transition. Some incorporate Yule customs into Christmas celebrations, while others observe Yule as a standalone holiday. Here are some ways to celebrate Yule in the modern world, connecting with its ancient wisdom and creating meaningful traditions:

1. **Create a Yule Altar**: Set up an altar with symbols of Yule, such as evergreens, pinecones, candles, and seasonal fruits. This altar can be a focal point for meditation, reflection, and honoring nature's beauty. Use it to set intentions, light candles for warmth and light, and connect with the energy of the winter solstice.

2. **Hold a Winter Solstice Meditation**: Meditation on the night of the winter solstice can help you connect with Yule's themes of rebirth and renewal. Visualize yourself embracing both light and darkness, letting go of the past, and welcoming new beginnings. This meditation encourages inner peace, introspection, and a deeper connection with nature's cycles.

3. **Light a Yule Candle**: Lighting a candle on Yule symbolizes the return of the Sun and invites warmth into your home. As you light the candle, reflect on the year's journey, express gratitude, and set intentions for the year to come. Let the candle burn as a symbol of hope, illuminating your path forward.

4. **Decorate a Yule Tree or Wreath**: Decorate a Yule tree with natural ornaments, such as dried oranges, cinnamon sticks, and pinecones. These decorations honor nature's abundance and the promise of growth. A Yule wreath, often made of evergreens, can be hung as a symbol of eternity, resilience, and the cycle of life.

5. **Prepare a Yule Feast**: Gather friends and family for a Yule-inspired feast, featuring seasonal foods like root vegetables, nuts, grains, and spiced drinks. Share stories, express gratitude, and celebrate the warmth of community. The feast is an opportunity to honor the abundance of the Earth and the bonds of companionship.

6. **Make Offerings to Nature**: Yule is an ideal time to give back to nature. Make offerings to wildlife, such as seeds or nuts for birds, or set out food for animals during the winter months. This practice honors the interconnectedness of life, expressing gratitude and fostering respect for the natural world.

Final Thoughts: Yule as a Celebration of Light, Renewal, and Connection

Yule, with its ancient roots and timeless wisdom, serves as a beacon of hope, a celebration of the cycles that shape our lives, and a reminder of the beauty found in both light and darkness. By embracing Yule's themes of renewal, community, and reverence for nature, we honor our ancestors and deepen our connection to the Earth and the cosmos.

As you celebrate Yule, allow its messages of rebirth, resilience, and unity to fill your heart. May the returning light bring warmth, joy, and inspiration as you journey through winter, carrying forward the wisdom of Yule into the year ahead. Embrace this season as a time of transformation, a reminder that just as the Sun returns, so too will brighter days and new beginnings.

Chapter 25: Comet Appearances and Their Festive Significance

Comets, with their bright, mysterious tails and sudden appearances, have long fascinated and inspired humanity. Often seen as omens or signs of great change, comets hold a special place in the lore of the night sky and are particularly significant during the holiday season. From their connection to the Christmas Star to their association with transformation, rebirth, and new beginnings, comets have woven themselves into the tapestry of festive celebrations and symbolism. This chapter explores the unique qualities of comets, their appearances throughout history, and how they have come to represent both wonder and significance in holiday traditions.

For ancient stargazers, the sight of a comet was a profound and often unnerving event. Unlike the fixed stars and predictable movements of planets, comets would suddenly appear in the sky, their bright tails cutting through the heavens before disappearing as quickly as they had come. This unpredictable behavior made comets symbols of cosmic messages, divine intervention, and powerful change, qualities that align with the themes of the holiday season, a time of reflection, renewal, and hope. By understanding the symbolism and cultural significance of comets, we can appreciate their impact on both ancient traditions and modern holiday celebrations.

The Celestial Nature of Comets

A comet is a small celestial body made up of ice, dust, and rock, which orbits the Sun in an elongated, elliptical path. As comets approach the Sun, they begin to heat up, releasing gas and dust that create a glowing coma and a long tail, which can stretch for millions of miles. This tail always points away from the Sun, driven by the solar wind, giving comets their distinctive appearance.

Comets are believed to be remnants from the formation of the solar system, preserved in regions like the Kuiper Belt and the Oort Cloud. When gravitational forces disturb these bodies, they are sent on trajectories that bring them closer to the Sun, making them visible from Earth. Because of their icy composition and long orbits, comets can take anywhere from a few years to thousands of years to return, making each appearance a rare and memorable event.

The unpredictable and transient nature of comets has long inspired myths and legends, as their sudden arrival was often seen as a divine message. For ancient astronomers and astrologers, comets defied the orderly nature of the cosmos, introducing an element of mystery and transformation. Their association with major events and changes has imbued comets with powerful symbolism, especially during the holiday season, when themes of rebirth, new beginnings, and divine guidance are prevalent.

Historical Comet Appearances and Their Cultural Significance

Throughout history, comets have been interpreted as signs of great change, often linked to both joyful and foreboding events. Ancient civilizations recorded comet appearances, attributing them to the birth of kings, the fall of empires, or divine messages. Some of the most famous comets have appeared near the holiday season, adding to their association with Christmas and celebrations of light.

1. **Halley's Comet**: Halley's Comet, one of the most famous comets, has been recorded by various civilizations throughout history, often as an omen of significant change. Its appearance in 12 BCE is sometimes linked to the birth of Jesus, leading some historians to speculate that it may have been interpreted as the Christmas Star. Halley's Comet has inspired awe and fascination for centuries, symbolizing cosmic cycles and the eternal return of light and knowledge.

2. **The Christmas Comet of 1680 (Kirch's Comet)**: In 1680, a particularly bright comet appeared close to Christmas, visible even during daylight. Known as Kirch's Comet or the Great Comet of 1680, it was one of the most spectacular comets of the 17th century. Its appearance inspired artists, poets, and theologians, who saw it as a divine sign during a time of religious significance. Kirch's Comet became known as the "Christmas Comet" and was linked to themes of spiritual awakening, wonder, and cosmic intervention.

3. **The Comet of 1577**: Another famous comet observed by Tycho Brahe, the Danish astronomer, appeared in 1577. This comet was visible for several weeks, sparking widespread interest and speculation. Brahe's observations helped shift astronomical understanding, revealing that comets were celestial phenomena far beyond Earth's atmosphere. The comet of 1577 inspired many interpretations, including predictions of change, renewal, and the coming of a new era.

4. **Comet Hale-Bopp (1997)**: Although Hale-Bopp did not appear around the holiday season, its brilliance and duration in the night sky made it one of the most observed comets of the 20th century. Hale-Bopp appeared during a period of renewed interest in celestial phenomena and spirituality, and its extended visibility inspired a sense of cosmic wonder. Observers across the globe saw it as a sign of new beginnings and collective reflection, themes that resonate with the holiday spirit of introspection and connection.

5. **The Star of Bethlehem Theories**: Some astronomers and historians propose that the Star of Bethlehem, which guided the Wise Men to Jesus's birthplace, may have been a bright comet. This theory suggests that a comet, with its tail pointing toward the Earth, would have appeared as a divine sign to ancient observers. If this was indeed the case, the Christmas Star represents a moment of cosmic guidance, aligning with the festive themes of hope, wonder, and the arrival of something new and divine.

Comets and Their Symbolic Meaning in Holiday Traditions

The symbolism of comets aligns with many of the themes celebrated during the holiday season: rebirth, divine intervention, and transformation. Their sudden appearances and bright tails evoke wonder, mystery, and a sense of cosmic guidance. Here's how comets have come to symbolize the spiritual essence of the holidays:

1. **Symbol of New Beginnings**: Just as comets reappear after long journeys, their arrival symbolizes cycles, renewal, and the start of new phases. During the holiday season, a time of reflection and preparation for the New Year, comets remind us of the opportunity for change, growth, and transformation.

2. **Celestial Messengers**: Throughout history, comets were often seen as messages from the heavens, signaling significant events or shifts in the world. During the holidays, a season often associated with spirituality and divine connection, comets serve as reminders that we are part of a vast, interconnected universe, with forces beyond our understanding guiding our paths.

3. **Hope and Light in Darkness**: Comets, with their bright, glowing tails, bring light into the darkness of the night sky. Their appearance aligns with the holiday theme of light overcoming darkness, symbolizing hope, joy, and the enduring nature of the human spirit. Just as holiday lights brighten the darkest time of year, comets represent the triumph of light and hope over uncertainty.

4. **Inspiration for Generations**: The awe that comets inspire transcends time and culture, creating a sense of shared wonder. During the holidays, this unifying experience is mirrored in the celebration of community, connection, and shared traditions. Comets encourage us to come together, celebrate life's mysteries, and appreciate the beauty of the cosmos.

5. **Cycles of the Cosmos**: Comets remind us of the natural cycles that govern the universe. Their periodic appearances, after years or centuries of absence, symbolize continuity, resilience, and the inevitability of change. The holiday season, especially New Year celebrations, reflects these themes of cycles and the anticipation of what lies ahead.

Modern Holiday Celebrations Inspired by Comets

Today, comets continue to inspire wonder and a sense of cosmic connection, especially during the festive season. Here are a few ways that comet symbolism and imagery have found their way into modern holiday celebrations:

1. **Comet-Themed Decorations**: In some cultures, comet-shaped ornaments, lights, and stars are used to decorate homes and trees, symbolizing the guidance and hope associated with celestial bodies. These decorations serve as reminders of the mysteries of the universe and the beauty of cosmic events that have been celebrated since ancient times.

2. **Comet-Inspired Star of Bethlehem Decorations**: The image of the Christmas Star, often depicted with a tail, resembles a comet in its shape and glow. Many holiday decorations—whether tree-toppers, candles, or wreaths—reflect this interpretation, symbolizing divine guidance and the journey toward enlightenment. The "shooting star" motif brings an added layer of mysticism to holiday decor.

3. **Astronomical Events and Stargazing Traditions**: Some families celebrate the holiday season by observing the night sky, keeping an eye out for meteor showers, planets, or comets. This tradition creates a sense of wonder and awe, connecting modern stargazers with ancient peoples who looked to the skies for guidance. Observing the night sky during the holidays reminds us of our connection to the cosmos and our shared history of fascination with celestial phenomena.

4. **Storytelling and Folklore**: Comets inspire stories of adventure, prophecy, and hope, adding a mythical dimension to holiday gatherings. Sharing tales of famous comets, or reading about the Christmas Star's possible comet origins, enhances the magic of the season. These stories remind us of humanity's enduring relationship with the stars and the myths that bind us.

5. **Intention-Setting Inspired by Comet Cycles**: Comets, with their long orbits and eventual returns, symbolize patience, endurance, and the promise of renewal. During the holiday season, people often set intentions for the New Year, inspired by the cycles of celestial bodies. Just as a comet returns after its journey, intention-setting for the coming year encourages us to stay true to our goals, trusting in the process and the cosmic rhythm of life.

Observing Comets and Other Celestial Events During the Holidays

While comets are unpredictable, other celestial events, such as meteor showers, planetary conjunctions, and the winter constellations, provide ample opportunity for holiday stargazing. Here are a few tips and ideas for observing the holiday night sky:

1. **Look for Meteor Showers**: The Geminid meteor shower, one of the most active meteor showers, occurs in mid-December and can produce bright, colorful meteors. Observing meteor showers during the holidays connects us with the thrill of cosmic beauty, as meteors streak across the night sky, like tiny reminders of the universe's wonders.
2. **Watch for Planetary Conjunctions**: Planetary alignments and conjunctions, when planets appear close to one another in the sky, can also be visible around the holiday season. These alignments echo the theories about the Christmas Star, offering a glimpse of the same cosmic phenomena that inspired ancient astronomers and theologians.
3. **Identify Winter Constellations**: Winter constellations such as Orion, Taurus, and Gemini provide a beautiful backdrop for holiday stargazing. Their mythology and seasonal symbolism enhance the holiday experience, allowing stargazers to connect with ancient stories of strength, connection, and perseverance.
4. **Check for Comet Sightings**: Though comets are less predictable than other celestial events, keeping an eye on astronomy news or star-gazing apps can help you track any comets visible during the holiday season. The appearance of a comet can make for a memorable holiday experience, bringing a real-life cosmic wonder to holiday traditions.

Final Thoughts: Comets as Messengers of Mystery and Wonder

Comets, with their radiant tails and rare appearances, symbolize transformation, renewal, and the vastness of the cosmos. They remind us that the universe is full of mysteries yet to be discovered and that, despite life's challenges, cycles of growth and rebirth are inevitable. The holiday season, a time for reflection and connection, aligns beautifully with the themes comets embody.

As we celebrate the holidays, let the symbolism of comets inspire us to embrace change, set intentions for the future, and find wonder in life's mysteries. Just as comets bring unexpected beauty to the night sky, so too can we find joy and hope in the unexpected moments and transformations of our lives. Whether observing the stars, decorating with comet-inspired motifs, or sharing stories of celestial wonders, we honor the timeless allure of comets and their festive significance.

Part 5: **Meteor Showers**

Chapter 26: The Geminids - December's Showers of Light

The Geminid meteor shower, known for its breathtaking display of bright, colorful meteors, is one of the most anticipated celestial events of the year. Occurring annually in mid-December, the Geminids offer a natural holiday light show, filling the sky with dozens of meteors per hour, often streaking in colors of yellow, green, and blue. This meteor shower, unique in both origin and brilliance, is widely regarded as one of the most reliable and vivid meteor showers. Observing the Geminids during the holiday season allows us to connect with the vastness of the cosmos, marveling at the beauty of these "shooting stars" that cross our skies during one of the darkest, yet most festive, times of the year.

Unlike other meteor showers, which are usually caused by debris from comets, the Geminids are linked to an asteroid, making them unique among the major meteor showers. This connection adds to the allure and mystery surrounding the Geminids, as they offer a different glimpse into the interplay of celestial bodies and the debris they leave in their wake. For those who take a moment to step outside and gaze up, the Geminids provide a truly magical and awe-inspiring spectacle, bringing a sense of wonder and light into the holiday season.

Origins and Unique Nature of the Geminids

The Geminid meteor shower is named after the constellation Gemini, from which the meteors appear to radiate. Known as the "radiant," this point in the sky lies near the bright stars Castor and Pollux in Gemini, giving the meteor shower its name. Though the meteors originate from Gemini's direction, they can be seen streaking across the sky in many directions, often appearing as quick, vibrant flashes against the darkness of a winter night.

What sets the Geminids apart from other meteor showers is their unusual source: an asteroid called **3200 Phaethon**. Most meteor showers are caused by comets, which shed icy particles as they near the Sun. These particles burn up upon entering Earth's atmosphere, creating the familiar sight of shooting stars. In the case of the Geminids, however, the debris comes from Phaethon, a rocky asteroid rather than an icy comet.

1. The Mystery of Phaethon

Asteroid 3200 Phaethon was discovered in 1983, and astronomers quickly noted its unusual properties. Phaethon orbits the Sun in a highly elliptical path, coming closer to the Sun than any other named asteroid in our solar system. When Phaethon nears the Sun, it heats up dramatically, causing its surface to crack and release dust and debris, which trails behind it in a path that Earth intersects each December. This process of shedding material is atypical for an asteroid, leading some astronomers to describe Phaethon as a "rock comet" because it behaves somewhat like a comet, though without ice.

Phaethon's path near the Sun and its resulting debris field provide the material that produces the Geminids. When Earth passes through this field each December, particles from Phaethon enter our atmosphere and burn up, creating the vibrant meteors we observe. The asteroid's close pass to the Sun heats it enough to release these particles, which makes Phaethon a truly unique parent body among meteor showers. This combination of characteristics has made Phaethon a subject of intrigue in the astronomical community, as it challenges the clear-cut distinction between comets and asteroids.

2. Why the Geminids Are So Active

The Geminid meteor shower is known for its high activity rate, often producing up to 120 meteors per hour at its peak, which occurs around December 13-14 each year. The Geminids have grown more active over the centuries, likely due to the Earth passing through increasingly dense parts of Phaethon's debris field. This build-up of material has created a dense and relatively wide trail, which Earth intersects each December, resulting in a particularly rich and reliable meteor shower.

In addition to their high frequency, the meteors in the Geminid shower are relatively slow-moving compared to those in other meteor showers, traveling at about 35 kilometers per second. This "slow" speed (for meteors) allows the meteors to be brighter and more visible as they burn up in the atmosphere, often resulting in long, colorful streaks that last a few moments in the night sky. The combination of high frequency, brightness, and vibrant colors makes the Geminids a remarkable and accessible meteor shower, visible even from areas with moderate light pollution.

The Best Conditions for Observing the Geminids

The Geminids reach their peak around December 13-14 each year, but meteors can be seen in lower frequencies for several days before and after the peak. To observe the Geminids at their best, it's essential to consider factors like timing, location, and visibility:

1. **Time of Night**: The Geminids are visible throughout the night, but the best time for viewing is typically after midnight, when the radiant in Gemini is higher in the sky. However, because of the Geminids' high activity rate, some meteors can often be seen as early as 9 or 10 p.m., making them more accessible for early-evening viewing.

2. **Location**: To see the Geminids in their full glory, find a location away from artificial lights and urban areas. The more rural and dark the environment, the more meteors will be visible. Open areas with an unobstructed view of the sky, such as fields, hilltops, or beaches, are ideal.

3. **Weather Conditions**: Clear skies are essential for meteor viewing. Cold winter nights often offer clear visibility, but clouds, fog, or snow can obscure the sky. Check local weather forecasts in advance to find an evening with good visibility, and be prepared for cold conditions by dressing warmly.

4. **Moonlight**: The moon phase plays a significant role in meteor visibility. When the moon is full or nearly full, its brightness can wash out fainter meteors, reducing the impact of the shower. New moon or crescent moon phases create ideal conditions for Geminid viewing, as the darker sky allows more meteors to be seen.

5. **Adjusting to the Dark**: To fully appreciate the Geminids, allow your eyes 20-30 minutes to adjust to the dark. Avoid looking at bright lights, screens, or flashlights, as they can interfere with night vision. Once adjusted, your eyes will be better equipped to spot fainter meteors in the sky.

The Symbolic Significance of the Geminids During the Holiday Season

The Geminids, with their vibrant colors and frequent streaks of light, offer more than just a visual spectacle—they also carry a symbolic resonance that aligns beautifully with the holiday season. Here are some of the deeper meanings and associations that make the Geminids particularly special in December:

1. Light in the Darkness

The Geminids appear during one of the darkest times of the year, near the winter solstice, when nights are longest and daylight is shortest. Their presence serves as a reminder of light's beauty and power, illuminating the dark sky like a shower of tiny stars. This symbolism of light shining through darkness reflects themes of hope, joy, and renewal, which are central to many holiday traditions.

In ancient cultures, light was a symbol of life and hope, and celestial events like meteor showers would have been seen as auspicious signs, especially during winter. The Geminids, by bringing light to December's darkest nights, embody this timeless idea of light overcoming darkness and serve as a celestial celebration of resilience and renewal.

2. Connection with the Cosmos

Meteor showers remind us of our connection to the cosmos, as they are visible signs of the interactions between celestial bodies. The particles that create the Geminids come from Phaethon, an asteroid with its own unique story and journey. Observing the Geminids allows us to feel a sense of cosmic kinship, reminding us that we are part of a vast, interconnected universe.

During the holiday season, which often brings thoughts of family, community, and unity, the Geminids highlight our shared place in the cosmos. Watching these meteors can be a contemplative experience, evoking awe and reminding us of the beauty and mystery of life beyond Earth.

3. Themes of Transformation and Rebirth

As fragments of Phaethon enter Earth's atmosphere, they transform from tiny particles of dust into bright, colorful streaks across the sky. This transformation from ordinary space debris to dazzling meteor mirrors the themes of transformation, renewal, and rebirth celebrated in December. The holiday season is often a time for reflection on the past year and preparation for new beginnings in the New Year, making the Geminids an inspiring reminder of the potential for change and growth.

The metamorphosis of each particle, igniting as it encounters Earth's atmosphere, can serve as a metaphor for personal transformation. Just as meteors become brilliant lights, we too can find moments of clarity, inspiration, and transformation amid life's challenges.

4. Traditions of Wonder and Storytelling

Meteor showers have inspired wonder and storytelling across cultures for centuries. The Geminids, with their unique origins and dramatic display, invite us to connect with this tradition of cosmic storytelling. Sharing stories about meteors, Phaethon, and the mythology of the constellation Gemini can enhance the experience of watching the Geminids, adding a layer of myth and meaning to the spectacle.

During the holiday season, a time often associated with storytelling and tradition, observing the Geminids can create new memories and family traditions. Whether alone, with family, or with friends, taking a moment to watch the meteors can become a cherished annual ritual, symbolizing both the magic of the universe and the warmth of shared experiences.

Preparing for a Geminid Viewing Experience

Watching the Geminids can be a transformative experience, offering a unique way to connect with the night sky during the holiday season. Here are some tips for planning and making the most of your Geminid viewing experience:

1. **Dress for Warmth and Comfort**: December nights can be frigid, so dress in layers, and bring blankets or sleeping bags if you plan to lie down for an extended viewing. Consider packing hot drinks like tea or cocoa to stay warm and comfortable.
2. **Choose a Relaxed Viewing Position**: Meteors can appear anywhere in the sky, so lying on your back or using a reclining chair will allow you to comfortably take in a wide field of view without straining your neck.
3. **Bring Binoculars or a Telescope (Optional)**: While you don't need binoculars or a telescope to enjoy the Geminids, having one on hand can enhance the experience by allowing you to see more stars and the radiant point in Gemini more clearly. However, meteors move quickly, so binoculars may not capture individual meteors well.
4. **Plan for a Group Experience**: Watching the Geminids with family or friends can add a social and celebratory element to the experience. Sharing the moment when a bright meteor streaks across the sky can be a bonding experience, bringing people together in awe and joy.
5. **Set Intentions or Reflect**: Consider using the Geminids as an opportunity for reflection or intention-setting. Watching the meteors can be a peaceful, meditative experience, reminding us of the beauty of life's fleeting moments and the cycles of growth and renewal.

Final Thoughts: The Geminids as a Gift of Light and Wonder

The Geminid meteor shower, with its radiant bursts of color and light, is a celestial gift during December's darkest nights, bringing wonder and magic to the holiday season. As we watch these meteors, we are reminded of our connection to the universe, the beauty of transformation, and the enduring power of light to overcome darkness. The Geminids encourage us to pause, look up, and appreciate the grandeur of the cosmos, creating a sense of awe that resonates with the themes of joy, renewal, and unity celebrated in December.

Each Geminid meteor is a fleeting yet brilliant moment, a reminder of the fragility and wonder of existence. As you watch this December light show, allow yourself to be swept up in the beauty of the moment, letting it inspire reflection, hope, and a deep appreciation for the mysteries of the universe. This holiday season, let the Geminids illuminate your path, filling your heart with the timeless magic of the stars.

Chapter 27: Meteor Showers in Holiday Mythology

Meteor showers have long been viewed with awe, wonder, and reverence, their fleeting brilliance filling the sky with mystery and magic. As shooting stars streak across the night sky, they captivate onlookers, evoking dreams, wishes, and deep reflections. During the holiday season, when many cultures celebrate themes of light, rebirth, and the cyclical nature of life, meteor showers like the Geminids and the Ursids hold special significance. Ancient myths, spiritual beliefs, and holiday traditions from around the world are infused with the symbolism of these celestial events, often linking them to divine intervention, blessings, and messages from the heavens.

The seasonal timing of meteor showers, particularly in December, aligns with a period when many cultures look toward the stars with hope, seeking guidance, joy, and renewal as they prepare for the coming year. In this chapter, we will explore how meteor showers have influenced holiday mythology, how ancient cultures interpreted these displays, and the meanings we can draw from them today. From symbols of spiritual blessings to messengers of fate, meteors have inspired stories and traditions that resonate deeply with the spirit of the holiday season.

Meteor Showers in Ancient Cultures: Myths and Legends

Ancient civilizations often viewed meteor showers as omens or signs from the divine, interpreting the sudden arrival of "falling stars" as messages from gods, spirits, or ancestors. These beliefs were reinforced by the unpredictability and brilliance of meteor showers, which made them stand out against the typically stable night sky. As a result, meteor showers became associated with festivals, rituals, and stories that emphasized their role as symbols of connection between the earthly and the celestial realms.

1. **Greek and Roman Mythology**: In ancient Greece, meteors were often seen as signs of divine favor or warning. The Greeks believed that Zeus, the king of the gods, could send meteors as omens or to communicate important messages to humanity. In some stories, Zeus would send meteors to show approval of a particular event or as a form of guidance. The Romans, similarly, associated meteors with Mars, the god of war, interpreting their sudden appearance as harbingers of battles or significant change. Both cultures saw meteors as divine messages that could signify everything from blessings to warnings, depending on the context of their appearance.

2. **Norse Mythology**: In Norse legends, meteor showers were believed to be sparks from the chariot of the sun god Sol, who rode across the heavens each day. Some legends even connected meteors to the mythological forge of the dwarves, who were believed to create weapons and tools in the heart of the earth, with meteors representing the fiery sparks of their labor. In a winter setting, meteors symbolized the endurance of light through the darkness, mirroring the winter solstice themes of Yule. For the Norse, these sparks were also seen as signs of power, courage, and the presence of the gods.

3. **Chinese and East Asian Beliefs**: In ancient China, meteors were regarded as omens from heaven, often seen as harbingers of change, both positive and negative. The sudden streaks of light were thought to be messages from celestial spirits or ancestors, prompting communi-

ties to perform rituals honoring their ancestors and seeking guidance. Meteor showers during winter festivals, which coincided with the holiday season, were seen as blessings, believed to bring good fortune for the coming year. Similarly, in Japan, meteors were associated with the deities of the Shinto religion, viewed as indicators of divine attention and intervention.

4. **Native American Myths**: Many Native American tribes have myths that celebrate the connection between stars and spirits. For some tribes, meteors were believed to be spirits of ancestors or warriors, traveling across the sky to communicate with the living. The Zuni people, for example, interpreted meteors as symbols of good luck, while the Lakota Sioux viewed them as messengers from the spirit world. The Iroquois would make offerings to meteors, seeing them as representatives of the divine. During the holiday season, when many tribes celebrated winter festivals, meteor showers were seen as sacred displays that reinforced the presence and guidance of the spiritual world.

5. **Mesoamerican Cultures**: The ancient Aztecs and Maya also held strong beliefs about celestial events, including meteors. The Maya linked meteors to their gods, especially their god of war and sacrifice, viewing them as signs of important events or warnings. The Aztecs believed that meteors were fire serpents, associating them with their god Quetzalcoatl, the feathered serpent. Meteor showers during the winter festivals held a special place, seen as displays of divine power and messages from the gods to celebrate or prepare for change.

The Symbolism of Meteor Showers in Holiday Mythology

Meteor showers evoke powerful themes that align closely with the spirit of the holiday season. As symbols of hope, renewal, divine guidance, and fate, meteors are perfect representations of the mystery and magic that many holiday traditions celebrate. Here are some of the most enduring symbolic meanings of meteors within holiday mythology:

1. **Messages from the Divine**: Across cultures, meteor showers are viewed as messages from gods, spirits, or ancestors, offering guidance, blessings, or warnings. During the holiday season, when many people reflect on their lives and seek meaning, meteor showers serve as reminders of the divine forces at play in the universe. The appearance of meteors, especially during winter festivals, reinforces the idea that life is guided by unseen forces and that our actions are part of a larger cosmic story.

2. **Wishes and Dreams**: The tradition of "wishing on a star" is closely associated with meteors, as people have long believed that shooting stars have the power to make dreams come true. This tradition likely arose from the rarity and beauty of meteors, which made them seem magical. During the holidays, a time when people often set intentions or resolutions for the new year, the act of wishing upon a meteor aligns with themes of hope, aspiration, and the pursuit of one's dreams.

3. **Renewal and Rebirth**: Meteor showers often coincide with seasonal changes, particularly winter, which represents both an end and a beginning. The arrival of meteors during December embodies the concept of rebirth, as their light illuminates the night and suggests a transition from the old year to the new. In holiday mythology, meteors symbolize the shedding of

the past and the welcoming of new possibilities, mirroring the themes of the winter solstice, Yule, and other winter celebrations.

4. **The Light in Darkness**: Meteor showers bring light to the darkest times of the year, an act that has deep symbolic resonance. The sudden flashes across the night sky reflect the themes of hope, light overcoming darkness, and resilience. Many holiday traditions celebrate the return of light, warmth, and life, making meteor showers a perfect symbol for this time of year. The Geminids, which reach their peak close to the winter solstice, particularly embody this theme, as they brighten the longest nights of the year.

5. **Connection to the Cosmos**: Observing meteor showers connects us with the cosmos, reminding us of our place within a vast and wondrous universe. This sense of cosmic connection is celebrated in many holiday traditions, which emphasize unity, community, and a shared human experience. Meteor showers during the holiday season remind us that, despite the challenges of the year, we are all part of a greater whole, tied to the stars and the mysteries beyond.

Modern Holiday Traditions Inspired by Meteor Showers

Today, meteor showers continue to inspire wonder and hope, particularly during the holiday season. For some, watching the Geminids or Ursids has become a seasonal tradition, a time to marvel at the sky and reflect on the year. Here are some ways meteor showers influence modern holiday traditions:

1. **Holiday Stargazing and Meteor-Watching Gatherings**: For those who live in areas where winter nights are clear, watching the December meteor showers has become a holiday tradition. Families and friends gather under blankets, sipping hot cocoa, and watching the Geminids or Ursids together. These gatherings bring a sense of community and celebration, reinforcing the themes of unity, warmth, and joy that define the holiday season.

2. **Wish-Making and Resolutions**: Making a wish on a shooting star is a tradition that has deep roots, and the December meteor showers provide the perfect opportunity to set intentions or make resolutions for the coming year. Whether individually or with loved ones, making wishes on meteors can be a meaningful way to mark the holiday season, symbolizing hope, renewal, and the power of dreams.

3. **Storytelling and Mythology**: Sharing stories and myths about meteors is a way to connect with ancient traditions and add depth to the holiday experience. Families and friends can gather around a fire or under the stars to share tales of celestial wonders, weaving the lore of meteors into the spirit of the season. These stories remind us of the timeless fascination humans have with the night sky and the myths that have been inspired by meteor showers over the centuries.

4. **Gift-Giving Inspired by Shooting Stars**: Some holiday gifts are inspired by the symbolism of shooting stars and meteors. Jewelry, art, and decorations featuring stars or meteors can serve as symbolic gifts, representing wishes, guidance, and the hope for new beginnings.

These gifts embody the spirit of holiday mythology, connecting the recipient with the themes of wonder and inspiration symbolized by meteors.

5. **Reflection and Meditation Under the Stars**: For many, the holiday season is a time of quiet reflection and gratitude. Observing a meteor shower can enhance this reflective experience, offering a time for introspection and spiritual connection. Watching meteors can be a meditative practice, encouraging thoughts on the mysteries of life, the beauty of nature, and the light that guides us through dark times.

The Ursids: December's Second Meteor Shower

In addition to the Geminids, the Ursid meteor shower, peaking around December 22, offers a second display of meteors for holiday stargazers. Named after the constellation Ursa Minor, from which they appear to radiate, the Ursids provide a quieter, more subtle celestial display than the Geminids, but they carry the same symbolism of light, mystery, and connection to the cosmos.

1. **The Constellation Ursa Minor**: Ursa Minor, or the Little Bear, is the constellation that holds Polaris, the North Star, which has been used for navigation and guidance for centuries. The Ursid meteor shower's association with Ursa Minor reinforces themes of direction, guidance, and constancy, qualities that align with the holiday themes of hope and resilience.

2. **Symbolism of a Winter Meteor Shower**: The Ursids, while smaller than the Geminids, are an added gift during the holiday season, a second shower of light that reminds us of the abundance of the universe. Observing both meteor showers in December creates a sense of cosmic generosity, as the heavens provide two opportunities to witness the magic of "falling stars" during the darkest time of the year.

3. **A Celestial Reminder of the Season's Themes**: Like the Geminids, the Ursids carry the message of light emerging from darkness, the promise of renewal, and the connection between Earth and the cosmos. Observing the Ursids reinforces the symbolism of meteor showers as celestial gifts, inviting us to pause, reflect, and find beauty in the transitory moments of life.

Final Thoughts: Meteor Showers as Holiday Messengers of Light and Wonder

Meteor showers, with their fleeting beauty and symbolic power, have inspired myths, traditions, and a sense of wonder that aligns perfectly with the holiday season. As December brings both the Geminids and the Ursids, these celestial events illuminate the night sky and the hearts of those who watch them, serving as reminders of hope, rebirth, and connection to something greater.

This holiday season, let the light of the meteors inspire your reflections, wishes, and dreams. Whether observed alone or shared with loved ones, meteor showers offer a timeless reminder of the beauty and mystery that surrounds us, encouraging us to celebrate, seek guidance, and hold onto hope as we journey through the year's end and into new beginnings.

Chapter 28: Observing Meteor Showers as a Festive Tradition

Observing meteor showers has become a beloved tradition for stargazers, families, and friends, particularly during the holiday season when the Geminid and Ursid meteor showers light up December's long, cold nights. As these meteors streak across the sky, they bring an element of natural wonder to the festivities, inviting observers to pause, reflect, and enjoy a cosmic light show. Watching a meteor shower can be a meditative experience, a bonding event with loved ones, or even a spiritual practice, providing an opportunity to reconnect with nature, find inspiration, and set intentions for the new year.

Incorporating meteor shower viewing into holiday traditions offers a unique way to honor the season's themes of light, hope, and renewal. Just as holiday lights brighten dark winter evenings, meteor showers bring their own magic, reminding us of our connection to the cosmos and the beauty of fleeting moments. This chapter explores how observing meteor showers can be integrated into holiday traditions, the practical aspects of planning a successful meteor-watching experience, and the deeper significance of celebrating celestial events as part of the holiday season.

The Magic of Meteor Showers During the Holiday Season

Meteor showers carry a unique sense of magic, particularly when they coincide with the holiday season. The December sky, with its long nights and crisp air, provides an ideal backdrop for observing meteors, which often appear brighter and clearer in winter. The holiday season's themes of light overcoming darkness, reflection, and renewal resonate deeply with the symbolism of meteor showers, which bring fleeting flashes of brilliance to the quiet and stillness of winter.

1. **Light in Darkness**: Winter meteor showers, especially the Geminids, peak close to the winter solstice, the longest night of the year. This connection to the solstice enhances the symbolism of light in darkness, a theme that is celebrated in many holiday traditions. Observing meteors during this time can serve as a reminder of resilience, the promise of brighter days, and the beauty that emerges from the dark.

2. **Unity and Togetherness**: Watching a meteor shower can be a bonding experience, bringing families, friends, or communities together to share in the wonder of the night sky. During the holidays, which often emphasize unity and celebration, gathering to observe meteors fosters a sense of shared experience and connection. This ritual can create lasting memories and strengthen relationships, reinforcing the spirit of the season.

3. **Contemplation and New Beginnings**: The sight of meteors flashing across the sky often inspires reflection, encouraging us to pause and consider the passing year. Observing meteors provides a meditative moment to set intentions for the new year, connect with nature, and embrace the mystery of the universe. This contemplative aspect aligns with holiday traditions of reflection, gratitude, and renewal.

4. **Inspiration from the Cosmos**: Meteor showers offer a reminder of the vastness of the cosmos and our place within it. The experience of watching meteors reminds us of the interconnectedness of all life and the wonder of existence, inspiring awe and gratitude. This per-

spective can enhance the meaning of the holiday season, deepening our appreciation for the beauty of life and the mysteries of the universe.

Planning a Successful Meteor Shower Viewing Experience

Successfully incorporating a meteor shower into holiday traditions requires a bit of preparation, especially during the colder winter months. With the right approach, however, you can create a comfortable, memorable experience that allows you to fully enjoy the celestial display. Here are some essential steps to planning a successful meteor-watching outing:

1. Timing and Location

- **Choose the Right Time**: The peak of the Geminid meteor shower usually occurs around December 13-14, while the Ursid meteor shower peaks around December 21-22. While these dates offer the highest meteor activity, meteors can also be observed in the days before and after the peak. Aim to view the shower after midnight, when the radiant (the point in the sky from which meteors appear to originate) is higher, increasing meteor visibility.
- **Select a Dark Location**: Light pollution can obscure fainter meteors, so choosing a location away from city lights is essential. Rural areas, parks, beaches, or elevated locations with an open view of the sky are ideal. The darker the sky, the more meteors you'll be able to see, making the experience more immersive and magical.

2. Preparing for Cold Weather

- **Dress in Layers**: Winter meteor showers require cold-weather preparation. Dress in multiple layers, including thermal undergarments, sweaters, insulated jackets, hats, scarves, and gloves. Keeping warm is key to enjoying the experience without discomfort, as watching meteors typically involves staying still for extended periods.
- **Bring Blankets or Sleeping Bags**: Blankets and sleeping bags add extra warmth and comfort, especially if you plan to lie on the ground or sit in a reclining chair. Layering blankets or using a thermal sleeping bag can create a cozy spot, allowing you to relax and focus on the sky without the distraction of cold.
- **Warm Drinks**: Bringing hot drinks such as cocoa, tea, or coffee adds a comforting touch to the experience. Thermoses filled with warm beverages can help you stay warm and enjoy the festive atmosphere. Sharing hot drinks also creates a communal element, making the experience more enjoyable for groups.

3. Choosing Equipment and Setup

- **Reclining Chairs or Ground Mats**: Reclining chairs allow you to comfortably view the sky without straining your neck, while ground mats or blankets create a comfortable base if you choose to lie down. This setup ensures that you can fully relax and enjoy the meteors without the discomfort of sitting in an awkward position.

- **Binoculars and Telescopes (Optional)**: While you don't need binoculars or a telescope to watch meteor showers, these tools can enhance the experience by allowing you to explore other parts of the night sky. Telescopes and binoculars are useful for viewing constellations, planets, and even the radiant area in Gemini for the Geminids. However, keep in mind that meteors move quickly, and viewing them with the naked eye is generally the most effective approach.
- **Red Flashlights or Headlamps**: Red flashlights or headlamps are ideal for preserving night vision while allowing you to navigate in the dark. Red light has a minimal impact on night vision, so using these instead of regular flashlights ensures that your eyes remain adjusted to the dark sky, making it easier to spot meteors.

4. Creating a Festive Atmosphere

- **Decorations and Lighting**: Add a festive touch to your meteor-watching setup by incorporating subtle holiday decorations. String lights with a red or warm glow (or dim battery-powered lights) can create a cozy ambiance that won't interfere with night vision. These small touches bring a holiday feel to the event, combining the festive atmosphere with the wonder of stargazing.
- **Music and Stories**: Light background music or storytelling can enhance the experience. Sharing myths, legends, or holiday stories about stars and meteors adds depth to the event, connecting you to the historical and cultural significance of meteor showers. Some families enjoy sharing personal reflections or memories, creating a tradition of storytelling under the stars.
- **Wish-Making and Intention-Setting**: Many people associate meteors with wishes, and making a wish on a shooting star is a simple yet meaningful way to celebrate the holiday season. Encourage everyone to make a wish or set an intention when they see a meteor, turning the experience into a moment of personal reflection and hope.

The Deeper Significance of Meteor-Watching as a Holiday Tradition

Meteor showers carry symbolic meanings that align closely with the holiday season's spirit of light, renewal, and unity. Observing meteor showers can deepen our understanding of these themes, bringing a sense of peace, inspiration, and connection to the festivities.

1. Reflection and Gratitude

The holiday season is often a time of reflection on the past year, and observing a meteor shower offers a perfect opportunity to pause and contemplate life's fleeting moments. Each meteor represents a small but beautiful fragment of space, burning brightly for a brief moment before disappearing. This symbolism can inspire us to reflect on the transience of life, the preciousness of each experience, and the gratitude we feel for our own moments of light.

2. Hope and New Beginnings

Meteor showers are connected to themes of new beginnings and transformation, as the meteors are fragments of comets or asteroids burning up in Earth's atmosphere. Watching meteors in December, as we approach the New Year, serves as a reminder of the potential for change, growth, and renewal. Just as meteors bring bursts of light into the night, we too can bring new light and energy into our lives.

3. A Connection to the Cosmos

Watching a meteor shower offers a moment to connect with the vastness of the universe. This experience can be humbling and uplifting, reminding us of our place within the cosmic order. The sight of meteors streaking through the sky evokes a sense of wonder, inspiring thoughts about the interconnectedness of life and the mysteries beyond our understanding. This cosmic perspective adds depth to holiday traditions, encouraging us to find unity and meaning in shared experiences.

4. The Spirit of Giving and Generosity

Meteor showers, as spontaneous and generous displays from the cosmos, evoke the spirit of giving. Their appearance is a gift of beauty that can't be owned or possessed, reminding us of the importance of sharing joy and wonder with others. This sentiment aligns with holiday values of generosity, kindness, and gratitude. Watching meteors encourages us to be mindful of the gifts we give and receive, fostering a spirit of gratitude and abundance.

Creating Personal and Family Traditions with Meteor Showers

Incorporating meteor showers into holiday traditions can create meaningful experiences that are unique to each family or group. Here are some ideas for establishing your own meteor-watching tradition:

1. **Annual Viewing Ritual**: Make it a holiday tradition to gather each December to watch the Geminids or Ursids. By marking this time each year, families and friends can create a sense of continuity and look forward to a shared experience that celebrates both the holiday season and the beauty of nature.

2. **Wish-Making Ceremonies**: Encourage each participant to make a wish on the first meteor they see, symbolizing hope and dreams for the coming year. Alternatively, everyone can write down their wishes or intentions before the viewing, then reflect on these wishes as they watch the sky, creating a personal connection to the meteors.

3. **Personal Reflections and Resolutions**: Use the time under the stars to reflect on the past year, share personal milestones, and set intentions for the future. Each person can share a memory from the past year or a hope for the new one, bringing a deeper level of connection and meaning to the meteor-watching experience.

4. **Themed Storytelling or Myth Sharing**: Sharing myths, legends, or personal stories about meteors, stars, or the winter season adds a rich layer to the experience. By connecting the celestial event to cultural lore or family history, each meteor becomes a part of a larger story, linking participants to both ancient traditions and personal memories.

5. **Moment of Gratitude**: End the evening by sharing what each person is grateful for. This simple act can deepen the sense of peace and joy, reinforcing the holiday's themes of gratitude and unity. Expressing gratitude for each meteor seen, each shared memory, and each hope for the future turns the event into a heartwarming tradition.

Final Thoughts: Meteor Showers as a Celebration of Nature and Life

Observing meteor showers as a festive tradition during the holiday season brings a sense of awe, beauty, and wonder to the celebrations. Watching meteors cross the night sky reminds us of the vastness of the universe, the interconnectedness of life, and the fleeting nature of existence. These cosmic visitors inspire us to pause, reflect, and embrace the mystery of life, adding a profound dimension to holiday traditions.

Incorporating meteor-watching into the holiday season allows us to celebrate nature's gifts, marvel at the universe's beauty, and share meaningful experiences with loved ones. As each meteor blazes briefly across the sky, we are reminded that moments of light, joy, and connection are precious, encouraging us to carry these sentiments forward into the new year. This holiday season, let the magic of meteor showers illuminate your path, filling your heart with wonder, gratitude, and a sense of belonging to something far greater than ourselves.

Part 6: **Solar Flares and Christmas Energy**

Chapter 29: Solar Activity's Effect on Holiday Moods

The Sun, our nearest star, not only provides the Earth with light and warmth but also significantly influences our planet's atmosphere and magnetic field through a phenomenon known as solar activity. Solar flares, coronal mass ejections (CMEs), and changes in the solar wind create disturbances in Earth's magnetic field, often producing the beautiful auroras but also impacting human emotions, health, and even behavior. During the holiday season, these solar influences can subtly shape our moods and interactions, influencing feelings of joy, stress, or introspection. As we gather with family and friends, understanding the effects of solar activity on our moods and well-being can help us navigate the holiday season with greater awareness and mindfulness.

This chapter explores how solar activity affects mood and energy, the science behind these effects, and how understanding this connection can enhance our holiday experience. From seasonal changes in sunlight to the impact of geomagnetic storms, we'll look at the various ways the Sun influences our emotional states and how we can align with these rhythms to make the most of the holiday season.

Understanding Solar Activity and Its Mechanisms

Solar activity refers to the various dynamic processes that occur on the Sun's surface and in its corona, the outermost layer. The Sun experiences an approximately 11-year solar cycle, alternating between solar minimum (low activity) and solar maximum (high activity). During periods of high solar activity, phenomena such as solar flares, CMEs, and solar wind bursts become more frequent and intense, affecting Earth's magnetic field and atmosphere.

1. **Solar Flares**: Solar flares are sudden, intense bursts of radiation from the Sun's surface, usually near sunspots. They release massive amounts of energy in the form of X-rays and ultraviolet radiation, which can disrupt communications and satellite systems on Earth. Solar flares can also affect human physiology, including hormonal regulation and sleep patterns, potentially influencing mood.

2. **Coronal Mass Ejections (CMEs)**: CMEs are large expulsions of plasma and magnetic fields from the Sun's corona. When directed toward Earth, CMEs can cause geomagnetic storms by disturbing Earth's magnetosphere. These storms create auroras near the poles but also affect human biology, including the production of melatonin, the hormone responsible for regulating sleep-wake cycles. Changes in melatonin levels can influence mood, energy levels, and even immune function.

3. **Solar Wind**: The solar wind is a stream of charged particles emitted by the Sun. Variations in the solar wind can amplify or quiet geomagnetic activity, depending on its intensity and direction. When intense, it can trigger mild geomagnetic storms, affecting both electronic systems and human physiology.

Solar Activity and Its Influence on Human Mood and Well-Being

Studies have shown that solar activity, particularly geomagnetic storms, can impact mood, behavior, and even health. While the exact mechanisms are still being explored, researchers suggest that geomagnetic storms disrupt the Earth's magnetic field, which in turn may affect the brain, heart, and immune system. During the holiday season, these subtle but powerful influences can shape our experiences and interactions, amplifying both positive and challenging emotions.

1. **Mood Fluctuations and Sensitivity**: Solar activity is known to influence mood, causing some people to experience heightened sensitivity, irritability, or anxiety. Geomagnetic storms, in particular, can disrupt the body's circadian rhythm and melatonin production, leading to disrupted sleep and increased stress. During the holiday season, these mood changes can make some people feel more emotionally sensitive or reactive, especially in social settings.

2. **Enhanced Emotional Intensity**: High solar activity is associated with increased production of serotonin, the "feel-good" neurotransmitter. This can lead to heightened emotional intensity, amplifying feelings of joy, excitement, or even frustration. When holiday gatherings coincide with geomagnetic storms, some people may feel these emotions more strongly, making festive moments feel more memorable but also increasing the likelihood of emotional ups and downs.

3. **Increased Empathy and Connection**: Some studies suggest that geomagnetic storms can enhance interpersonal sensitivity, making people feel more attuned to others' emotions and needs. During the holiday season, this heightened empathy can help foster deeper connections and understanding, allowing people to bond more easily. However, it can also lead to feeling overwhelmed, as heightened empathy may make it challenging to manage intense social interactions.

4. **Stress and Fatigue**: Solar activity disrupts the regulation of cortisol, the body's primary stress hormone, which may lead to feelings of stress or fatigue. This is particularly true during geomagnetic storms, which have been linked to increased heart rate variability and changes in blood pressure. During the holidays, which are already filled with bustling activities, high solar activity may add to feelings of exhaustion, making it essential to prioritize rest and self-care.

5. **Sleep Disruptions and Energy Levels**: Changes in solar activity can alter melatonin levels, which are closely tied to sleep quality. Melatonin helps regulate our internal clock, and fluctuations in its levels due to geomagnetic disturbances may lead to insomnia or disrupted sleep patterns. During the holidays, poor sleep can impact energy levels, affecting mood and even

immune function, which can make it harder to enjoy festivities or fully engage with loved ones.

Seasonal Changes and Solar Influence on Holiday Moods

Apart from solar activity, the holiday season falls during winter in the Northern Hemisphere, when days are shorter and exposure to natural sunlight is limited. This seasonal lack of sunlight impacts mood by altering levels of melatonin and serotonin, often contributing to a condition known as Seasonal Affective Disorder (SAD). While solar activity itself plays a role, the interplay between sunlight, seasonal rhythms, and individual sensitivity creates a complex emotional landscape during the holidays.

1. **Seasonal Affective Disorder (SAD)**: SAD is a form of depression that typically occurs in winter, characterized by low mood, fatigue, and difficulty concentrating. Reduced sunlight affects the hypothalamus, which regulates melatonin and serotonin production, leading to mood disturbances. People with SAD may experience challenges during the holidays, finding it difficult to feel festive or enjoy activities they typically love.

2. **The Importance of Natural Light Exposure**: Sunlight exposure is essential for maintaining mood stability, as it helps regulate serotonin and melatonin. During the holiday season, making an effort to spend time outdoors during daylight hours can counteract the effects of both reduced sunlight and the influences of solar activity. Natural light can help stabilize mood, improve energy levels, and increase feelings of well-being, making it easier to enjoy the holiday festivities.

3. **Circadian Rhythms and Holiday Social Schedules**: The holiday season often involves gatherings and events that disrupt natural sleep patterns, which can exacerbate the effects of solar activity on mood. Late nights, increased socialization, and changes in routine can make people more vulnerable to mood fluctuations, especially when geomagnetic storms are in play. Maintaining a balanced sleep schedule during the holidays can help mitigate these effects, ensuring that the influence of solar activity is less likely to disrupt mood or well-being.

Enhancing Holiday Well-Being Through Awareness of Solar Activity

Understanding the effects of solar activity and seasonal changes on mood can empower us to navigate the holidays with greater self-awareness and resilience. By paying attention to our body's responses to solar activity, we can make choices that enhance well-being, reduce stress, and maximize enjoyment of the holiday season.

1. **Practicing Mindfulness and Emotional Regulation**: Heightened solar activity can amplify emotions, making it easier to feel joyful but also more susceptible to stress or irritability. Practicing mindfulness techniques, such as deep breathing or meditation, can help calm the nervous system, countering the effects of solar-induced stress. This mindful approach can make holiday interactions more harmonious and allow for a deeper sense of connection with others.

2. **Prioritizing Sleep and Rest**: Given the impact of solar activity on sleep, prioritizing rest becomes even more essential during the holiday season. Try to maintain a consistent sleep routine, avoid excessive caffeine, and create a relaxing bedtime ritual to support good-quality rest. Using blackout curtains, reducing blue light exposure before bed, and incorporating relaxation techniques like reading or gentle stretching can help counteract the sleep-disruptive effects of geomagnetic storms.

3. **Embracing Nature and Outdoor Time**: Exposure to natural light, especially in the morning, helps regulate melatonin and boosts serotonin production, improving mood and energy levels. Plan outdoor activities like winter walks, snow play, or even just sitting by a window to soak up sunlight. The combination of fresh air and sunlight exposure can counteract feelings of fatigue or low mood associated with both solar activity and seasonal changes.

4. **Setting Boundaries During Social Gatherings**: When heightened solar activity amplifies emotional intensity, it's helpful to be mindful of personal boundaries. Socializing during the holidays can be wonderful but also overwhelming, especially if you're more sensitive to others' emotions. Practice self-care by setting time limits, allowing for moments of solitude, and communicating boundaries. Being mindful of emotional needs can help create a balanced holiday experience.

5. **Staying Hydrated and Nourished**: Solar activity, especially geomagnetic storms, has been linked to fluctuations in blood pressure and heart rate. Staying hydrated and maintaining balanced blood sugar levels through nutritious meals can help regulate mood and reduce stress. Foods rich in magnesium, B vitamins, and omega-3 fatty acids support mental health and can mitigate stress-related symptoms. Incorporating grounding foods like warm soups, herbal teas, and complex carbohydrates can promote relaxation and a stable mood.

6. **Using Light Therapy**: For those particularly affected by reduced sunlight during the winter season, light therapy can provide a boost to mood and energy levels. Using a light therapy box that simulates natural daylight for 20-30 minutes each morning can help stabilize circadian rhythms, reduce symptoms of SAD, and counteract the mood-destabilizing effects of solar activity.

Making Solar Awareness Part of the Holiday Tradition

Incorporating an awareness of solar and seasonal influences into holiday traditions can enrich the season by adding a layer of mindfulness and self-compassion. Whether through shared rituals, moments of introspection, or personal self-care, honoring our connection to the rhythms of nature can deepen the holiday experience.

1. **Creating a Solar Reflection Ritual**: Set aside a few moments to reflect on the Sun's influence on mood and energy, discussing how sunlight and the changing seasons shape our emotional experiences. Consider creating a tradition of gratitude for the Sun's warmth and light, recognizing its essential role in supporting life and well-being.
2. **Setting Intentions Based on Solar Cycles**: Use the holiday season as an opportunity to align intentions with the natural rhythms of solar activity and the year's cycle. During a calm, reflective gathering, set intentions for the coming year that emphasize balance, resilience, and mindfulness, honoring both the Sun's energy and the winter season's call for introspection.
3. **Holiday Outdoor Gatherings**: Embrace the holiday season with outdoor gatherings, weather permitting. Sunlit winter activities, like skating, hiking, or simply walking together in nature, can offer both exposure to natural light and an opportunity to connect with loved ones. This tradition fosters gratitude for sunlight, grounding the season in a sense of harmony with nature.
4. **Tracking Solar Activity Together**: For those interested in astronomy, consider tracking solar activity together as a family or group, using online resources or apps that report on solar flares, geomagnetic storms, and solar cycles. This activity can become a shared holiday ritual, helping everyone stay mindful of the Sun's influence on mood and energy while building a sense of connection with the cosmos.

Final Thoughts: Solar Activity as a Guide for Holiday Well-Being

The Sun's influence extends far beyond providing light and warmth; it impacts our moods, sleep, and overall well-being, subtly shaping our holiday experiences. By becoming aware of the effects of solar activity, we gain insights into the ways these cosmic forces shape our emotions, interactions, and health. During the holiday season, when emotions run high, and gatherings are frequent, understanding these influences can help us make choices that support harmony, mindfulness, and joy.

This holiday season, let solar awareness enhance your festivities, guiding you toward a more balanced and grounded experience. Embrace the Sun's influence as a reminder of the cyclical nature of life, finding peace in its rhythms and gratitude for its light, even during the cold winter months. By aligning with these natural cycles, we can deepen our sense of connection, resilience, and wonder, creating a holiday season that is both meaningful and attuned to the cosmic forces that shape our world.

Chapter 30: December's Solar Flares and Cosmic Energy

December, with its long, dark nights and cold winter air, provides a unique atmosphere for exploring the powerful forces of the cosmos. Among these celestial phenomena are solar flares, intense bursts of energy from the Sun that release streams of charged particles into space. While solar flares occur throughout the year, their effects during December can be particularly intriguing, as they influence Earth's magnetic field and subtly impact our mood, health, and even spiritual awareness during the holiday season. This chapter delves into the nature of December's solar flares, the science behind their impact on Earth and human experience, and how we can align with this cosmic energy to enhance our holiday season with greater mindfulness and balance.

Solar flares, with their bursts of energy and far-reaching impacts, are a potent symbol of change and transformation. They remind us of the Sun's dynamic nature and its ability to affect life on Earth, even across millions of miles. Understanding the energy of solar flares and learning to harmonize with their rhythms can deepen our connection to the cosmos, helping us to integrate the Sun's powerful influence into our holiday traditions and celebrations.

What Are Solar Flares?

Solar flares are sudden eruptions of energy on the Sun's surface, usually occurring in areas with complex magnetic fields near sunspots. When these magnetic fields realign, they release a massive amount of energy in the form of radiation, which includes X-rays, gamma rays, and particles like protons and electrons. Solar flares are classified based on their intensity, with five primary classes: A, B, C, M, and X, each representing a higher level of energy output, with X-class flares being the most intense.

1. The Mechanics of Solar Flares

- Solar flares occur when magnetic energy that has built up in the solar atmosphere is suddenly released. This energy heats plasma to millions of degrees, causing the emission of high-energy radiation and accelerating particles that travel outward from the Sun.
- The energy from a solar flare can reach Earth in as little as eight minutes, disrupting radio communication, satellite operations, and sometimes even power grids. Larger flares are often accompanied by **coronal mass ejections (CMEs)**, which release solar plasma and magnetic fields that can cause geomagnetic storms on Earth.

2. December's Solar Flares

- The occurrence and intensity of solar flares vary based on the Sun's approximately 11-year solar cycle, which alternates between solar minimum and solar maximum. During solar maximum, when sunspot activity is highest, solar flares are more frequent and intense. The current solar cycle, Solar Cycle 25, began in 2019, with increasing activity expected to peak around 2025.
- December often aligns with increased solar activity as the Sun's cycle intensifies, and the effects of these flares are felt more profoundly as geomagnetic disturbances occur. These De-

cember solar flares add a unique layer to the cosmic energy of the holiday season, subtly influencing both our external environment and internal experiences.

The Impact of Solar Flares on Earth's Magnetic Field

When solar flares occur, they release streams of charged particles that interact with Earth's magnetic field, resulting in geomagnetic storms and auroras near the poles. These disturbances, while visually spectacular, also affect Earth's atmosphere and magnetic field in ways that can have subtle but significant impacts on human biology and psychology.

1. **Geomagnetic Storms and Auroras**: When charged particles from solar flares collide with Earth's magnetosphere, they produce a phenomenon known as auroras, or the northern and southern lights. These colorful displays are most visible near the polar regions, where the magnetic field directs charged particles into the atmosphere. Auroras are a beautiful visual reminder of the Sun's energetic influence on Earth and a cosmic symbol of interconnectedness during the holiday season.
2. **Disruptions to Communication and Navigation**: Solar flares emit high levels of radiation that can interfere with radio signals, GPS systems, and even power grids. These disruptions serve as a reminder of how closely linked we are to the Sun's rhythms, as a single flare can affect technologies integral to modern life.
3. **Earth's Magnetic Field and Human Health**: The human body has its own electromagnetic field, which interacts with Earth's magnetic field. When geomagnetic storms occur, they can disrupt this natural balance, influencing our heart rate, blood pressure, and circadian rhythm. These disturbances can impact mood, energy, and mental clarity, often leading to increased sensitivity, anxiety, or physical fatigue. During the holiday season, these effects can amplify the emotional highs and lows already present in this festive period.

Solar Flares' Influence on Mood and Behavior

Solar flares don't just affect technology and Earth's magnetic field; they also impact human physiology and mood. Research has shown that fluctuations in geomagnetic activity, especially during geomagnetic storms, can influence the human nervous system, disrupting sleep, affecting cognitive function, and intensifying emotional responses. December's solar flares, combined with the holiday season's social and emotional demands, can create unique challenges and opportunities for inner growth and connection.

1. **Emotional Sensitivity and Stress**: Increased solar activity has been linked to heightened sensitivity and emotional reactivity. Solar flares can disrupt the balance of melatonin and serotonin, two hormones that regulate mood and sleep. This imbalance can lead to emotional intensity, mood swings, and, for some, increased stress. During the holiday season, when gatherings, travel, and family interactions are common, these effects can make it harder to stay calm and centered.

2. **Enhanced Creativity and Inspiration**: On a positive note, the increased energy of solar flares can also stimulate the creative and intuitive centers of the brain. This boost of cosmic energy often results in heightened mental clarity, deeper insights, and bursts of inspiration. For those celebrating the holidays, this can translate into creative activities, such as decorating, cooking, crafting, or storytelling, allowing for a more meaningful holiday experience.

3. **Impact on Sleep and Energy Levels**: Solar flares can interfere with sleep patterns by altering melatonin production. Many people report difficulty falling asleep or staying asleep during periods of heightened solar activity, leading to fatigue and irritability. During the holiday season, this disruption can impact energy levels, making it harder to enjoy festivities. Practicing relaxation techniques, maintaining a regular sleep schedule, and avoiding excessive caffeine can help mitigate these effects.

4. **Spiritual Sensitivity and Insight**: Some people report feeling more spiritually aware during times of heightened solar activity, as solar flares are thought to increase sensitivity to subtle energies. This heightened awareness can inspire personal reflection, meditation, and a deeper connection to the meaning of the holiday season. Solar flares, in this sense, serve as catalysts for introspection, allowing people to align with the themes of peace, gratitude, and unity that the holidays represent.

Embracing Solar Flares as Part of the Holiday Experience

By understanding and working with the energies of solar flares, we can integrate their influence into our holiday celebrations, turning potential stressors into opportunities for growth and connection. Here are some ways to harmonize with December's solar energy to create a more fulfilling holiday experience:

1. **Practicing Grounding and Energy-Balancing Techniques**: Grounding, or connecting with Earth's energy, can help offset the effects of solar flares on mood and energy. Techniques such as walking barefoot outdoors, meditating with visualizations of being rooted in the Earth, or practicing yoga can stabilize the body's energy field, helping to maintain calm and balance during times of heightened solar activity.

2. **Using Meditation and Breathwork for Centering**: Meditation, particularly techniques focused on breath awareness and visualization, can counteract the disruptive effects of solar flares on mood and energy. Visualizing a calming, protective light around the body or focusing on slow, deep breathing can create a sense of peace and inner stillness. This practice is especially valuable during holiday gatherings, allowing for greater emotional resilience and clarity.

3. **Engaging in Reflective and Spiritual Practices**: Solar flares often enhance intuition and spiritual awareness, making December an ideal time for reflective and spiritual practices. Journaling, setting intentions for the coming year, or engaging in gratitude practices can deepen the holiday experience, allowing for a meaningful exploration of the themes of love, connection, and renewal that characterize the season.

4. **Setting Boundaries and Prioritizing Rest**: Solar flares can heighten emotions and create a need for more personal space. Practicing self-care by setting boundaries and prioritizing rest can prevent overwhelm, especially during the busy holiday season. If gatherings become too intense or social interactions too taxing, taking breaks, going for a walk, or finding a quiet place to recharge can help maintain balance.

5. **Expressing Creativity and Channeling Energy**: The amplified energy of solar flares can enhance creativity and enthusiasm, making December a wonderful time to engage in creative holiday traditions. Baking, decorating, crafting, and even gift-giving can become expressions of joy and gratitude. By channeling cosmic energy into creative projects, we can transform the effects of solar flares into memorable holiday experiences.

Solar Flares as Symbols of Transformation and Renewal

Solar flares, with their dynamic bursts of energy, symbolize transformation, release, and renewal—concepts that align beautifully with the spirit of the holiday season. December's solar flares remind us of the cyclical nature of energy, encouraging us to release what no longer serves us and to embrace growth and change as we approach the new year.

1. **Releasing Old Patterns and Embracing New Intentions**: The energy of solar flares supports the process of letting go of old patterns and setting intentions for the future. This symbolic release can be integrated into holiday traditions by creating rituals that honor the closing of one chapter and the beginning of another. Writing down intentions or participating in a holiday ceremony dedicated to renewal can help align with the transformative energy of the Sun.

2. **Celebrating Light and Cosmic Energy**: Solar flares serve as reminders of the Sun's power and its vital role in sustaining life. As we celebrate the holidays, incorporating symbols of light and warmth can honor this cosmic energy. Lighting candles, using warm colors in decorations, or sharing stories about the Sun and stars can help connect holiday traditions to the broader theme of cosmic influence, adding depth and significance to celebrations.

3. **Reflection on Inner and Outer Light**: Solar flares, as bursts of outer light, remind us to nurture our own inner light. The holiday season provides an opportunity to reflect on what brings us joy, meaning, and inspiration. By aligning with the Sun's energy, we can focus on cultivating our inner light, sharing warmth, kindness, and compassion with others as part of the holiday spirit.

4. **Connecting with Nature's Rhythms**: Solar flares remind us of our interconnectedness with the cosmos and the natural world. Taking time to connect with nature—whether through winter walks, watching the stars, or observing the sky—can reinforce this sense of connection and bring a sense of peace and grounding during the holiday season. Aligning with the rhythms of nature allows us to feel more in sync with the world, enhancing well-being and perspective.

Final Thoughts: Integrating Solar Energy into the Holiday Season

December's solar flares offer more than just cosmic light shows; they influence our emotions, inspire creativity, and invite us to reflect on our place in the universe. By embracing the energy of solar flares as part of the holiday season, we can connect with the Sun's power in a way that enriches our lives, brings peace, and inspires growth. Solar flares serve as powerful symbols of renewal, transformation, and interconnectedness, qualities that resonate with the themes of the holiday season.

This December, as solar energy pulses through the cosmos and reaches Earth, let its dynamic influence remind you of the cycles of release and renewal, light and darkness, and the energy within and beyond. Whether through mindful reflection, creative expression, or simple acts of kindness, may the Sun's energy illuminate your holiday season, filling it with warmth, wonder, and a deep appreciation for the beautiful, ever-changing dance of the cosmos.

Chapter 31: Harnessing Solar Power for Festive Inspiration

As the holidays approach, the spirit of warmth, joy, and creativity fills the air, inviting us to celebrate, reflect, and connect with loved ones. Solar power, a clean and renewable energy source derived from the Sun, offers a unique way to add depth to our holiday season by connecting with the very source of light and warmth that sustains life. Integrating solar power into holiday celebrations is both environmentally conscious and spiritually significant, allowing us to align with nature, reduce our carbon footprint, and inspire others to embrace sustainability.

In this chapter, we'll explore how solar power can enhance holiday traditions and provide ideas for using solar energy creatively during the season. From solar-powered decorations and outdoor lighting to thoughtful eco-friendly gift ideas and renewable holiday traditions, harnessing solar power for festive inspiration can bring an added sense of purpose and meaning to holiday celebrations. We'll also look at the symbolic significance of solar energy, which aligns beautifully with the themes of light, renewal, and giving back to the Earth.

The Symbolism of Solar Energy in Holiday Celebrations

Throughout history, the winter holiday season has centered around themes of light, warmth, and rebirth, often celebrated with candles, fires, and now, electric lights. Solar power provides a unique way to honor these timeless themes, as it captures energy directly from the Sun—a universal symbol of life, vitality, and continuity.

1. **Light and Warmth in Dark Times**: As winter days grow shorter and nights grow longer, solar power becomes a powerful symbol of light overcoming darkness. By incorporating solar-powered lights and decorations, we can celebrate the return of the Sun and embrace the warmth and joy that solar energy brings into our homes and communities.

2. **Renewal and Sustainability**: Solar energy represents a commitment to sustainability, encouraging us to use renewable resources and reduce our reliance on fossil fuels. During a season that often emphasizes gratitude, generosity, and hope for the future, using solar power aligns with the idea of giving back to the planet and conserving resources for future generations.

3. **Connection to the Cosmos and Nature**: The Sun, as the central source of life and energy, reminds us of our connection to the cosmos and the natural world. By integrating solar power into holiday traditions, we honor the Sun's essential role in life on Earth and reinforce a sense of interconnectedness. This awareness can deepen our appreciation for the environment and inspire practices that benefit both people and the planet.

Solar-Powered Holiday Decorations

Incorporating solar-powered decorations into holiday celebrations is an easy and effective way to bring festive spirit into the home or garden while reducing energy consumption. From solar string lights to illuminated ornaments and pathway lights, solar-powered decorations offer a wide range of creative options.

1. **Solar String Lights**: Solar string lights are a popular and versatile option for holiday decorating, available in various colors, lengths, and styles. These lights can be used indoors or outdoors, providing a warm, festive glow powered by the Sun. Solar string lights work well for decorating trees, porches, fences, windows, and even indoor spaces that receive ample sunlight during the day. By using these lights, you can create a magical, cozy atmosphere while conserving energy.

2. **Illuminated Ornaments and Garden Sculptures**: Solar-powered ornaments and sculptures can add a unique touch to holiday decor. Garden sculptures, solar-powered lanterns, and illuminated animal figures can bring charm and whimsy to outdoor spaces. Solar ornaments are ideal for gardens, balconies, or windows, where they can soak up sunlight during the day and shine in the evening, creating an enchanting holiday display without the need for electric cables.

3. **Pathway and Driveway Lights**: Solar-powered pathway lights are a practical and decorative way to brighten walkways and driveways during the holiday season. Many designs are available, from classic lanterns to star-shaped or holiday-themed lights, providing both safety and style. These lights create a welcoming glow that guides guests to your home, emphasizing the spirit of hospitality while using clean energy.

4. **Solar-Powered Tree Toppers and Window Stars**: Solar-powered tree toppers and window stars are a unique way to bring a solar touch to traditional decorations. These can be placed near a window or in an area that receives ample sunlight, illuminating at night and reminding us of the connection between holiday lights and the Sun's radiant energy. Solar window stars add a soft, festive glow to interiors, perfect for embracing the holiday spirit sustainably.

5. **DIY Solar Jar Lights and Lanterns**: For a personal touch, try creating solar jar lights or lanterns using mason jars and small solar-powered LED lights. Simply place a small solar light inside a jar, add decorative elements like holiday charms, glitter, or pine cones, and let it soak up sunlight. These DIY solar lanterns are perfect for setting on windowsills, mantels, or tables and make beautiful, eco-friendly decorations that can be reused year after year.

Solar-Powered Holiday Gifts

Giving solar-powered gifts not only promotes sustainability but also encourages recipients to explore renewable energy. These gifts are thoughtful and practical, serving as a reminder of the importance of clean energy throughout the year. Here are some ideas for solar-powered holiday gifts:

1. **Solar Chargers for Phones and Gadgets**: Solar chargers are practical gifts for anyone who uses a smartphone, tablet, or other portable electronics. These chargers harness solar energy to power devices, making them ideal for travelers, hikers, and anyone interested in reducing reliance on electrical outlets. Compact and efficient, solar chargers can be a valuable addition to any tech lover's toolkit.

2. **Solar-Powered Flashlights and Lanterns**: Solar-powered flashlights and lanterns are useful, eco-friendly alternatives to traditional battery-powered lights. These items are perfect for outdoor enthusiasts, campers, or emergency preparedness kits, as they provide reliable illumination without the need for disposable batteries. They are also a thoughtful gift option for friends and family who appreciate practical, energy-efficient solutions.

3. **Solar Cookers and Ovens**: For those who love cooking and sustainability, a solar cooker or solar oven is an innovative gift option. These devices harness solar energy to cook food without electricity, gas, or wood, making them perfect for outdoor picnics, camping, or emergency situations. Solar cookers are available in various sizes and styles, from compact models for small meals to larger designs for family gatherings.

4. **Solar Garden and Outdoor Décor**: Solar garden lights, wind chimes with solar lights, and solar-powered fountains make wonderful gifts for those who love gardening or outdoor decor. These items add beauty and functionality to outdoor spaces, providing gentle illumination and ambiance without requiring electric power. Solar-powered garden decor is a gift that keeps on giving, as it reduces energy costs and enhances outdoor aesthetics.

5. **Educational Solar Kits for Kids**: Solar kits designed for children are fun, educational gifts that introduce kids to the basics of solar energy and renewable resources. These kits typically include materials to build simple solar-powered devices like cars, robots, or small lights, fostering curiosity and creativity. Educational solar kits inspire the next generation to learn about sustainability in an interactive way, making them perfect gifts for children during the holiday season.

Solar-Powered Community and Family Activities

Harnessing solar power during the holidays can go beyond individual gifts and decorations. Engaging in solar-powered community activities or family traditions can inspire awareness, education, and togetherness, fostering a deeper connection to sustainable living.

1. **Solar-Powered Community Light Displays**: Community holiday light displays are a cherished tradition in many towns, and incorporating solar-powered lights into these displays reduces energy consumption while promoting awareness of renewable energy. Communities can organize solar-powered lighting installations in public parks, plazas, or gardens, showcasing the beauty of solar energy while celebrating the holiday season. These events also provide opportunities for educational talks or demonstrations about solar energy.

2. **Family Solar Crafting Day**: A family crafting day focused on creating solar-powered decorations, gifts, or DIY lights can be a fun and creative holiday activity. Families can gather to make solar jar lights, solar wreaths, or other handmade decorations, turning solar crafting into a festive, eco-friendly tradition. This hands-on activity is both educational and enjoyable, teaching children and adults alike about the possibilities of renewable energy.

3. **Hosting a Solar-Powered Holiday Feast Outdoors**: If weather permits, hosting a holiday meal outdoors during the day and using solar cookers can be a memorable and sustainable experience. Prepare food using solar ovens or cookers, and use solar-powered lights to create ambiance as the evening sets in. This unique celebration offers a chance to gather with loved ones while enjoying the Sun's energy and embracing eco-friendly practices.

4. **Organize a Solar-Powered Movie Night**: Set up an outdoor projector powered by a portable solar generator, and host a cozy movie night under the stars. Bring blankets, hot cocoa, and holiday treats, and enjoy a seasonal film with family and friends. A solar-powered movie night combines entertainment with sustainability, showcasing how solar energy can be used in creative ways beyond traditional lighting.

5. **Encouraging Solar Education and Awareness**: The holiday season is a great time to give back by hosting or participating in community workshops or presentations about solar energy. Local environmental organizations, schools, or community centers may be open to educational events that teach about the benefits of solar energy and sustainability. These events can include solar energy demonstrations, DIY solar projects, and discussions about the future of renewable energy.

Solar-Powered Traditions for a Sustainable Holiday Season

Establishing holiday traditions that incorporate solar power can help create a lasting commitment to sustainability, transforming the season into a time of environmental stewardship. These traditions remind us of the importance of reducing our ecological impact and can become meaningful parts of holiday celebrations for years to come.

1. **Solar Lighting Ceremony**: Begin the holiday season with a solar lighting ceremony, using only solar-powered lights to illuminate a tree, wreath, or outdoor space. This tradition symbolizes the arrival of light in the dark season and honors the Sun's contribution to life on Earth. A solar lighting ceremony can become a cherished part of holiday celebrations, marking the start of festivities with a mindful focus on sustainability.

2. **Eco-Friendly Solar Gift Exchange**: Host a solar-powered or eco-friendly gift exchange with family or friends, where each person gives a gift that supports sustainable living. Solar-powered gadgets, sustainable home goods, or reusable items encourage eco-friendly habits and inspire recipients to think more consciously about energy use. This type of gift exchange highlights the spirit of giving while promoting positive change for the planet.

3. **Nature Walk with Solar Lanterns**: Create a family tradition of taking a nature walk with solar lanterns to appreciate the beauty of winter landscapes. This outdoor activity, conducted around dusk or nightfall, allows families to enjoy fresh air and nature's tranquility while using sustainable lighting. Solar lanterns add a festive touch to the experience, combining exploration with a focus on clean energy.

4. **Solar-Powered New Year's Intentions**: As part of New Year celebrations, set intentions related to sustainable living, renewable energy, or conservation. Use a solar-powered light or lantern as a symbolic reminder of the commitment to sustainability, letting it shine throughout the night as a symbol of hope and change. This tradition can help foster long-term dedication to environmental stewardship.

5. **Celebrating Winter Solstice with Solar Rituals**: The winter solstice, the shortest day of the year, holds significance as a turning point when the Sun's light begins to return. Create rituals that celebrate the Sun's power and recognize the importance of renewable energy. Lighting solar candles, reflecting on the year's achievements, and setting intentions for the future can honor the solstice's themes of renewal and light.

Final Thoughts: Bringing Solar Power into Holiday Traditions

Harnessing solar power for festive inspiration allows us to celebrate the holidays in a way that respects the Earth, honors the Sun, and aligns with the spirit of giving. Solar-powered decorations, gifts, and traditions not only reduce our carbon footprint but also inspire others to think creatively about renewable energy and sustainable living. By integrating solar power into holiday celebrations, we bring a sense of purpose and mindfulness into a season that is already rich with meaning.

This holiday season, let the warmth and light of the Sun illuminate your celebrations, reminding you of the power of renewable energy and the importance of sustainability. Whether through simple solar decorations, thoughtful gifts, or community traditions, embracing solar power creates a festive experience that honors nature and nurtures hope for a brighter, greener future. As you harness the Sun's energy in your holiday festivities, may its light inspire you to carry these values forward, creating a season of joy, harmony, and lasting impact.

Part 7: **Lunar Eclipses & Christmas**

Chapter 32: Lunar Eclipses' Influence on Emotions in December

A lunar eclipse, an event when the Earth passes between the Sun and the Moon, casting its shadow over the Moon, is one of the most awe-inspiring celestial phenomena visible from Earth. When this event occurs in December, it holds special significance, especially as it coincides with the holiday season, a time already rich with reflection, celebration, and heightened emotions. Many cultures and spiritual traditions believe that lunar eclipses intensify our emotions, bringing feelings to the surface and encouraging us to explore the depths of our subconscious. This chapter explores the nature of lunar eclipses, how they affect emotional well-being, and how we can mindfully navigate their influence to enhance our holiday season.

December's long nights provide an ideal backdrop for lunar events, allowing for uninterrupted views of the Moon's transformation during an eclipse. As we observe the Moon being cloaked in shadow, it serves as a powerful symbol of introspection, cycles of change, and the duality of light and darkness—qualities that resonate deeply during the winter months. By understanding the emotional and psychological impact of a lunar eclipse, we can harness its energy to reflect, connect, and find balance as we navigate the holiday season.

The Mechanics of a Lunar Eclipse

A lunar eclipse occurs when the Earth's shadow falls on the Moon, temporarily obscuring its light. This phenomenon can only happen during a full moon, as that is when the Sun, Earth, and Moon are aligned. There are three types of lunar eclipses, each creating a distinct visual and symbolic experience.

1. **Total Lunar Eclipse**: During a total lunar eclipse, the Earth's shadow completely covers the Moon, causing it to appear red or orange—a phenomenon often called the "Blood Moon." This effect is due to Earth's atmosphere filtering out blue light and scattering the red hues, which reach the Moon's surface. A total eclipse creates a powerful visual transformation, symbolizing deep introspection and intense emotional processing.
2. **Partial Lunar Eclipse**: In a partial eclipse, only a part of the Moon enters Earth's shadow, leaving a portion of it visible. This type of eclipse often represents partial revelation, where certain aspects of our emotions or subconscious come to light while others remain hidden.
3. **Penumbral Lunar Eclipse**: The least dramatic visually, a penumbral eclipse occurs when the Moon passes through the Earth's outer shadow, the penumbra, causing only a subtle shading. While this eclipse might not create a striking image in the sky, its influence on emotions and reflection can still be significant, representing subtle changes and gradual realizations.

During a lunar eclipse, the absence of the Moon's usual brightness in the night sky can feel unsettling or unusual, stirring our inner worlds and bringing unresolved feelings or thoughts to the forefront. This dynamic makes lunar eclipses a potent time for introspection, release, and emotional transformation.

The Emotional and Psychological Impact of Lunar Eclipses

Lunar eclipses are known to heighten emotional sensitivity, often prompting deep self-reflection, revealing hidden emotions, and encouraging us to confront aspects of ourselves that we may have ignored. The Moon, associated with emotions, intuition, and the subconscious, becomes "shadowed" during an eclipse, symbolizing the exploration of our inner shadows—our fears, suppressed desires, and unresolved memories.

1. **Intensified Emotions and Sensitivity**: Many people report feeling more emotionally sensitive or vulnerable during a lunar eclipse. This heightened sensitivity can bring up unresolved feelings, allowing us to address them. During December, a time when we may already be reflecting on the year's experiences, a lunar eclipse can amplify these feelings, prompting us to examine our emotional landscape more closely.

2. **Release and Letting Go**: Eclipses, especially total lunar eclipses, are often seen as catalysts for letting go of old patterns, relationships, or mindsets that no longer serve us. This sense of release aligns with the themes of the holiday season, as we prepare to transition into a new year. The energy of a lunar eclipse can encourage us to release emotional baggage, making room for renewal and growth.

3. **Heightened Intuition and Psychic Awareness**: Lunar eclipses are believed to open doors to the subconscious, making it easier to access intuition and insights. During an eclipse, people may experience vivid dreams, sudden realizations, or a stronger connection to their inner guidance. This intuitive boost can be particularly valuable during the holiday season, helping us make meaningful decisions and approach relationships with greater empathy and understanding.

4. **Exploration of Shadows and Inner Healing**: The shadowed Moon symbolizes the exploration of our inner "shadows"—the parts of ourselves we may try to hide, ignore, or suppress. Lunar eclipses offer an opportunity to confront these hidden aspects and address unresolved issues. By embracing this period of introspection, we can work through limiting beliefs, fears, or doubts, creating a stronger foundation for personal growth.

5. **Impact on Relationships and Family Dynamics**: The holiday season often brings family gatherings and social events, which can become more emotionally charged during a lunar eclipse. The heightened emotional sensitivity can lead to increased empathy and understanding, but it may also bring old conflicts or unresolved family issues to the surface. Lunar eclipses provide an opportunity to address these dynamics with compassion, helping to clear misunderstandings and foster deeper connections.

Harnessing the Energy of a December Lunar Eclipse

Navigating the influence of a lunar eclipse requires mindfulness, self-compassion, and a willingness to explore inner emotions. When harnessed constructively, the energy of a lunar eclipse can promote healing, growth, and renewal. Here are some practices for making the most of this powerful time:

1. **Reflection and Journaling**: Journaling during a lunar eclipse can help clarify emotions and uncover hidden thoughts or desires. Begin by writing about recent experiences, relationships, or challenges, allowing your thoughts to flow freely. This process of reflection can bring insight into unresolved feelings and highlight areas in need of healing or release. Consider questions like, "What am I ready to let go of?" or "What has this past year taught me about myself?"

2. **Embracing Solitude and Quiet Time**: Lunar eclipses are ideal for introspection, making it beneficial to spend some time in solitude. Create a quiet space free from distractions, where you can connect with your inner self. This dedicated time for reflection allows you to process emotions, listen to your intuition, and embrace any realizations that arise.

3. **Releasing Rituals for Emotional Clearing**: Rituals are powerful tools for acknowledging and releasing emotions, especially during a lunar eclipse. Consider writing down anything you want to release—old habits, limiting beliefs, or unresolved emotions—and then safely burn or bury the paper as a symbolic act of letting go. These rituals help to create closure, allowing you to move forward with a lighter heart and a renewed sense of clarity.

4. **Meditation and Visualization**: Meditation during a lunar eclipse can deepen your connection to the subconscious mind, facilitating healing and insight. Try a guided meditation focused on releasing old patterns or visualizing yourself letting go of what no longer serves you. Visualization exercises, such as imagining the shadow on the Moon dissolving with each breath, can also be powerful in supporting emotional cleansing.

5. **Working with the Symbolism of Light and Shadow**: A lunar eclipse is a dance between light and shadow, symbolizing the balance between our conscious and subconscious minds. Embrace this duality by acknowledging both the positive and challenging aspects of your emotions. Recognize that both light and shadow have valuable lessons to teach, and that embracing both aspects of the self leads to greater wholeness and self-acceptance.

6. **Setting Intentions for the Coming Year**: As a time of transition, a lunar eclipse in December provides a powerful opportunity to set intentions for the new year. Reflect on the insights gained during the eclipse and consider what you want to invite into your life in the coming months. These intentions can serve as a guide for personal growth, encouraging you to nurture the qualities and experiences that align with your higher self.

The Influence of Lunar Eclipses on Social and Family Gatherings

Lunar eclipses, with their capacity to heighten emotions, can influence the dynamics of social and family gatherings during the holiday season. Being aware of this effect can help you navigate interactions with greater compassion and sensitivity, creating an atmosphere of understanding and harmony.

1. **Increased Empathy and Understanding**: The emotional sensitivity that arises during a lunar eclipse can enhance empathy, making it easier to understand and connect with others on a deeper level. This heightened awareness allows for more meaningful conversations and creates an environment of mutual support and care. Taking time to listen actively and respond with compassion can foster stronger bonds, especially during family gatherings.

2. **Navigating Emotional Triggers and Family Patterns**: Family gatherings often bring up past dynamics and emotional patterns, which can feel amplified during a lunar eclipse. If unresolved issues surface, approach them mindfully, recognizing that the eclipse's influence may be making emotions more intense. Take breaks if necessary, and use grounding techniques to stay calm and centered. This mindful approach can help you handle sensitive topics with grace and maintain a positive atmosphere.

3. **Creating Space for Reflection in Group Settings**: Holiday gatherings offer a chance for collective reflection, which can be especially meaningful during a lunar eclipse. Encourage group activities that promote introspection, such as sharing stories of the past year, expressing gratitude, or setting intentions together. These reflective moments can deepen connections and create a shared sense of purpose, making the holiday season more meaningful and supportive.

4. **Balancing Celebration with Mindfulness**: While the holiday season is often filled with festivities and excitement, a lunar eclipse calls for a more balanced approach. Allow space for both celebration and quiet reflection, honoring the emotional undercurrents that may arise. By integrating mindfulness into your holiday plans, you create a harmonious blend of joy and introspection, aligning with the natural rhythms of the lunar cycle.

Lunar Eclipses and Spiritual Reflection During the Holiday Season

The spiritual significance of a lunar eclipse can deepen our understanding of the holiday season, encouraging us to reflect on the interconnectedness of life, change, and renewal. During a December lunar eclipse, we are reminded of the cyclical nature of life, the importance of letting go, and the promise of new beginnings.

1. **Honoring Cycles of Change and Transformation**: A lunar eclipse symbolizes the closing of one chapter and the beginning of another, much like the transition from one year to the next. Embrace this period as a time of spiritual transformation, releasing anything that no longer aligns with your purpose. This process of letting go can be a powerful way to honor the cyclical nature of life and set the stage for growth.

2. **Connecting to the Collective Consciousness**: Lunar eclipses are collective experiences, shared by people around the world. Reflecting on this shared event can create a sense of unity and interconnectedness, reminding us that we are all part of something larger than ourselves. Take time to consider how your actions, thoughts, and intentions contribute to the collective well-being, reinforcing the values of compassion, empathy, and service that define the holiday season.

3. **Exploring Inner Wisdom and Spiritual Insight**: The introspective energy of a lunar eclipse provides an ideal environment for exploring inner wisdom and spiritual insights. Engage in practices such as meditation, dream journaling, or divination to connect with your intuition. Use this time to gain clarity about your life's path and purpose, setting intentions that align with your highest self as you prepare for the new year.

4. **Celebrating the Light and Embracing the Shadow**: Just as the Moon is temporarily obscured by Earth's shadow during a lunar eclipse, we are invited to explore our own shadows. Recognize that both light and darkness have valuable lessons to teach. Embracing the shadow aspects of ourselves can lead to self-acceptance, healing, and empowerment. This balanced perspective allows us to enter the new year with a more complete understanding of who we are and what we aspire to become.

Final Thoughts: Navigating December's Lunar Eclipse with Awareness and Grace

A lunar eclipse in December provides a unique opportunity to explore emotions, deepen self-awareness, and align with the themes of renewal that define the holiday season. By understanding the influence of a lunar eclipse, we can navigate this time with mindfulness, compassion, and grace, embracing both the challenges and gifts that it brings.

This holiday season, let the energy of the lunar eclipse guide you toward greater introspection, healing, and personal growth. Whether through quiet reflection, connecting with loved ones, or engaging in mindful rituals, embrace the transformative power of the eclipse as a catalyst for emotional release and spiritual renewal. As you honor the cycles of light and shadow, may you find clarity, peace, and inspiration to carry into the new year, creating a season of meaning, purpose, and profound inner harmony.

Chapter 33: The Eclipse and Reflection During the Festive Season

An eclipse—whether lunar or solar—has long been a symbol of profound transformation, a time when the usual patterns of the sky are disrupted, inviting us to pause, reflect, and reconnect with our inner worlds. Eclipses have a unique ability to disrupt the flow of life, revealing the shadow aspects of ourselves and the world around us. When an eclipse aligns with the festive season, it deepens our experience of this time of year, adding layers of introspection and symbolism to our celebrations. This chapter explores how eclipses encourage reflection during the holidays, how they affect us emotionally and spiritually, and how we can use their energy to gain insight, heal, and set intentions for the future.

December, with its colder, darker days, encourages us to slow down and look inward. The holiday season brings with it themes of togetherness, gratitude, and new beginnings, all of which are magnified by the presence of an eclipse. The interplay of light and shadow in an eclipse reflects the human journey of self-discovery, making this celestial event a powerful opportunity for mindful reflection, personal growth, and deeper connection during the festive season.

The Symbolism of Eclipses: Light, Shadow, and Transformation

Eclipses have fascinated and inspired humanity for millennia. Ancient cultures viewed them as powerful omens, messages from the divine, or times when the veil between worlds was thinnest. Both solar and lunar eclipses offer symbolic meaning, representing cycles of change, balance, and transformation.

1. **Solar Eclipses**: During a solar eclipse, the Moon passes between the Earth and the Sun, momentarily blocking the Sun's light. This rare event is often associated with new beginnings, breakthroughs, and a fresh perspective. Symbolically, solar eclipses represent the temporary obscuring of consciousness (the Sun) by our emotions and subconscious (the Moon). They encourage us to look within and consider what we may not be seeing in our lives, providing a period of clarity after the light returns.

2. **Lunar Eclipses**: In a lunar eclipse, the Earth comes between the Sun and the Moon, casting its shadow over the Moon. Lunar eclipses are associated with endings, revelations, and emotional release. They bring to light the hidden aspects of our emotions, encouraging us to confront our inner shadows and resolve unfinished business. Lunar eclipses are seen as times for letting go, healing, and preparing for a new chapter.

3. **The Dance of Light and Shadow**: Both types of eclipses highlight the balance between light and shadow, reflecting the duality within us all. Light represents our conscious mind, the aspects of ourselves that are visible to the world, while shadow symbolizes the subconscious, the hidden or suppressed aspects of our psyche. Eclipses remind us that true growth comes from embracing both light and shadow, integrating our whole selves for greater clarity and wholeness.

The Eclipse's Influence on Emotional Reflection

Eclipses, with their powerful energies, affect us on an emotional level, amplifying feelings and bringing long-buried issues to the surface. This heightened emotional state can lead to breakthroughs, insights, and resolutions, but it may also bring up feelings of vulnerability, sensitivity, and introspection. Understanding these influences allows us to embrace the eclipse as an opportunity for healing and self-awareness during the holiday season.

1. **Heightened Emotional Awareness**: Eclipses create a surge in emotional energy, often bringing unresolved emotions to the forefront. This heightened sensitivity can intensify our reactions, making us more aware of what needs attention or release. During the holiday season, this can lead to deeper family conversations, honest self-reflection, or insights into what we truly value.

2. **Revelation and Realization**: Eclipses, especially lunar ones, reveal hidden truths and encourage revelations. During the festive season, this can take the form of realizing what is truly important, recognizing patterns that no longer serve us, or gaining clarity about relationships, goals, and values. These realizations often act as a catalyst for growth, helping us make decisions that align with our higher purpose.

3. **Emotional Cleansing and Letting Go**: Lunar eclipses are known for their ability to facilitate emotional release, offering a chance to let go of past hurts, fears, or patterns that are holding us back. The holiday season's themes of renewal and gratitude are magnified during an eclipse, allowing us to clear away emotional burdens and make space for new experiences. Engaging in practices that honor this release can create a powerful sense of freedom and emotional clarity.

4. **Increased Empathy and Intuition**: Eclipses amplify our sensitivity to others' emotions, making us more attuned to the feelings and needs of those around us. This heightened empathy can be especially meaningful during the holidays, helping us connect with loved ones on a deeper level. However, it's also essential to set boundaries and practice self-care, as heightened empathy can lead to emotional overwhelm.

Mindful Reflection and Practices During an Eclipse

An eclipse invites us to slow down, look inward, and listen to our inner voice. Mindful practices such as meditation, journaling, and intention-setting can help us harness the eclipse's energy for personal growth and spiritual insight. Here are some ways to embrace an eclipse during the festive season:

1. **Meditation and Visualization**: Meditation during an eclipse can deepen your connection to your subconscious mind, allowing for greater insight and clarity. Try visualizing the eclipse as it unfolds, imagining your inner self bathed in light and then shadow, symbolizing the process of self-discovery. This meditation can help you explore both the conscious and subconscious aspects of yourself, facilitating balance and integration.

2. **Journaling for Reflection and Release**: Writing is a powerful way to process emotions, gain insight, and let go of what no longer serves you. During an eclipse, take time to journal about the past year, your current emotions, and what you hope to release. Consider questions like, "What have I learned this year?" or "What patterns am I ready to let go of?" By putting thoughts into words, you can gain perspective and create space for new beginnings.

3. **Setting Intentions for the Future**: Eclipses represent transitions, making them ideal times for setting intentions that align with your highest aspirations. As you reflect on the past, consider what you want to cultivate in the coming year. Whether it's personal growth, relationships, career, or health, set clear, heart-centered intentions that will guide your actions and decisions.

4. **Practicing Gratitude and Forgiveness**: The eclipse's transformative energy makes it an ideal time for gratitude and forgiveness practices. Reflect on the people, experiences, and lessons that have shaped you, expressing gratitude for their role in your journey. Additionally, consider what or whom you need to forgive to move forward with an open heart. These practices help release emotional burdens and reinforce a sense of peace and compassion.

5. **Engaging in Rituals of Release**: Eclipses encourage letting go of old patterns and habits, and rituals can provide a symbolic way to facilitate this release. Consider writing down anything you want to release on a piece of paper, then burn or bury it as an act of letting go. Lighting candles, creating a vision board, or engaging in mindful movement can also enhance this sense of release, aligning with the eclipse's energy of transformation.

Eclipses and Holiday Gatherings: Navigating Emotional Sensitivity

The holiday season often involves gatherings with family and friends, which can become more emotionally charged during an eclipse. Navigating these interactions mindfully can help you create a harmonious environment that honors both connection and personal boundaries.

1. **Creating Space for Open Conversations**: Eclipses bring hidden emotions to the surface, making them ideal times for open, heartfelt conversations. If old family dynamics or unresolved issues arise, approach them with empathy and a willingness to listen. This openness can lead to healing conversations, creating a more supportive and understanding atmosphere.
2. **Setting Personal Boundaries**: The heightened emotional energy of an eclipse can lead to feelings of overwhelm, especially in social settings. Setting boundaries, such as taking breaks, setting time limits, or finding a quiet place to recharge, can help you manage your energy and stay balanced. Remember that it's okay to prioritize your well-being during the holidays, especially during an eclipse.
3. **Engaging in Collective Reflection**: If you feel comfortable, consider organizing a reflective activity for your family or friends, such as sharing personal highlights of the year, expressing gratitude, or setting intentions for the coming year. These practices can create a sense of unity and shared purpose, aligning with the holiday season's themes of connection and renewal.
4. **Mindful Celebration and Self-Care**: While the holiday season is often full of celebration, an eclipse encourages a balance between activity and introspection. Allow space for both celebration and quiet reflection, recognizing that the emotional intensity of an eclipse may call for extra self-care. Practices such as grounding exercises, breathwork, or a quiet walk in nature can help you stay centered.

The Eclipse as a Catalyst for Spiritual Growth

An eclipse offers a unique opportunity for spiritual growth, encouraging us to reflect on life's mysteries, embrace change, and connect with the deeper aspects of our being. When this event aligns with the holiday season, it amplifies themes of transformation, unity, and renewal, allowing us to approach the new year with a clear mind and open heart.

1. **Honoring the Cycle of Light and Shadow**: The eclipse's dance of light and shadow mirrors the spiritual journey of embracing both the known and unknown aspects of ourselves. Use this time to reflect on what light and shadow mean to you, considering how both contribute to personal growth. Recognizing the value in both aspects helps us cultivate inner balance, wisdom, and self-acceptance.
2. **Connecting with the Collective Consciousness**: Eclipses are universal experiences, viewed by people around the world. Reflecting on this shared moment can deepen your sense of connection with humanity and the greater universe. Consider how your actions, thoughts, and intentions contribute to the collective well-being, reinforcing a sense of unity and compassion that resonates with the spirit of the holiday season.

3. **Exploring Inner Wisdom and Spiritual Insight**: The energy of an eclipse enhances intuition, making it an ideal time for spiritual practices such as meditation, dream journaling, or divination. Use this time to connect with your inner wisdom, seeking clarity about your life path and purpose. Embrace any insights that arise as guiding messages, helping you align with your highest self as you enter the new year.

4. **Embracing the Theme of Renewal**: Eclipses symbolize transition, endings, and new beginnings—concepts that align with the holiday season's themes of renewal and hope. Use this energy to reflect on the areas of your life that are ready for change, and welcome the opportunity to start fresh. As you release old patterns, recognize that each ending brings with it the promise of something new, reinforcing a sense of optimism and resilience.

Final Thoughts: Embracing the Eclipse's Energy During the Festive Season

Eclipses are powerful times of reflection, transformation, and spiritual insight, offering us a chance to pause, look within, and reconnect with our true selves. When an eclipse occurs during the festive season, it magnifies the holiday's themes of gratitude, renewal, and connection, encouraging us to approach celebrations with mindfulness and intention.

This holiday season, let the energy of the eclipse guide you toward greater clarity, compassion, and self-awareness. Embrace the interplay of light and shadow as a symbol of your own inner journey, allowing both to coexist in harmony. Whether through reflection, conversations with loved ones, or rituals of release and intention, may the eclipse inspire you to honor the past, celebrate the present, and welcome the future with an open heart and a clear mind. As you navigate this unique moment in time, may the eclipse serve as a catalyst for personal growth, healing, and a renewed sense of purpose in the new year.

Chapter 34: How Past Lunar Eclipses Shaped Holiday Astrology

Lunar eclipses have long captivated astrologers, inspiring interpretations that blend celestial phenomena with human experiences. These awe-inspiring events, where Earth's shadow temporarily darkens the Moon, were traditionally seen as powerful omens that influenced personal lives, communities, and the world at large. In the context of holiday astrology, lunar eclipses take on a special significance, shaping themes of reflection, transformation, and renewal that align with the holiday season's spirit of introspection and new beginnings. As we explore the history of lunar eclipses and their astrological interpretations, we'll see how past events have influenced holiday astrology, coloring our understanding of family, connection, and the emotional and spiritual growth associated with the end of the year.

This chapter delves into the legacy of past lunar eclipses during the holiday season, examining how they shaped astrological interpretations and influenced how people celebrated, set intentions, and navigated the end-of-year energies. By understanding the impact of these celestial events on holiday astrology, we gain insight into the cyclical nature of growth, the role of lunar eclipses in revealing hidden emotions, and the importance of releasing old patterns to make way for new beginnings.

The Astrological Significance of Lunar Eclipses

In astrology, the Moon is associated with emotions, intuition, the subconscious, and cycles of growth and change. When a lunar eclipse occurs, it brings these qualities to the forefront, symbolizing heightened emotional intensity, hidden truths, and moments of revelation. Lunar eclipses act as cosmic mirrors, reflecting our inner world and urging us to confront our shadows—the hidden parts of ourselves that may need healing or transformation.

1. **Emotional and Psychological Reflection**: Lunar eclipses intensify emotions, amplifying feelings and thoughts that may have been buried. Astrologers view them as opportunities for emotional cleansing and self-discovery, encouraging us to let go of patterns or relationships that no longer serve us.
2. **Cycles of Closure and New Beginnings**: Lunar eclipses mark an end to one phase and the beginning of another, particularly in the context of personal and emotional growth. This cyclical quality aligns with holiday astrology's themes of closure and renewal, as we release the past and prepare for the new year.
3. **Collective Influence on Societal Patterns**: Eclipses are believed to have a collective influence, affecting not only individuals but also the social and cultural environment. Historically, holiday lunar eclipses were viewed as signs of transformation within communities or shifts in societal values. They highlight the interconnectedness of individuals within a collective experience, adding a layer of depth to holiday gatherings and celebrations.

Historical Holiday Lunar Eclipses and Their Astrological Impact

Throughout history, lunar eclipses that coincided with the holiday season have been viewed as significant events, shaping astrological interpretations for years to come. These eclipses were seen as markers of change, influencing both individual and societal values. Let's look at some notable holiday lunar eclipses and the astrological meanings attributed to them.

1. The Lunar Eclipse of December 29, 1944

The lunar eclipse of December 29, 1944, occurred during a time of intense global change near the end of World War II. This eclipse, occurring in the sign of Cancer (a zodiac sign closely associated with home, family, and emotional security), symbolized a moment of reflection, particularly around themes of familial connections and collective security. Astrologers interpreted this eclipse as a call to reconnect with loved ones, emphasizing the importance of unity, resilience, and compassion during times of hardship.

- **Astrological Influence**: Cancer's influence brought themes of protection, nurturing, and emotional bonding, aligning perfectly with the holiday season's focus on family. This eclipse encouraged people to find comfort and support in their communities, shaping an astrological perspective that placed an emphasis on emotional healing and creating safe spaces within families.

- **Legacy in Holiday Astrology**: The 1944 lunar eclipse's themes of security, resilience, and emotional closeness became associated with holiday astrology, reinforcing the idea that the end of the year is a time to reconnect with family, heal emotional wounds, and find strength in unity.

2. The Lunar Eclipse of December 19, 1964

The lunar eclipse of December 19, 1964, occurred in Gemini, a sign associated with communication, intellect, and adaptability. This eclipse highlighted themes of truth-seeking, curiosity, and open communication, prompting people to examine their relationships, express their true feelings, and seek understanding in their social circles. In the context of holiday astrology, this eclipse encouraged conversations and revelations, emphasizing that the holiday season is an ideal time for sharing thoughts, clarifying misunderstandings, and forging stronger connections.

- **Astrological Influence**: With Gemini's influence, the 1964 eclipse brought an energy of exploration and curiosity. Astrologers interpreted it as a time to embrace open-mindedness, engage in meaningful dialogue, and question old beliefs. Gemini's influence encouraged adaptability, symbolizing that growth often comes from being willing to learn and embrace new perspectives.

- **Legacy in Holiday Astrology**: This eclipse introduced themes of communication, intellectual curiosity, and flexibility to holiday astrology. It emphasized the importance of open conversations during the holiday season, fostering a tradition of heartfelt discussions, reconnecting with loved ones, and reflecting on the year's lessons.

3. The Lunar Eclipse of December 9, 1992

The lunar eclipse of December 9, 1992, occurred in Gemini, during a time of cultural and technological shifts. Astrologers interpreted this eclipse as a call to embrace change and transformation, particularly in areas of communication and connection. The eclipse invited people to adapt to new forms of socialization and interaction, highlighting the holiday season as a time to adapt traditions and embrace a changing world.

- **Astrological Influence**: This Gemini eclipse encouraged flexibility, creative thinking, and adaptability, reflecting the rapid advancements in technology and globalization. Astrologers saw it as a time to experiment with new ways of connecting, aligning with the holiday season's themes of unity and togetherness.
- **Legacy in Holiday Astrology**: The 1992 eclipse added themes of adaptability, technological advancement, and open-mindedness to holiday astrology, emphasizing that the season can be a time of innovation, new traditions, and finding creative ways to connect across distances.

4. The Lunar Eclipse of December 21, 2010

The lunar eclipse of December 21, 2010, coincided with the winter solstice, making it a particularly powerful event. Occurring in the sign of Gemini, this eclipse highlighted themes of transformation, duality, and introspection, aligning with the solstice's symbolism of rebirth and renewal. Astrologers saw this eclipse as a turning point, encouraging people to embrace new beginnings and release the past as they entered a new year.

- **Astrological Influence**: The 2010 eclipse encouraged self-reflection, transformation, and new beginnings. The duality of Gemini symbolized the integration of past and future, light and shadow, encouraging people to find balance in their lives. This eclipse became a powerful reminder of the interconnectedness of personal and collective transformation.
- **Legacy in Holiday Astrology**: The 2010 eclipse emphasized the themes of rebirth, self-discovery, and balance during the holiday season. It inspired a more introspective approach to the holidays, focusing on aligning with one's true self and making resolutions that reflect personal growth and transformation.

Themes and Lessons from Past Holiday Lunar Eclipses in Holiday Astrology

The legacy of past holiday lunar eclipses has shaped key themes in holiday astrology, creating a framework that encourages reflection, connection, and growth. Here are some of the central themes and lessons inspired by these historical eclipses:

1. **Reconnecting with Family and Community**: Many holiday eclipses emphasize the importance of family and community, underscoring the value of support and unity. These themes remind us to prioritize relationships, heal family dynamics, and celebrate the joy of togetherness. Eclipses during the holiday season encourage us to strengthen these bonds, creating a foundation of love and mutual support.

2. **Embracing Change and Letting Go**: Lunar eclipses, with their symbolism of endings and beginnings, encourage us to release old patterns and make space for growth. The holiday season, with its transition into a new year, is an ideal time for letting go of what no longer serves us. This process of release allows us to move forward with clarity and intention, aligning with the eclipse's energy of transformation.

3. **Balancing Tradition and Adaptability**: Eclipses that fall in Gemini or other mutable signs highlight the importance of balancing tradition with adaptability. These influences remind us that while traditions bring comfort and stability, it's also essential to remain open to change. The holiday season can be a time to honor customs while exploring new ways to connect, celebrate, and grow.

4. **Fostering Open Communication and Emotional Clarity**: Eclipses often bring hidden emotions and truths to the surface, encouraging honesty and transparency. During the holiday season, this can lead to deeper conversations, the resolution of misunderstandings, and greater emotional closeness. These eclipses remind us to approach relationships with authenticity, using the festive season to reconnect on a deeper level.

5. **Setting Intentions for Transformation and Renewal**: Many holiday lunar eclipses emphasize the themes of self-reflection and intention-setting. The end of the year is a powerful time to set goals, focus on personal growth, and envision the future. Eclipses amplify this process, allowing us to connect with our inner truth and align our intentions with our highest aspirations.

Practical Ways to Integrate Eclipse Wisdom into Holiday Celebrations

Understanding the astrological legacy of past holiday lunar eclipses can inspire new ways to celebrate and reflect during the festive season. Here are some practices to help integrate eclipse wisdom into holiday traditions:

1. **Year-End Reflection and Journaling**: Use the energy of the eclipse to reflect on the past year's experiences, lessons, and challenges. Journaling allows you to process emotions, clarify insights, and identify areas of growth. Consider questions like, "What am I ready to release?" or "What intentions do I want to set for the new year?" This practice aligns with the eclipse's themes of transformation and renewal.

2. **Family Bonding and Communication Rituals**: Host a family gathering centered around sharing gratitude, personal highlights, and hopes for the future. Encourage open communication, allowing family members to express themselves freely. This ritual fosters connection, understanding, and a sense of unity, echoing the themes of past eclipses that emphasize family and community.

3. **Creating a Release Ritual**: A release ritual allows you to symbolically let go of old patterns, habits, or emotions. Write down what you want to release on a piece of paper, then burn or bury it as a symbolic act of closure. This ritual can be done alone or with loved ones, creating a shared experience of release and renewal.

4. **Setting Intentions with Loved Ones**: Gathering with friends or family to set intentions for the new year can be a meaningful way to honor the eclipse's transformative energy. Light candles, share intentions, and support each other's goals. This collective act aligns with the holiday season's spirit of hope and inspiration, reinforcing a sense of purpose and mutual encouragement.

5. **Creating an Altar or Reflection Space**: Design a space in your home dedicated to reflection, meditation, and intention-setting. Include symbols of transformation, such as candles, crystals, or objects that hold personal meaning. This space serves as a reminder of the eclipse's energy and provides a sanctuary for contemplation during the holiday season.

Final Thoughts: Honoring the Legacy of Past Eclipses in Holiday Astrology

The legacy of past lunar eclipses during the holiday season has shaped holiday astrology, enriching our understanding of family, community, and personal growth. These eclipses remind us that the end of the year is not only a time for celebration but also an opportunity for introspection, healing, and renewal. By embracing the wisdom of these celestial events, we deepen our connection to the themes of light, transformation, and hope that define the holiday season.

This year, let the lessons of past holiday lunar eclipses inspire you to celebrate with mindfulness, connect with loved ones, and set intentions for growth. As you navigate the season, may the eclipse's energy encourage you to release what no longer serves you, embrace change, and welcome the possibilities of a new year with an open heart and a clear vision. Through honoring the cosmic rhythms that guide us, we create a holiday experience that is both meaningful and aligned with the timeless cycles of transformation and renewal.

Part 8: **Planetary Alignments and Festivities**

Chapter 35: Jupiter and Saturn - The Christmas Conjunction

One of the most awe-inspiring celestial events associated with the holiday season is the conjunction of Jupiter and Saturn, often called the "Christmas Conjunction." Occurring approximately every 20 years, this alignment brings the two largest planets in our solar system close together in the night sky, creating a brilliant point of light visible to the naked eye. During December 2020, this phenomenon took on added significance, as Jupiter and Saturn aligned closer than they had in nearly 400 years, resulting in a dazzling "Great Conjunction" that was referred to as the "Christmas Star."

In astrology, a conjunction between Jupiter and Saturn is seen as an event of immense importance, marking the end of one cycle and the beginning of another. Known for their symbolic roles as the planets of expansion (Jupiter) and structure (Saturn), their alignment brings together contrasting energies, creating a powerful moment for transformation, reflection, and vision for the future. This chapter explores the astrological meaning of the Christmas Conjunction, its historical significance, and how it impacts the holiday season's themes of reflection, connection, and new beginnings.

The Celestial Mechanics of a Jupiter-Saturn Conjunction

A conjunction between Jupiter and Saturn occurs when the two planets align closely in the same part of the sky from our viewpoint on Earth. While this phenomenon takes place approximately every 20 years, the intensity of the 2020 event was unique due to the close alignment, making it the most visually striking conjunction in centuries.

1. **Orbital Cycles of Jupiter and Saturn**: Jupiter, with its orbit of around 12 years, and Saturn, which orbits every 29.5 years, come together once every two decades. This rhythm results in what is known as the "Great Conjunction," a recurring event that astronomers and astrologers alike have observed for centuries.

2. **The 2020 Conjunction**: The conjunction that occurred on December 21, 2020, coincided with the winter solstice, a moment already rich with symbolism as the day with the longest night and the promise of returning light. During this event, Jupiter and Saturn appeared just 0.1 degrees apart, closer than they had since the 1600s, creating a nearly single point of light in the sky that many likened to the Star of Bethlehem.

3. **Significance of the Christmas Conjunction**: Given its timing near the winter solstice and the holiday season, the Christmas Conjunction resonates deeply with themes of hope, renewal, and unity. The alignment of these two planetary giants symbolizes both the culmination of a long cycle and the start of a new phase, providing a cosmic backdrop for reflection and intention-setting during the holiday season.

The Astrological Meaning of Jupiter and Saturn's Conjunction

In astrology, Jupiter and Saturn are both "social planets," influencing the collective energies that shape society, culture, and values. Their conjunction is seen as a major event, representing shifts in collective consciousness, societal structures, and even generational themes. Let's explore the qualities of each planet and how their alignment affects our lives.

1. **Jupiter - Expansion, Wisdom, and Hope**: Jupiter, known as the planet of abundance and growth, represents optimism, vision, and expansion. It is associated with philosophical thought, higher learning, and the pursuit of meaning. In the context of a conjunction, Jupiter brings a sense of hope, joy, and aspiration, encouraging us to broaden our horizons and seek fulfillment.

2. **Saturn - Structure, Discipline, and Responsibility**: Saturn, by contrast, is the planet of boundaries, discipline, and responsibility. It represents authority, structure, and the lessons we learn through perseverance. Saturn's influence encourages self-discipline, patience, and accountability, often prompting us to work within limitations to achieve lasting results.

3. **Jupiter-Saturn Conjunction - The Balance of Expansion and Structure**: When Jupiter and Saturn align, their contrasting energies blend, creating a moment of balance between growth and restriction, vision and responsibility. This conjunction invites us to integrate optimism with practicality, dreams with reality, and personal aspirations with social responsibilities. Astrologically, it signals a time to align our goals with a solid foundation, making it possible to build something enduring and meaningful.

4. **Influence on Personal and Collective Transformation**: On a personal level, the conjunction urges individuals to take stock of their lives, consider long-term goals, and focus on personal growth grounded in real-world commitments. Collectively, it encourages society to reconsider values, shift perspectives, and rebuild structures that may have become outdated. This dual focus on the individual and society aligns beautifully with holiday themes of reflection, connection, and the spirit of renewal.

Historical and Cultural Significance of the Christmas Conjunction

Throughout history, the conjunction of Jupiter and Saturn has been associated with significant cultural and societal shifts. Ancient astrologers considered these alignments to be harbingers of change, often linking them to the rise of new leaders, the start of influential movements, or changes in collective values. Let's look at how some of these historical conjunctions have been interpreted and their impact on society.

1. **Ancient Babylonian and Medieval Beliefs**: The Babylonians were among the first to record the Jupiter-Saturn conjunctions, believing them to signal shifts in kingship and authority. In medieval Europe, astrologers viewed these conjunctions as significant indicators of religious and political changes, as well as markers of influential events that would shape the future of civilizations.

2. **The Conjunction of 7 BCE - The Star of Bethlehem**: Some astronomers and historians suggest that the Star of Bethlehem, described in the Bible, may have been a conjunction of Jupiter and Saturn. This 7 BCE conjunction occurred in the sign of Pisces, which was often associated with spirituality and compassion. For early Christians, the appearance of the "Christmas Star" symbolized hope, guidance, and divine presence—a theme that continues to resonate during the holiday season.

3. **The Great Conjunction of 1623 and the Age of Enlightenment**: The conjunction of Jupiter and Saturn in 1623, which closely followed the Scientific Revolution, is often associated with a shift in consciousness that led to the Enlightenment. Astrologers saw it as a time of intellectual awakening, where old structures of belief were questioned, leading to advancements in science, philosophy, and human rights.

4. **The 2020 Christmas Conjunction**: The conjunction of Jupiter and Saturn on December 21, 2020, was seen as marking the beginning of a new era, with astrologers interpreting it as the start of the "Air Era" as it occurred in Aquarius, an air sign associated with innovation, social reform, and collective progress. This conjunction is believed to symbolize a shift toward a more interconnected, technology-driven, and humanitarian society, aligning with the holiday season's themes of unity, hope, and new beginnings.

The Christmas Conjunction's Influence on Holiday Themes

The symbolic qualities of the Jupiter-Saturn conjunction enrich the themes traditionally celebrated during the holiday season. These alignments offer a time for both reflection on the past and optimism for the future, encouraging us to consider how we can create a fulfilling, balanced life aligned with our values and responsibilities.

1. **Hope and Renewal**: Jupiter's influence in the conjunction inspires hope and a sense of possibility, encouraging us to set ambitious goals and envision a brighter future. This optimism aligns with the holiday season's themes of renewal and new beginnings, reminding us that growth and change are always possible, even during challenging times.

2. **Reflection and Accountability**: Saturn's grounding energy brings an element of reflection and responsibility, urging us to take stock of our lives and assess the foundations on which we build our dreams. This influence encourages holiday introspection, making it an ideal time to review personal goals, acknowledge achievements, and consider where we may need to make adjustments for lasting fulfillment.

3. **Unity and Collective Responsibility**: The conjunction represents the union of individual aspirations (Jupiter) and social structures (Saturn), encouraging us to find harmony between personal goals and collective well-being. This balance is reflected in holiday traditions that emphasize connection, compassion, and the importance of giving back, reminding us that we are part of a larger whole.

4. **Setting Foundations for the Future**: Jupiter and Saturn's alignment symbolizes the start of a new chapter, where we are encouraged to lay down practical, meaningful foundations for the future. This aligns with holiday practices of setting intentions or resolutions, focusing not just on immediate gratification but on goals that will foster growth and stability in the long term.

Practical Ways to Embrace the Christmas Conjunction's Energy During the Holidays
Harnessing the energy of the Jupiter-Saturn conjunction during the holiday season can bring both inspiration and practical insights, helping us align with the themes of hope, balance, and renewal. Here are some ways to integrate this celestial event into holiday traditions and personal practices:

1. **Setting Long-Term Goals with Intention**: Use the energy of the conjunction to set realistic, long-term goals for the coming year. Reflect on areas of your life where you'd like to grow, focusing on aspirations that can be achieved with dedication and patience. Consider setting goals that balance personal desires with social or family responsibilities, as the conjunction encourages aligning individual ambitions with the greater good.

2. **Creating a Vision Board for the Future**: Gather images, words, and symbols that represent your intentions for the new year, and arrange them on a vision board. This creative exercise channels Jupiter's expansive energy and Saturn's focus on structure, helping you visualize and manifest your dreams in a grounded, realistic way. Place your vision board somewhere you can see daily, reminding you of your commitment to both personal growth and stability.

3. **Gratitude and Reflection Rituals**: Reflect on the past year and acknowledge the lessons learned, challenges faced, and achievements accomplished. Write down what you are grateful for and consider how these experiences have helped shape your path. This practice aligns with Saturn's reflective energy, providing a sense of closure and a grounded foundation as you move into the new year.

4. **Balancing Celebration with Mindfulness**: While the holiday season is a time for joy and celebration, the conjunction's influence encourages a balanced approach. Embrace both social activities and quiet reflection, recognizing the value of both. Use this time to connect deeply with loved ones, engaging in meaningful conversations that foster understanding and strengthen relationships.

5. **Embracing Tradition and Innovation**: The conjunction of Jupiter and Saturn in Aquarius, the sign of innovation, encourages a blend of tradition with fresh perspectives. Try incorporating new elements into holiday celebrations, such as eco-friendly practices, alternative rituals, or creative ways to connect with distant loved ones. This blend of old and new honors the holiday season's themes of continuity and renewal.

The Christmas Conjunction as a Symbol of Hope and Possibility

The rare alignment of Jupiter and Saturn as the "Christmas Conjunction" offers a profound symbol of hope, unity, and the potential for growth rooted in stability. As we celebrate the holiday season, this conjunction reminds us of the power of balance, inviting us to blend dreams with discipline, optimism with responsibility, and personal goals with collective well-being.

This unique celestial event, visible to all under the night sky, reminds us that we are part of something larger, connected to each other and to the cosmos in ways that transcend time and distance. The Christmas Conjunction encourages us to look beyond the present moment, envisioning a future that reflects our highest aspirations and values. As we observe the brilliance of Jupiter and Saturn in their close embrace, we are reminded that even the smallest acts of kindness, compassion, and resilience contribute to a better world.

Final Thoughts: Honoring the Christmas Conjunction in Holiday Traditions

As you celebrate the holiday season, let the energy of the Christmas Conjunction inspire you to approach life with both optimism and intention. Embrace the spirit of hope that Jupiter brings, coupled with Saturn's wisdom of responsibility and structure. May this celestial event guide you to align with your true purpose, honor your commitments, and create a future that reflects both your dreams and your dedication.

This holiday season, let the brilliance of Jupiter and Saturn serve as a reminder of the power within each of us to create, connect, and grow. Whether through reflection, setting intentions, or simply marveling at the beauty of the night sky, may the Christmas Conjunction encourage you to celebrate life's journey, cherish the present, and look forward to a future filled with possibility and purpose.

Chapter 36: Venus - Love and Festive Relationships

Venus, the planet of love, beauty, and harmony, holds a special place in astrology, influencing our relationships, aesthetic sense, and desires for connection and pleasure. During the holiday season, Venus's influence takes on added significance, as this time of year is often centered around family gatherings, social events, and deepening bonds with those we cherish. Known as the "planet of love," Venus governs how we relate to others, the nature of our connections, and our ability to find joy in shared experiences. Exploring Venus's impact on festive relationships can help us approach the holiday season with greater awareness, sensitivity, and an open heart.

This chapter delves into the astrological significance of Venus in the context of holiday relationships, examining how its energies shape our experiences of love, friendship, and harmony. By understanding Venus's role in holiday astrology, we gain insights into nurturing meaningful connections, balancing personal needs with collective harmony, and making the most of Venusian energy to create joyful, memorable moments.

The Astrological Influence of Venus

Venus is associated with love, affection, pleasure, and the arts. It governs the way we express love, our tastes, our values, and the things that bring us joy. As the planet closest to Earth after Mercury, Venus represents the energy of attraction and desire, drawing us to people, experiences, and aesthetics that resonate with our hearts. In the context of the holiday season, Venus influences how we approach relationships, make peace, and share warmth with others.

1. **Love and Relationships**: Venus's influence on love goes beyond romantic relationships; it also includes friendships, family bonds, and the connections we build within our communities. In holiday astrology, Venus encourages a spirit of compassion, understanding, and celebration of those we hold dear.

2. **Harmony and Aesthetics**: Venus governs beauty and harmony, shaping our appreciation for aesthetics and our desire to create beautiful spaces. During the holidays, Venus's influence enhances our appreciation for festive decorations, traditions, and experiences that bring people together in celebration.

3. **Values and Gratitude**: Venus influences our values and the things we hold dear, encouraging us to reflect on what truly matters in our relationships and lives. During the holidays, Venus reminds us of the importance of gratitude, generosity, and the spirit of giving, enhancing the season's themes of connection and appreciation.

4. **Desire for Pleasure and Joy**: Venus inspires our desire for pleasure, comfort, and joy. The holiday season, with its festive meals, celebrations, and gift-giving, aligns with Venusian values, allowing us to indulge in experiences that bring happiness, satisfaction, and love.

Venus and Holiday Love: Celebrating Connections and Family Bonds

During the holiday season, Venus's influence highlights the importance of nurturing and cherishing our relationships. Whether it's romantic love, family connections, or friendships, Venus brings a spirit of compassion, warmth, and joy to the season, encouraging us to celebrate and deepen our bonds.

1. **Strengthening Family Bonds**: Venus reminds us to value our family connections, fostering an environment of mutual appreciation, forgiveness, and understanding. Holiday gatherings often bring families together, creating opportunities to reinforce family ties, resolve conflicts, and create lasting memories. Venus's energy encourages empathy and compassion, helping to heal rifts and reinforce family unity.

2. **Cultivating Romantic Relationships**: For couples, the holiday season offers a chance to share meaningful experiences and express love. Venus inspires romantic gestures, quality time, and a focus on intimacy, allowing partners to reconnect and celebrate their bond. Whether through shared traditions, thoughtful gifts, or spending quiet moments together, Venus encourages couples to prioritize their connection and embrace the warmth of togetherness.

3. **Building Friendships and Social Connections**: The festive season is a time for connecting with friends and social circles, fostering bonds that bring joy and companionship. Venus enhances our desire for social harmony, making it easier to bridge gaps, form new friendships, and rekindle old connections. This energy encourages a spirit of camaraderie and inclusion, making holiday gatherings more enjoyable and meaningful.

4. **Practicing Forgiveness and Compassion**: The holiday season, with Venus's influence, is an ideal time to practice forgiveness and compassion. Venus encourages us to let go of past conflicts, heal misunderstandings, and approach others with empathy. This willingness to forgive can create a sense of peace and harmony, allowing us to enter the new year with a lighter heart and strengthened relationships.

Venusian Harmony in Holiday Aesthetics and Traditions

Venus's influence extends beyond relationships; it also shapes our appreciation for beauty, comfort, and harmony. During the holiday season, Venus inspires our desire to create aesthetically pleasing environments, indulge in festive traditions, and celebrate the season's warmth through art, decoration, and shared experiences.

1. **Creating Beautiful Spaces**: Venus enhances our desire to create beautiful, welcoming spaces that foster connection and celebration. Decorating for the holidays—whether with lights, ornaments, or natural elements like pine, berries, and candles—can become a ritual that embodies Venusian beauty and warmth. Venus encourages us to surround ourselves with beauty, creating an atmosphere that uplifts and inspires joy.

2. **Embracing Holiday Traditions**: Traditions are an essential part of holiday celebrations, bringing people together through shared customs, foods, and rituals. Venus's influence highlights the importance of these traditions, encouraging us to honor cultural practices, family customs, and activities that create a sense of continuity and connection. Whether it's baking treats, decorating the tree, or lighting candles, Venus reminds us that traditions are powerful ways to bond and express love.

3. **The Art of Giving and Receiving**: Venus values generosity and the act of giving as expressions of love and appreciation. The holiday season, with its focus on gift-giving, provides a natural opportunity to show gratitude and affection. Venus encourages thoughtful, heart-centered giving, reminding us that gifts are meaningful when they come from a place of genuine care. Similarly, Venus invites us to receive gifts with gratitude, recognizing them as tokens of connection and appreciation.

4. **Indulging in Festive Pleasures**: Venus inspires our desire for pleasure, urging us to embrace the sensory delights of the holiday season. From savoring seasonal foods and drinks to enjoying music, laughter, and festive gatherings, Venus encourages us to celebrate with all our senses. By engaging in the pleasures of the season, we nurture our spirit, creating joyful memories that resonate with Venus's energy of love and abundance.

Navigating Venusian Energy in Holiday Relationships

While Venus brings harmony and connection, its influence can also bring challenges if imbalances arise in relationships. During the holiday season, heightened emotions and social expectations can sometimes lead to stress, misunderstandings, or tension. Navigating Venusian energy with awareness and mindfulness can help us maintain harmony and compassion in our interactions.

1. **Balancing Social Obligations with Self-Care**: Venus encourages us to connect and socialize, but it's important to balance these obligations with personal needs. The holiday season can be socially demanding, making it essential to set boundaries and prioritize self-care. Recognizing when to take breaks, recharge, or spend time alone can help us stay balanced and prevent burnout, allowing us to fully enjoy Venus's energy of connection.

2. **Embracing Authenticity in Relationships**: Venus's influence can sometimes lead to people-pleasing tendencies, where we prioritize others' needs over our own to maintain harmony. During the holidays, it's important to embrace authenticity in relationships, expressing our true feelings and needs with kindness and honesty. Authenticity strengthens bonds, allowing us to connect on a deeper level and experience relationships that are built on mutual respect and understanding.

3. **Practicing Gratitude and Acknowledgement**: Venus thrives in an environment of gratitude and appreciation. Taking the time to acknowledge the people who enrich our lives—whether through words, gestures, or acts of kindness—reinforces the bonds of love and friendship. Practicing gratitude during the holiday season nurtures positive relationships, creating a foundation of mutual respect and appreciation.

4. **Finding Peace in Imperfection**: Venus values beauty and harmony, but these ideals can sometimes lead to unrealistic expectations, especially during the holidays when there may be pressure to create a "perfect" celebration. Embracing imperfection and letting go of the need for everything to be flawless can reduce stress and help us focus on what truly matters—connection, love, and shared experiences.

Venus and Personal Reflection: Self-Love and Inner Harmony

While Venus is often associated with external relationships, it also governs self-love and personal values. During the holiday season, Venus encourages us to reflect on our relationship with ourselves, nurturing inner harmony, self-compassion, and self-appreciation. This self-reflection can enhance our ability to connect with others, as true love begins with self-love.

1. **Reflecting on Self-Worth and Personal Values**: Venus invites us to consider our values and how they shape our relationships and goals. Taking time during the holiday season to reflect on what truly matters—whether it's family, creativity, health, or spirituality—can provide clarity and reinforce a sense of purpose. Venus encourages us to embrace our self-worth, recognizing that we deserve love, respect, and fulfillment.

2. **Practicing Self-Compassion and Forgiveness**: Venusian energy encourages self-compassion, reminding us to treat ourselves with kindness and understanding. During a season that often emphasizes giving to others, it's essential to also give to ourselves, practicing forgiveness and letting go of self-criticism. This self-compassion nurtures inner harmony, allowing us to show up in relationships with authenticity and an open heart.

3. **Embracing Self-Care and Indulgence**: The holiday season is an ideal time to embrace self-care and indulge in activities that bring joy and relaxation. Whether it's taking a warm bath, enjoying a favorite meal, or dedicating time to creative expression, Venus encourages us to honor our needs and embrace experiences that nourish our soul. Self-care helps us recharge and stay grounded, enhancing our ability to connect with others from a place of love and balance.

4. **Setting Intentions for Personal Growth and Connection**: Venus's influence provides a meaningful opportunity to set intentions for growth and connection in the new year. Consider what aspects of your relationships you'd like to nurture, what qualities you'd like to bring into your interactions, and how you can foster a deeper sense of love and appreciation in your life. These intentions create a foundation of positivity and purpose, supporting both personal growth and fulfilling connections.

Practical Venus-Inspired Practices for a Heartfelt Holiday Season

Incorporating Venusian practices into holiday celebrations can help create an atmosphere of love, beauty, and harmony, making the season more meaningful and joyful. Here are some ways to honor Venus's energy during the holidays:

1. **Create a Gratitude Jar**: Place a gratitude jar in a common area where family members can write down what they appreciate about one another or memories they cherish. At the end of the holiday season, read these notes together as a reminder of the love and connection that binds you.
2. **Host a Festive Meal with Intention**: Plan a holiday meal that celebrates love and harmony, inviting guests to share something they're grateful for or a wish they have for the new year. This gathering can become a ritual of gratitude and connection, aligning with Venus's themes of love, unity, and appreciation.
3. **Practice Loving-Kindness Meditation**: Engage in a loving-kindness meditation, sending love and compassion to yourself, loved ones, and the world. This practice fosters a sense of peace and unity, amplifying Venus's influence and enhancing the holiday spirit of warmth and goodwill.
4. **Gift Thoughtfully and Meaningfully**: Venus values heartfelt gestures, so consider choosing gifts that reflect your appreciation for each recipient. A handwritten letter, a handmade item, or a personalized gift can hold more meaning than a material present, reinforcing the bonds of love and friendship.
5. **Create a Beautiful Space for Reflection**: Dedicate a corner of your home to Venusian beauty and reflection, decorating it with candles, flowers, or art. Use this space to meditate, journal, or simply relax, allowing you to connect with Venus's energy of peace, harmony, and self-love.

Final Thoughts: Honoring Venus in Holiday Relationships

As we celebrate the holiday season, Venus's influence invites us to approach relationships with love, compassion, and appreciation. By nurturing our bonds with family, friends, and ourselves, we embrace the true spirit of the holidays, creating an environment of warmth and connection. Venus reminds us that love is the foundation of meaningful relationships, and by honoring this energy, we can create lasting memories filled with joy, unity, and a sense of shared purpose.

This holiday season, let Venus inspire you to approach each moment with an open heart and a spirit of generosity. Whether through a kind gesture, a heartfelt conversation, or simply being present with loved ones, may Venus's energy guide you to celebrate the beauty of connection and the power of love. As you embrace the season with Venusian grace, may your relationships flourish, your heart expand, and your holidays be filled with harmony, joy, and a deep sense of belonging.

Chapter 37: Mars - Drive, Energy, and Holiday Ambition

Mars, the planet of action, motivation, and assertiveness, is often associated with power, energy, and the pursuit of personal goals. While the holiday season is typically a time for rest, reflection, and connection, Mars's influence brings a unique and dynamic energy that can amplify our sense of purpose, drive, and ambition. Mars is the source of our inner fire, governing our desires, competitiveness, and ability to take decisive action. During the holidays, when gatherings, gift-giving, and end-of-year obligations are high, Mars's influence can be both motivating and challenging, encouraging us to stay productive while balancing the season's demands.

This chapter delves into Mars's role in holiday astrology, exploring how its energy shapes our drive, ambitions, and actions. By understanding Mars's influence, we can channel its power to achieve our goals, approach holiday activities with vigor, and maintain balance in our relationships. We'll also examine how to navigate Mars's assertive energy during social gatherings, manage stress, and use its dynamic qualities to fuel positive change.

The Astrological Influence of Mars

In astrology, Mars represents action, determination, and courage. It is the planet that propels us forward, giving us the energy and motivation to pursue our desires, overcome obstacles, and assert ourselves. Mars is associated with physical activity, competition, and even conflict, as it governs the way we handle challenges, assert boundaries, and protect our interests. Mars also relates to our sense of independence and personal power, encouraging us to be bold, resilient, and self-assured.

1. **Ambition and Drive**: Mars fuels our ambition and drive, inspiring us to set and achieve goals. During the holiday season, its energy can be a motivating force for finishing projects, organizing events, and making the most of the year's end.
2. **Physical Energy and Activity**: Mars governs physical energy and stamina, making it essential for engaging in activities that require strength, movement, or endurance. Its influence can encourage us to stay active, participate in holiday traditions, and bring energy to gatherings and festivities.
3. **Assertiveness and Boundaries**: Mars governs assertiveness, helping us stand up for our needs and set boundaries. During the holidays, when social interactions are heightened, Mars's influence can help us communicate openly and protect our energy when needed.
4. **Independence and Confidence**: Mars is associated with independence and self-confidence, qualities that inspire us to pursue our own path and make decisions aligned with our true desires. Its influence can encourage us to stay true to ourselves and avoid overextending to please others.

Mars and Holiday Ambition: Achieving Goals and Managing Holiday Stress

The holiday season is a busy time, often filled with a mix of personal, professional, and social obligations. Mars's assertive energy can be an asset, helping us manage these responsibilities and channel our ambition toward completing tasks and pursuing meaningful goals. Here are some ways Mars influences holiday ambition:

1. **Setting and Achieving Year-End Goals**: The end of the year is a time for reflection and goal-setting, and Mars's influence can add determination and focus to this process. Whether it's meeting work deadlines, organizing holiday events, or finalizing personal projects, Mars provides the energy to stay committed and see tasks through to completion.

2. **Handling Holiday Preparations with Energy**: Mars's physical energy can be particularly helpful during the holiday season, as many tasks—shopping, cooking, decorating, or hosting—require sustained effort. Mars enhances our stamina, making it easier to handle multiple tasks, stay active, and keep up with the demands of the season.

3. **Managing Holiday Stress and Avoiding Burnout**: While Mars brings energy, its assertive nature can also lead to stress if not balanced. During the holidays, there's often pressure to meet expectations, attend events, and fulfill obligations. Mars's influence encourages us to stay productive, but it's essential to recognize when to take breaks and recharge. Prioritizing tasks, setting limits, and taking moments to rest can prevent burnout and ensure that Mars's energy remains positive.

4. **Channeling Mars Energy into Healthy Competition**: Mars rules competition, inspiring friendly contests, challenges, and games that can add fun to holiday gatherings. Whether it's playing sports, board games, or friendly cooking contests, channeling Mars's energy into fun, healthy competition can create memorable experiences that bring people together.

Mars in Relationships: Assertiveness, Boundaries, and Holiday Interactions

Mars's energy in relationships encourages us to communicate assertively, protect our boundaries, and navigate social interactions with confidence. However, Mars can also bring intensity to relationships, sometimes leading to conflict or misunderstandings if emotions run high. Navigating Mars's influence with mindfulness can help us create harmony, balance, and mutual respect in our holiday relationships.

1. **Communicating Assertively**: Mars's influence encourages direct and assertive communication, which is helpful for expressing needs, setting expectations, and avoiding misunderstandings. During holiday gatherings, assertiveness can help address issues openly, fostering honest conversations that bring clarity and strengthen connections.

2. **Setting and Respecting Boundaries**: Mars encourages self-protection and boundary-setting, making it easier to assert limits. Holiday gatherings can sometimes be emotionally charged, with the potential for conflict or overstepped boundaries. Mars's energy empowers us to communicate our needs clearly and respectfully, ensuring that interactions remain respectful and positive.

3. **Navigating Conflict with Calm Assertiveness**: Mars's influence can sometimes lead to impatience or impulsivity, which may increase the likelihood of conflict. During holiday interactions, staying mindful of Mars's intensity can help us respond thoughtfully rather than reactively. If tensions arise, taking a moment to breathe and communicate calmly can prevent misunderstandings and keep the focus on resolving issues constructively.

4. **Encouraging Mutual Respect and Independence**: Mars values independence and self-respect, qualities that enhance holiday relationships by encouraging mutual respect. During holiday gatherings, allowing each person to express their individuality, interests, and ideas can create a harmonious environment where everyone feels valued.

Embracing Mars's Energy for Physical Activity and Wellness

Mars is associated with physical vitality, stamina, and the drive to stay active. Embracing Mars's influence during the holiday season can support physical wellness, encourage self-care, and provide a constructive outlet for stress.

1. **Staying Active with Seasonal Activities**: The holiday season provides opportunities to engage in seasonal activities that embrace Mars's love for physical energy. Activities like ice skating, hiking, skiing, or even a family walk after a meal can help channel Mars's vitality into enjoyable experiences. Staying active supports both physical health and mental well-being, helping us feel energized and balanced.

2. **Prioritizing Physical Wellness**: Mars reminds us to prioritize physical health, even amidst holiday indulgences. Making time for exercise, eating nutritious meals, and getting adequate sleep are ways to honor Mars's influence and maintain balance. Physical wellness helps us manage stress and keep energy levels stable, allowing us to fully enjoy the season.

3. **Channeling Energy into Physical Self-Care**: Physical self-care, such as stretching, yoga, or massage, can help manage Mars's energy constructively. These practices provide relaxation while honoring the body, helping to relieve tension and maintain flexibility. Engaging in physical self-care during the holidays can reduce stress, enhance mood, and align with Mars's focus on vitality.

4. **Setting Personal Challenges and Goals**: Mars is driven by achievement and personal challenges. Setting small, achievable fitness or wellness goals during the holiday season—such as taking daily walks, drinking more water, or completing a physical challenge—can keep us motivated and focused. Mars's energy thrives on progress, making these small accomplishments satisfying and confidence-boosting.

Using Mars to Cultivate Holiday Ambition and Drive

Mars's influence can be an asset for setting intentions, achieving goals, and cultivating motivation for the new year. By harnessing its ambitious energy, we can approach the holiday season with a sense of purpose and clarity, setting a strong foundation for the months to come.

1. **Setting New Year's Intentions with Determination**: Mars's ambitious energy makes it an ideal time to set New Year's intentions that reflect personal growth and achievement. Consider areas of life where you'd like to make progress and use Mars's focus to create realistic, actionable goals. Setting intentions during the holidays, while Mars's energy is strong, adds a sense of commitment and purpose to the new year.

2. **Breaking Down Large Goals into Actionable Steps**: Mars is a planet of action and thrives on movement. Rather than feeling overwhelmed by large goals, breaking them down into smaller, actionable steps can make them manageable. This approach helps maintain momentum and motivation, allowing us to work steadily toward meaningful achievements without burnout.

3. **Using Visualization for Motivation**: Mars responds well to visualization, as it inspires action through clear mental imagery. Visualizing desired outcomes, whether in personal or professional life, can enhance motivation and help us connect emotionally with our goals. Creating a vision board, journaling intentions, or setting daily reminders can keep Mars's energy aligned with our ambitions.

4. **Celebrating Small Wins and Progress**: Mars values achievement, so acknowledging and celebrating small accomplishments can keep motivation high. During the holiday season, take time to recognize your progress, whether in personal goals, work, or wellness. Celebrating small wins builds confidence and reinforces Mars's energy, helping you maintain momentum.

Managing Mars's Challenges During the Holidays

While Mars brings energy, it can also intensify emotions, leading to impatience, irritability, or impulsive behavior. Recognizing these tendencies and using them constructively can help keep Mars's influence balanced during the holiday season.

1. **Practicing Mindfulness to Temper Impulsivity**: Mars's intensity can sometimes lead to impulsive reactions or decisions. Practicing mindfulness, such as pausing before responding, breathing deeply, or considering the bigger picture, can help us make thoughtful choices. This approach is especially helpful during social gatherings, where heightened emotions may lead to misunderstandings.

2. **Channeling Excess Energy into Physical Activity**: Mars's energy can sometimes feel restless or overwhelming. Engaging in physical activities that release energy—like exercise, dancing, or even going for a walk—can help channel this intensity in a positive way. Physical movement reduces stress, improves mood, and helps us stay calm and focused.

3. **Using Breathing Techniques for Calmness**: Simple breathing exercises can be effective for managing Mars's intensity, especially when feeling stressed or impatient. Techniques such as

deep belly breathing, counting breaths, or using affirmations can ground us and bring calmness, helping us navigate challenging situations with composure.

4. **Avoiding Overcommitment and Overwhelm**: Mars's ambitious nature can sometimes lead to overcommitting, especially during the busy holiday season. Staying aware of personal limits and avoiding unnecessary obligations can prevent overwhelm. Setting realistic goals and focusing on what truly matters helps maintain Mars's energy positively and prevents burnout.

Practical Mars-Inspired Practices for a Productive and Balanced Holiday

Incorporating Mars's energy into holiday activities can enhance productivity, support well-being, and encourage purposeful action. Here are some ways to align with Mars's influence during the season:

1. **Create a "Holiday Action Plan"**: Use Mars's organizational energy to plan holiday activities, tasks, and goals. List priorities, set deadlines, and break larger tasks into manageable steps. This approach adds structure to holiday preparations, helping you stay organized and enjoy the season with less stress.
2. **Set a "Holiday Wellness Challenge"**: Create a personal or family wellness challenge that aligns with Mars's physical energy. Whether it's a daily walk, a step-count goal, or a simple fitness challenge, engaging in physical activities can keep you energized and connected to Mars's vitality.
3. **Engage in "Holiday Self-Reflection"**: Mars values achievement, making the holiday season an ideal time for self-reflection on accomplishments, lessons learned, and areas for growth. Consider journaling about your progress over the past year, acknowledging both wins and challenges, and setting intentions for the new year.
4. **Establish a "Rest and Recharge Ritual"**: Balance Mars's high energy with intentional rest. Create a ritual that includes relaxation practices such as reading, meditating, or simply spending time in nature. This practice helps restore energy, maintains balance, and prevents Mars's influence from becoming overwhelming.

Final Thoughts: Honoring Mars's Energy During the Holiday Season

Mars, with its drive, ambition, and energy, provides a powerful influence that can help us navigate the holiday season with focus and purpose. While the holidays are often thought of as a time for rest and reflection, Mars encourages us to take action, pursue our goals, and bring vitality to our celebrations. By harnessing Mars's energy with mindfulness, we can achieve a sense of balance, embracing both productivity and rest, connection and independence.

This holiday season, let Mars inspire you to approach each moment with determination, resilience, and an open heart. Whether through completing year-end goals, connecting with loved ones assertively, or simply engaging in activities that bring joy, may Mars's influence guide you toward a season of purpose, energy, and fulfillment. As you align with Mars's dynamic power, may you find the confidence to pursue your aspirations, the courage to set boundaries, and the vitality to fully embrace the spirit of the holidays.

Chapter 38: Mercury - Communication and Festive Gatherings

Mercury, the planet of communication, intellect, and connection, plays a pivotal role in holiday gatherings, shaping how we interact, share stories, and strengthen bonds with loved ones. Known as the "messenger of the gods" in mythology, Mercury governs language, travel, ideas, and all forms of expression. During the holiday season, when gatherings, reunions, and social engagements are abundant, Mercury's influence becomes especially significant. It affects not only how we communicate but also our ability to listen, empathize, and navigate the complexities of group dynamics.

In this chapter, we explore the role of Mercury in holiday astrology, examining its impact on communication styles, interpersonal relationships, and social interactions. By understanding Mercury's energy, we can approach festive gatherings with greater mindfulness, enhancing connections, resolving misunderstandings, and making lasting memories. We'll also discuss how to navigate Mercury retrograde during the holiday season, an astrological event that can sometimes complicate communication but also offers valuable lessons in patience, introspection, and understanding.

The Astrological Influence of Mercury

In astrology, Mercury is associated with the mind, intellect, and all forms of communication. As the planet closest to the Sun, Mercury acts as a bridge between our inner world and outer expressions, governing how we think, speak, write, and interact with others. Mercury's energy is curious, agile, and adaptable, encouraging learning, exploration, and the exchange of ideas.

1. **Communication and Expression**: Mercury influences how we convey thoughts, share ideas, and connect with others. It shapes our communication style, from our choice of words to the tone of voice we use, making it an essential factor in how we relate to family and friends during the holidays.

2. **Social Connections and Networking**: Mercury governs social interactions, networking, and our ability to engage with diverse groups. Its influence is especially beneficial during holiday gatherings, when we connect with people from various parts of our lives, fostering a spirit of unity and shared celebration.

3. **Intellect and Curiosity**: Mercury's intellectual nature fuels our curiosity and desire to learn, encouraging lively conversations, storytelling, and discussions. During the holidays, this influence promotes meaningful exchanges, allowing us to share personal experiences, cultural traditions, and new ideas.

4. **Adaptability and Flexibility**: Mercury is highly adaptable, helping us navigate different social settings, understand others' perspectives, and adjust to various group dynamics. This flexibility is invaluable during holiday gatherings, where family traditions, expectations, and personalities may vary widely.

Mercury's Role in Enhancing Holiday Gatherings

Mercury's influence during the holiday season can help create memorable, heartwarming experiences. Its energy encourages openness, curiosity, and a willingness to connect on a deeper level, making it easier to bridge generational gaps, foster empathy, and strengthen relationships.

1. **Engaging in Meaningful Conversations**: Mercury inspires a love for communication, encouraging us to engage in conversations that go beyond small talk. The holiday season, with its focus on connection, is an ideal time to explore deeper topics, share stories, and ask questions that reveal the values, dreams, and experiences of our loved ones. Mercury's influence can transform ordinary conversations into meaningful exchanges that leave lasting impressions.

2. **Creating Traditions of Storytelling**: Storytelling is a timeless holiday tradition, and Mercury enhances our ability to share personal narratives, family histories, and cultural lore. Whether recounting fond memories, childhood adventures, or family legends, storytelling helps preserve traditions and fosters a sense of belonging. Mercury's energy enhances this tradition, making stories more vivid, engaging, and impactful.

3. **Bridging Generational Gaps**: Mercury encourages curiosity and open-mindedness, making it easier to connect across generations. By listening to the stories of elders, sharing our own experiences, and asking questions that reveal common values, Mercury's influence helps foster understanding between family members of different ages, strengthening intergenerational bonds.

4. **Facilitating Reconciliation and Healing**: Mercury's role in communication can also support healing conversations, particularly in family gatherings where misunderstandings or past conflicts may arise. Mercury encourages diplomacy, empathy, and clarity, creating a space for open dialogue that can help resolve lingering tensions and rebuild trust. By approaching conversations with patience and compassion, we can use Mercury's energy to foster reconciliation and harmony.

5. **Encouraging Light-Hearted Fun and Laughter**: Mercury's playful side brings humor and wit to social gatherings, encouraging light-hearted exchanges, games, and laughter. Its influence makes it easier to enjoy the moment, share jokes, and participate in activities that bring joy and entertainment. This energy helps balance the holiday season's reflective and sentimental moments with a spirit of fun and spontaneity.

Navigating Mercury Retrograde During the Holidays

Mercury retrograde occurs several times a year, including occasionally during the holiday season. During this period, Mercury appears to move backward in the sky from our perspective on Earth, often coinciding with disruptions in communication, technology, travel, and plans. While Mercury retrograde can present challenges, it also offers an opportunity for introspection, patience, and adaptability.

1. **Preparing for Travel and Plan Changes**: Mercury retrograde is notorious for causing delays, miscommunications, and travel mishaps. If you're traveling during this period, allow extra time for potential delays, double-check bookings, and have backup plans. Embracing flexibility and humor can turn unexpected detours into memorable experiences.

2. **Double-Checking Communication**: During Mercury retrograde, misunderstandings can arise more easily, making it essential to communicate with extra clarity. Taking a moment to think before speaking, double-checking written messages, and actively listening can prevent miscommunication. Approaching interactions with patience and open-mindedness helps ensure that intentions are understood and that conflicts are avoided.

3. **Embracing Patience and Flexibility**: Mercury retrograde teaches patience and the importance of going with the flow. Unexpected events or delays may arise, but remaining adaptable can help keep stress at bay. Use this time to focus on meaningful interactions, slow down, and approach each moment with mindfulness, allowing space for reflection and reconnection.

4. **Reflecting and Revisiting Memories**: Mercury retrograde is an ideal time for reflection and revisiting memories, making it a wonderful opportunity for holiday storytelling, reviewing family photo albums, and reminiscing about past celebrations. This reflective quality aligns well with the holiday spirit, encouraging us to connect with the past while creating new memories.

Practical Mercury-Inspired Tips for Festive Communication

Incorporating Mercury's qualities into holiday gatherings can help create harmonious, enjoyable, and meaningful experiences. By fostering open communication, active listening, and intellectual curiosity, we can deepen our connections and celebrate the holiday season with greater empathy and understanding.

1. **Practice Active Listening**: Mercury's influence encourages us to listen as much as we speak. Active listening—focusing on the speaker, avoiding interruptions, and responding with empathy—fosters deeper understanding and connection. During holiday gatherings, active listening allows family members and friends to feel heard, valued, and respected, strengthening bonds and creating a positive atmosphere.

2. **Engage in Open-Ended Conversations**: Mercury inspires curiosity, making open-ended questions a wonderful way to spark meaningful dialogue. Asking questions like, "What's been the highlight of your year?" or "What traditions mean the most to you?" encourages reflection and invites loved ones to share thoughts and stories. These conversations create a richer, more fulfilling holiday experience.

3. **Set Up a Holiday Storytelling Circle**: Dedicate time during gatherings for storytelling, allowing family members to share memories, personal experiences, or family history. This activity, guided by Mercury's love for expression, fosters a sense of continuity, tradition, and understanding. Storytelling circles also provide an opportunity to share laughs, wisdom, and heartfelt moments that make the holiday season memorable.

4. **Host a Game or Trivia Night**: Mercury loves mental stimulation and play, making a game night or trivia session a fun way to engage family and friends. Choose games that encourage laughter, teamwork, and creativity, such as trivia about family history, charades, or board games. These activities create a relaxed atmosphere, making it easy to bond over friendly competition and shared enjoyment.

5. **Create a Family or Friends Time Capsule**: Mercury's influence on memory and expression makes a time capsule a meaningful holiday activity. Invite everyone to contribute items, messages, or small mementos that capture the essence of the year or holiday season. Seal the capsule and plan to open it in the future, creating a tangible link between past and future gatherings.

Enhancing Relationships with Mercury's Communication Tools

Mercury's energy can also be harnessed to nurture relationships, resolve conflicts, and enhance understanding within families and social circles. By approaching holiday interactions with clarity, empathy, and openness, we can use Mercury's tools to build stronger, healthier relationships.

1. **Expressing Appreciation and Gratitude**: Expressing gratitude to family members and friends strengthens relationships, creating an atmosphere of appreciation and positivity. Mercury encourages thoughtful communication, making it a perfect time to share words of thanks, affirmations, or personal messages of appreciation. Simple gestures like writing a thank-you card or verbally expressing gratitude can leave a lasting impact.

2. **Navigating Difficult Conversations with Diplomacy**: Mercury's diplomacy supports respectful conversations, making it easier to address sensitive topics or resolve misunderstandings. If challenging conversations arise, approach them with patience, empathy, and a focus on finding common ground. Staying calm, validating others' feelings, and using "I" statements rather than "you" statements can help prevent defensiveness and foster mutual understanding.

3. **Sharing Cultural and Personal Traditions**: Mercury's curiosity about the world around us makes it an ideal time to share and learn about diverse traditions. During the holidays, encourage family members to share customs, foods, or practices that are meaningful to them. This exchange of traditions enriches the holiday experience, fostering respect, appreciation, and a sense of unity within diversity.

4. **Creating Opportunities for Connection with Introverted Guests**: Mercury's influence can sometimes favor extroverted expression, but introverted family members or friends may feel overwhelmed in social settings. Creating quiet spaces or offering low-key activities, such as one-on-one conversations, can make gatherings more inclusive and comfortable for everyone. Mercury's adaptability reminds us that each person has unique communication needs, and honoring them strengthens bonds.

Mercury's Influence on Travel and Holiday Planning

The holiday season often involves travel, organizing events, and coordinating schedules—all of which fall under Mercury's domain. By embracing Mercury's skills in planning and adaptability, we can navigate holiday logistics with greater ease and efficiency.

1. **Organize Travel Plans with Precision**: Mercury governs travel logistics, so planning ahead and double-checking details can help ensure smooth journeys. Confirm reservations, prepare for possible delays, and keep communication lines open with travel companions. This proactive approach allows you to respond calmly to unexpected events and make travel a stress-free part of the holiday experience.

2. **Streamline Communication with Family and Friends**: Coordinating gatherings often requires clear communication, especially when multiple people are involved. Use group messaging apps, email, or shared calendars to keep everyone informed of plans and expectations. Mercury's influence encourages clarity and consistency, making it easier to organize events and ensure everyone is on the same page.

3. **Practice Patience in Busy Environments**: Holiday travel and shopping can be chaotic, but Mercury encourages adaptability and patience. Recognize that delays or crowded environments are temporary, and use this time to practice mindfulness, read, or engage in light conversation with those around you. Mercury's flexibility helps us stay calm and make the most of each situation.

Practical Mercury-Inspired Reflections for a Meaningful Holiday

Mercury's influence during the holidays provides a perfect opportunity for reflection, both individually and as a family. By taking time to connect with ourselves and our loved ones, we can use Mercury's insights to create a holiday experience that is both thoughtful and fulfilling.

1. **Reflect on Communication Goals for the New Year**: Mercury's energy is ideal for setting intentions around communication, relationships, and self-expression. Reflect on areas where you'd like to improve communication, strengthen relationships, or become a better listener. These goals create a foundation for meaningful interactions in the new year, aligned with Mercury's principles of understanding and connection.

2. **Practice Gratitude and Express Appreciation**: Take time to reflect on the people who have enriched your life, and consider ways to express gratitude during the holidays. Writing a heartfelt note, sharing a memory, or verbally expressing appreciation can foster a deeper sense of connection and respect. This practice aligns with Mercury's value of communication, transforming appreciation into meaningful expressions of love.

3. **Engage in Mindful Communication Practices**: Mercury encourages thoughtful communication, making it an ideal time to practice active listening, empathy, and kindness. Approach each interaction with intention, listen fully, and speak with clarity. These practices foster a sense of connection and respect, creating a harmonious environment that reflects Mercury's influence.

4. **Explore New Ideas and Traditions Together**: Mercury values learning and curiosity, making it a wonderful time to explore new traditions, games, or cultural customs. Encouraging family members to share something they've learned or a tradition they enjoy adds variety to holiday gatherings, enriching the experience with diverse perspectives and meaningful exchanges.

Final Thoughts: Honoring Mercury in Holiday Gatherings

Mercury's influence during the holiday season reminds us of the importance of communication, connection, and shared experiences. By embracing Mercury's qualities of curiosity, empathy, and adaptability, we can approach each gathering with an open heart and a clear mind, making the holiday season a time of joy, understanding, and unity. Whether through heartfelt conversations, shared stories, or simple expressions of gratitude, Mercury's energy enhances our relationships, creating lasting memories filled with love and appreciation.

This holiday season, let Mercury inspire you to connect with others thoughtfully, share your authentic self, and listen with compassion. May Mercury's influence guide you to embrace the beauty of communication, celebrate the diversity of perspectives, and create a festive season that resonates with warmth, understanding, and true connection. As you navigate the celebrations, may Mercury's spirit of curiosity and openness make each interaction a meaningful part of your holiday experience, building bonds that will last far beyond the season.

Chapter 39: Neptune - Spirituality and Holiday Mysticism

Neptune, the planet of spirituality, dreams, and mysticism, governs the realms beyond the physical, inviting us to explore our intuition, imagination, and higher states of consciousness. Often referred to as the planet of dreams, Neptune's influence deepens our sense of connection to something greater than ourselves. During the holiday season—a time of celebration, reflection, and tradition—Neptune's energy brings a sense of enchantment, allowing us to access the magic and mystery of the season in profound ways. Its influence enhances holiday rituals, fuels spiritual reflection, and encourages a sense of unity, compassion, and transcendence that enriches the meaning of the holidays.

In this chapter, we explore Neptune's role in holiday astrology, examining how its mystical energy enhances our spiritual experiences, inspires acts of compassion, and fosters a sense of interconnectedness. By aligning with Neptune's energy, we can bring a touch of mysticism to our holiday celebrations, embracing the season's deeper meanings and connecting with loved ones on a soul level. We'll also delve into practical ways to integrate Neptune's influence through rituals, mindfulness, and practices that foster a sense of wonder and unity.

The Astrological Influence of Neptune

Neptune is associated with intuition, dreams, mysticism, and the spiritual dimension of life. It governs the imaginative, compassionate, and transcendent aspects of our nature, helping us connect with our inner wisdom and the mysteries of existence. Often linked to spiritual practices, artistic inspiration, and deep empathy, Neptune's influence guides us to look beyond the material world and explore our inner, spiritual selves.

1. **Spirituality and Transcendence**: Neptune represents our connection to the divine, helping us explore spirituality and the search for higher meaning. Its influence encourages us to look beyond the physical and embrace the unseen, making it an ideal energy for holiday reflections, rituals, and sacred practices.

2. **Intuition and Mysticism**: Neptune heightens our intuition, allowing us to sense energies, access our subconscious, and explore mystical practices. During the holidays, Neptune's influence can bring a magical, almost otherworldly quality to celebrations, inspiring us to engage in symbolic rituals and connect with our inner selves.

3. **Compassion and Unity**: Neptune fosters empathy, compassion, and a sense of unity, encouraging us to recognize the interconnectedness of all life. In the context of the holidays, Neptune's energy enhances the spirit of giving, charity, and kindness, reminding us that love and compassion are at the heart of the season.

4. **Creativity and Imagination**: Neptune is a source of artistic inspiration and creativity, inspiring imagination and fantasy. This energy brings a dreamlike quality to holiday celebrations, encouraging us to appreciate beauty, art, and the simple wonders of the season.

Neptune and the Spiritual Meaning of the Holiday Season
Neptune's influence brings a profound sense of spirituality to the holiday season, inviting us to connect with the deeper meanings behind holiday traditions, rituals, and gatherings. By embracing Neptune's energy, we can transform the holidays into a time of reflection, compassion, and unity, focusing on the values that transcend materialism and connect us to our higher selves.

1. **Exploring the Sacredness of Tradition**: Neptune's mystical energy encourages us to view holiday traditions as sacred rituals that connect us with the past, our families, and the collective spirit of humanity. Lighting candles, decorating trees, and gathering for meals can be seen as symbols of love, continuity, and reverence. By viewing these traditions as sacred, we deepen our appreciation for the season's beauty and significance.

2. **Connecting with the Divine and Inner Self**: The holiday season is an ideal time for spiritual reflection, meditation, and connecting with the divine. Neptune's energy encourages us to seek moments of stillness, allowing us to tap into our inner wisdom and higher consciousness. Whether through prayer, meditation, or simply sitting in silence, these moments bring a sense of peace and alignment, reminding us of the spiritual dimension of the season.

3. **Embracing the Spirit of Compassion and Kindness**: Neptune's influence fosters a deep sense of compassion and empathy, qualities that align beautifully with the holiday season's focus on giving, gratitude, and connection. Acts of charity, kindness, and selflessness are reflections of Neptune's energy, reminding us that the essence of the holidays lies in caring for others, sharing joy, and extending love to those in need.

4. **Experiencing the Holiday Season as a Time of Unity**: Neptune inspires a sense of unity and interconnectedness, encouraging us to view ourselves as part of a larger whole. The holidays, with their focus on gathering and togetherness, offer a natural opportunity to honor this unity, connecting not only with family and friends but also with humanity as a collective. This perspective fosters a sense of belonging and reinforces the idea that we are all connected through love and compassion.

Holiday Rituals and Practices Inspired by Neptune's Mysticism

Neptune's influence invites us to incorporate spiritual and mystical elements into our holiday celebrations, transforming them into soulful, meaningful experiences. Through mindful rituals, creative expression, and moments of stillness, we can honor Neptune's energy and infuse the holiday season with a sense of magic and depth.

1. **Creating a Sacred Space for Reflection**: Designate a space in your home for reflection and meditation, adorned with items that bring a sense of peace and spiritual connection, such as candles, crystals, incense, or holiday symbols. This space serves as a sanctuary where you can engage in Neptune-inspired practices, such as meditation, journaling, or simply quiet contemplation.

2. **Engaging in Candle or Light Rituals**: Lighting candles or string lights is a symbolic way to bring light into darkness, reflecting Neptune's mystical quality. Consider a ritual where each candle represents an intention or a prayer for the new year, honoring the hope, love, and peace that the holidays inspire. Candle lighting also creates a serene atmosphere, ideal for meditation or quiet reflection.

3. **Practicing Guided Meditation or Visualization**: Guided meditations or visualizations are powerful tools for connecting with Neptune's energy, as they engage the imagination and deepen the sense of spiritual connection. A meditation focused on gratitude, compassion, or unity can help center you in the present moment, fostering a sense of peace and purpose. Visualizing loving energy surrounding family and friends also enhances the holiday spirit of love and connection.

4. **Participating in a Gratitude or Compassion Ritual**: Neptune's compassion is beautifully expressed through acts of gratitude and kindness. Consider creating a gratitude ritual where each person shares something they're thankful for, or engage in acts of kindness for those in need. Donating time, resources, or gifts to a charitable cause or simply reaching out to someone who may feel lonely can make a profound impact and align with Neptune's energy of empathy.

5. **Using Symbols and Art in Holiday Decor**: Neptune's creativity can inspire the use of symbolic and artistic elements in holiday decorations. Incorporate items that hold personal or spiritual meaning, such as nature-inspired decor, handmade ornaments, or art that reflects beauty and unity. This approach to holiday decor brings a sense of intention and reverence, transforming spaces into sacred expressions of joy and connection.

Neptune-Inspired Reflections for a Deeper Holiday Experience

The holiday season offers a natural opportunity for introspection, allowing us to explore the deeper meanings behind our traditions, relationships, and personal growth. Neptune's influence encourages soulful reflections that connect us with our inner selves, helping us enter the new year with clarity, purpose, and alignment.

1. **Reflecting on the Year's Spiritual Lessons**: Neptune's influence can guide us to review the past year through a spiritual lens, considering the lessons learned, growth experienced, and values deepened. Take time to reflect on how challenges and blessings have shaped you, asking questions like, "What have I learned about compassion and resilience?" and "How can I bring more love and kindness into my life?"

2. **Journaling for Insight and Clarity**: Journaling provides a powerful outlet for self-discovery and healing, helping us connect with Neptune's introspective energy. During the holidays, consider journaling on topics such as gratitude, forgiveness, and spiritual goals. Neptune's influence enhances intuition, allowing you to explore emotions and insights that deepen your understanding of self and soul.

3. **Setting Spiritual Intentions for the New Year**: Neptune encourages setting intentions that go beyond material goals, focusing instead on spiritual growth, emotional healing, and inner peace. Reflect on intentions that nurture your spirit, such as practicing compassion, deepening mindfulness, or exploring creative or mystical interests. These intentions align with Neptune's energy, supporting a journey of self-discovery and fulfillment.

4. **Exploring Dream Work and Intuition**: Neptune governs dreams and the subconscious, making the holiday season an ideal time for dream work and intuitive exploration. Keep a dream journal, noting any symbols or themes that arise, or engage in practices that enhance intuition, such as tarot, meditation, or working with oracle cards. These practices provide insight into the subconscious and encourage a deeper connection to inner wisdom.

Holiday Mysticism and the Spirit of Giving

Neptune's energy reminds us that the true essence of the holidays lies in acts of compassion, kindness, and selflessness. Embracing the spirit of giving, both materially and spiritually, allows us to connect with others in meaningful ways, fostering a sense of unity and joy that transcends physical gifts.

1. **Giving from the Heart**: Neptune encourages giving that comes from a place of love and empathy, rather than obligation. Consider creating handmade gifts, writing personal messages, or giving experiences rather than material items. Gifts that hold personal significance or reflect thoughtfulness align with Neptune's spirit, enhancing the joy of both giving and receiving.
2. **Practicing Selflessness and Service**: Acts of service are powerful expressions of Neptune's compassion, reinforcing the holiday season's spirit of unity. Consider volunteering, supporting charitable causes, or simply being present for someone in need. Acts of kindness, even small ones, create ripples of positivity, reinforcing the idea that we are all connected.
3. **Offering Emotional Support and Empathy**: Neptune's energy fosters deep empathy, allowing us to connect with others' emotions and offer meaningful support. During the holidays, this can mean listening actively, offering comfort to those who may be struggling, or simply being present with an open heart. Empathy strengthens bonds, creating a holiday experience grounded in genuine love and connection.

Neptune's Role in Creative and Artistic Holiday Expressions

Neptune is closely associated with art, music, and creative expression, all of which add a magical quality to holiday celebrations. Whether through music, poetry, art, or dance, Neptune's influence enhances our ability to experience beauty and transcend the ordinary, allowing us to see the holidays as a celebration of both inner and outer beauty.

1. **Using Music to Create a Spiritual Atmosphere**: Music has a profound ability to evoke emotions and create a sacred space, and Neptune's influence enhances our receptivity to its power. Curate a playlist of calming, meditative, or spiritually uplifting music to set the tone for gatherings or personal reflection. Sacred or instrumental music can create a tranquil environment, perfect for meditation, relaxation, or simply enjoying a moment of peace.
2. **Creating Art as a Holiday Ritual**: Engaging in artistic expression is a wonderful way to honor Neptune's creative energy. Whether through painting, drawing, or crafting, creating holiday-themed art can be both meditative and joyful. Consider setting aside time for family art projects, or creating vision boards that capture hopes and dreams for the new year, infusing holiday gatherings with creativity and imagination.
3. **Writing Poetry, Stories, or Letters**: Neptune's influence enhances the poetic and imaginative, making writing a meaningful holiday practice. Writing poetry, stories, or heartfelt letters to loved ones can be a beautiful way to express emotions, reflect on memories, and convey appreciation. These written expressions become treasured keepsakes that carry the spirit of Neptune's compassion and beauty.
4. **Engaging in Symbolic or Thematic Decor**: Neptune's love for symbolism makes it meaningful to incorporate artistic, nature-inspired, or mystical themes in holiday decor. Using symbols that represent peace, love, or spiritual growth—such as feathers, stars, crystals, or nature elements—brings a deeper layer of meaning to festive decorations, creating an environment that reflects Neptune's soulful energy.

Final Thoughts: Embracing Neptune's Mysticism During the Holidays

Neptune's influence invites us to approach the holiday season with a sense of wonder, spirituality, and compassion, reminding us that the essence of this time lies in connection, reflection, and the celebration of inner beauty. By embracing Neptune's energy, we can transform holiday gatherings into moments of profound meaning, fostering unity, peace, and a shared sense of purpose.

This holiday season, let Neptune inspire you to explore the spiritual dimensions of the season, honor the beauty of simple moments, and connect with loved ones on a soul level. Through acts of kindness, mindful rituals, and a focus on gratitude, may Neptune's energy guide you toward a season that resonates with depth, compassion, and joy. As you celebrate, may Neptune's spirit of mysticism bring enchantment, unity, and spiritual fulfillment to each gathering, creating a holiday experience that transcends the ordinary and touches the heart of what truly matters.

Chapter 40: Uranus - Innovation and Unique Holiday Celebrations

Uranus, the planet of innovation, individuality, and unexpected change, is the cosmic force that encourages us to break from tradition, think outside the box, and explore new ways of being. Known as the "rebel" planet, Uranus represents freedom, creativity, and originality, challenging norms and inviting us to explore alternative perspectives. During the holiday season, Uranus's influence brings an exciting opportunity to reinvent old customs, add fresh ideas to family gatherings, and celebrate the season in ways that feel uniquely meaningful. Uranus's energy encourages us to experiment, celebrate diversity, and create traditions that reflect our individuality and values.

In this chapter, we explore how Uranus's innovative spirit can inspire unique holiday celebrations, helping us move beyond convention and embrace a holiday experience that is authentic, creative, and reflective of who we are. From introducing new traditions to incorporating technology in meaningful ways, Uranus offers endless possibilities for a dynamic and memorable season. We'll also delve into the ways Uranus's energy can help us stay flexible and open-minded, making it easier to navigate changes in plans and adapt to the unexpected.

The Astrological Influence of Uranus

In astrology, Uranus is associated with innovation, originality, freedom, and change. It governs sudden insights, technological advancements, and revolutionary thinking, encouraging us to challenge old systems and explore new perspectives. Uranus's energy is forward-thinking, seeking to liberate us from outdated patterns and inspire progress. It is also highly adaptable, helping us remain open to change and view the world through a lens of possibility.

1. **Innovation and Creativity**: Uranus encourages creativity and a willingness to experiment, allowing us to break from traditional molds and explore new ideas. This energy inspires us to infuse originality into our holiday celebrations, creating experiences that are uniquely meaningful.

2. **Individuality and Authenticity**: Uranus values authenticity and self-expression, helping us honor our individuality without feeling constrained by convention. Its influence encourages us to create holiday traditions that reflect our values, interests, and unique family dynamics.

3. **Adaptability and Flexibility**: Uranus is associated with change, allowing us to adapt to unexpected situations and view challenges as opportunities. During the holidays, this energy makes it easier to navigate disruptions in plans, handle surprises, and approach each moment with a sense of adventure.

4. **Technology and Modernization**: Uranus governs technology and innovation, making it a wonderful influence for incorporating modern elements into holiday traditions. Its energy encourages us to embrace digital tools, connect with loved ones virtually, and find new ways to make the season meaningful, regardless of physical distance.

Embracing Innovation in Holiday Traditions

Uranus's influence invites us to rethink holiday traditions, creating celebrations that align with our values, lifestyles, and unique preferences. From reimagining rituals to experimenting with new activities, embracing Uranus's energy can add a sense of excitement, creativity, and authenticity to the holiday season.

1. **Creating Personalized Traditions**: Uranus encourages us to move beyond "one-size-fits-all" traditions and create rituals that reflect our family's unique interests and values. Consider brainstorming as a family or group, allowing each person to contribute ideas for holiday activities or themes. Whether it's an annual outdoor adventure, a movie marathon, or a creative cooking challenge, personalized traditions make the season feel uniquely meaningful.

2. **Experimenting with New Holiday Foods and Recipes**: Holiday meals are often tied to tradition, but Uranus's influence invites us to explore new flavors, ingredients, and cultural cuisines. Trying fusion recipes, experimenting with plant-based dishes, or hosting a global potluck where each person brings a dish inspired by another culture are ways to add excitement and broaden culinary horizons. This open-minded approach to holiday meals encourages exploration and celebrates diversity.

3. **Rethinking Gift-Giving**: Traditional gift-giving can sometimes feel like an obligation, but Uranus's energy encourages alternative approaches that add meaning and originality. Consider experiences over material gifts, homemade or upcycled items, or "gifts of service" where family members offer time or talents. Creating a "Secret Santa" with a twist, where each person must create something or offer a unique experience, adds a sense of surprise and personalization.

4. **Engaging in Acts of Social or Environmental Impact**: Uranus's humanitarian spirit aligns beautifully with social responsibility, making the holiday season a wonderful time to give back in innovative ways. Consider incorporating eco-friendly practices, such as zero-waste gift wrapping, reusable decorations, or homemade gifts. Participating in charitable activities, supporting local businesses, or organizing a family volunteer project can transform the holiday season into an opportunity for meaningful impact.

Infusing Technology into Holiday Celebrations

As the ruler of technology and modernity, Uranus encourages us to embrace digital tools and creative innovations to stay connected and enhance holiday gatherings. Technology can add convenience, inclusivity, and creativity to celebrations, especially when distance or busy schedules are a factor.

1. **Virtual Gatherings and Digital Connections**: For families and friends separated by distance, virtual gatherings are an excellent way to stay connected. Consider hosting virtual holiday parties, game nights, or even a shared meal over video call. Create a group playlist or have a virtual movie night to make everyone feel involved, regardless of location.

2. **Creating Digital Scrapbooks or Family Videos**: Use technology to create and share memories, such as a digital scrapbook of family photos, a slideshow of holiday highlights, or a video message that can be sent to loved ones. These digital keepsakes allow family members to share moments, celebrate milestones, and feel connected in a tangible way, even across distances.

3. **Organizing an Online Recipe Swap or Cook-Along**: For families that love to cook, a virtual recipe swap or cook-along can be a fun and interactive way to share traditions. Choose a favorite family recipe or new holiday dish and cook together via video call, sharing stories and memories as you go. This activity preserves culinary traditions while adding a modern twist that keeps everyone connected.

4. **Using Social Media to Share and Celebrate Together**: Social media can be a useful tool for sharing holiday updates, photos, and stories. Create a private family group on social media or a messaging app where everyone can post photos, holiday wishes, and updates. This digital space serves as a virtual gathering place, allowing family and friends to stay connected and celebrate each other's moments throughout the season.

Celebrating Individuality and Unique Expressions of Holiday Spirit
Uranus encourages us to celebrate our individuality and honor each person's unique interests, personality, and style. By creating space for self-expression and encouraging each person to contribute in their own way, holiday gatherings become a reflection of everyone's unique spirit.

1. **Encouraging Creative Self-Expression in Decor**: Give each family member a space or area to decorate according to their personal style. Allowing creativity to flow in holiday decor adds diversity, color, and uniqueness to shared spaces. Whether through homemade ornaments, theme-based decorations, or symbolic items, this practice celebrates each person's creativity.

2. **Hosting a "Holiday Talent Showcase"**: For families with diverse talents, hosting a talent showcase can be a fun and uplifting way to celebrate individuality. Each person can share a skill, such as singing, dancing, storytelling, or a creative project. This event not only highlights unique talents but also builds confidence, making the gathering memorable and inclusive.

3. **Exploring Unique Themes for Holiday Gatherings**: Themed gatherings add excitement and encourage creative engagement. Consider themes like "International Holidays" where each person dresses or brings a dish from a different culture, or "Holiday in Space" with futuristic decorations and an imaginative twist. Themes inspire fun, creativity, and collaboration, bringing Uranus's love for originality into the celebration.

4. **Allowing for Flexible Participation**: Some people enjoy actively participating in holiday gatherings, while others may prefer quieter or less structured roles. Uranus values individuality and autonomy, so allowing each person to participate in a way that feels comfortable to them helps everyone feel respected. This could mean creating quieter spaces, offering multiple activity options, or simply encouraging each person to express their holiday spirit in their own way.

Staying Open to Change and Unexpected Surprises

Uranus, as the planet of unpredictability, teaches us to embrace change and adapt to unexpected events. During the holidays, plans can shift, last-minute challenges may arise, or new opportunities may present themselves. Uranus's influence helps us navigate these situations with flexibility, creativity, and a positive attitude.

1. **Adapting to Last-Minute Changes with Grace**: Holiday plans don't always go as expected, and Uranus's energy encourages us to remain open to change. If a gathering needs to be moved, a travel delay occurs, or other unexpected events arise, approach the situation with flexibility and a spirit of adventure. Often, these changes can lead to new experiences, discoveries, or connections that make the season even more memorable.

2. **Using Unexpected Events as Opportunities**: Uranus views challenges as opportunities for growth, creativity, and exploration. If plans fall through, consider it an invitation to try something different—like an impromptu picnic instead of a formal meal, or a night of stargazing if an indoor event is canceled. Embracing these opportunities can bring about spontaneous joy and help us create lasting memories.

3. **Embracing the Concept of Minimalist or "Unplugged" Holidays**: For those looking to simplify, a minimalist or "unplugged" holiday can be a refreshing change. Consider celebrating with fewer material items, focusing instead on quality time, experiences, and moments of peace. Uranus's influence supports the idea that meaningful celebrations don't require elaborate planning, only genuine connection and presence.

4. **Encouraging Openness to New Relationships and Connections**: Uranus's influence often brings new people into our lives, sometimes in unexpected ways. During the holiday season, remain open to new connections, whether it's welcoming friends of friends, neighbors, or strangers who may need company. Uranus encourages inclusivity and open-heartedness, reminding us that sometimes the most unexpected friendships are the most meaningful.

Practical Uranus-Inspired Activities for an Innovative Holiday Season

Incorporating Uranus's qualities into holiday activities adds a touch of innovation, freedom, and creativity to gatherings. Here are some ideas to help you create an exciting, dynamic holiday experience:

1. **Create a Family Vision Board for the New Year**: Use Uranus's forward-thinking energy to create a collective vision board that reflects shared goals, dreams, and aspirations for the new year. Each family member can add images, words, or symbols that represent their intentions. This activity encourages creativity, unity, and a shared vision for the future.
2. **Host a "Holiday Hackathon"**: If your group enjoys problem-solving, host a "holiday hackathon" where everyone brainstorms creative solutions to holiday challenges, such as eco-friendly wrapping, affordable gift ideas, or ways to stay connected. This playful activity harnesses Uranus's innovative spirit, encouraging teamwork and out-of-the-box thinking.
3. **Celebrate Nature with an "Outdoor Holiday"**: Uranus is connected to the environment, making an outdoor celebration an ideal way to honor nature. Consider hosting a winter picnic, a hiking adventure, or a stargazing night. Connecting with nature adds a grounding and refreshing element to the holidays, providing an experience that is both memorable and meaningful.
4. **Explore DIY Crafting with Recycled Materials**: Uranus values sustainability, so incorporating DIY crafts with recycled or upcycled materials can be both fun and eco-friendly. Create holiday decorations, gifts, or cards from items you already have, transforming ordinary objects into unique and meaningful creations. This approach to crafting aligns with Uranus's innovative spirit and reinforces environmental consciousness.

Final Thoughts: Celebrating with Uranus's Spirit of Innovation and Freedom

Uranus's influence encourages us to approach the holiday season with a sense of adventure, creativity, and a willingness to break from tradition. By embracing originality, flexibility, and inclusivity, we can create holiday celebrations that are uniquely our own—expressions of who we are and what we value. Uranus reminds us that there is no "right" way to celebrate and that each person's approach to the holidays can be as distinctive as they are.

This holiday season, let Uranus inspire you to try new things, explore alternative traditions, and celebrate the season in a way that feels truly authentic. Whether through innovative activities, meaningful connections, or simply allowing yourself to be open to the unexpected, may Uranus's spirit of freedom and originality bring excitement, joy, and connection to your holiday celebrations. As you embrace the spirit of Uranus, may your holiday season be filled with inspiration, discovery, and the delight of celebrating on your own terms.

Part 9: **Retrogrades During the Holidays**

Chapter 41: Mercury Retrograde - Miscommunications and Mishaps

Mercury Retrograde is one of the most well-known astrological events, often associated with delays, miscommunications, and unexpected challenges. When Mercury appears to move backward in the sky, its retrograde motion brings an energy shift that influences travel, communication, technology, and day-to-day operations. This period, which occurs about three to four times a year, is known for its tendency to disrupt plans and lead to misunderstandings, requiring patience, flexibility, and a good sense of humor. During the holiday season, when family gatherings, travel, and holiday preparations are in full swing, Mercury Retrograde can add an extra layer of complexity to celebrations.

In this chapter, we explore the influence of Mercury Retrograde on holiday gatherings, examining how it affects communication, travel, technology, and planning. By understanding the energies at play, we can approach Mercury Retrograde with awareness, minimizing its potential for disruption and even embracing its lessons in patience, adaptability, and reflection. We'll also provide practical tips for navigating this period smoothly, turning potential mishaps into opportunities for growth, laughter, and connection.

The Astrological Significance of Mercury Retrograde

Mercury is the planet of communication, travel, intellect, and technology. Its retrograde periods are times when these areas of life can experience delays, errors, or misunderstandings, often requiring a more thoughtful and deliberate approach. During Mercury Retrograde, we are encouraged to slow down, reflect, and revisit past actions or relationships rather than pushing forward with new plans. This introspective energy can feel frustrating when plans seem to go awry, but it offers valuable opportunities for clarity, understanding, and growth.

1. **Communication and Misunderstandings**: Mercury Retrograde is notorious for causing communication issues, from missed messages and misunderstandings to disagreements and impulsive reactions. This period challenges us to be mindful of our words, listen carefully, and avoid making assumptions.

2. **Travel and Delays**: Travel is often impacted during Mercury Retrograde, with delays, missed connections, and last-minute changes being common occurrences. Flexibility and patience are key, as is preparing for contingencies to handle unexpected changes.

3. **Technology and Disruptions**: Technology and electronics can be particularly unpredictable during Mercury Retrograde, leading to issues with devices, connectivity problems, and data loss. This is an ideal time to back up data, double-check online orders, and approach technology with caution.

4. **Reflection and Revisiting the Past**: While Mercury Retrograde can be challenging, it's also a period for introspection, allowing us to review, reassess, and reconnect. This energy encourages us to slow down, evaluate past choices, and address any unresolved issues that may benefit from a fresh perspective.

Navigating Miscommunications During Mercury Retrograde

Mercury Retrograde can often lead to misunderstandings and conflicts, especially during the holiday season, when family gatherings, social events, and high expectations can amplify emotions. Navigating this period with awareness and mindfulness can help minimize misunderstandings and foster a more harmonious holiday experience.

1. **Practice Active Listening**: Communication issues are more likely during Mercury Retrograde, so practicing active listening is essential. Make an effort to fully engage in conversations, avoiding distractions and giving your complete attention to the speaker. This reduces the likelihood of misinterpretations and helps build stronger connections.
2. **Clarify Messages and Confirm Plans**: Miscommunications and scheduling conflicts are common during Mercury Retrograde. Take extra steps to clarify messages, confirm arrangements, and double-check important details. If sending invitations or coordinating travel, follow up to ensure everyone has the correct information, and don't assume that messages were received or understood.
3. **Avoid Jumping to Conclusions**: Mercury Retrograde can heighten our tendency to assume or react impulsively, leading to unnecessary conflicts. If a conversation becomes heated or confusing, take a moment to pause, ask clarifying questions, and try to understand the other person's perspective. This approach can prevent misunderstandings and maintain peace during gatherings.
4. **Choose Words Carefully and Avoid Criticism**: During Mercury Retrograde, words can easily be taken out of context, leading to unintended offense or misunderstandings. Approach conversations with kindness, and think carefully before speaking, especially if discussing sensitive topics. Avoid criticism or sarcasm, as these can be misinterpreted, especially in high-stress environments.

Managing Travel Plans and Delays

Travel plans are often disrupted during Mercury Retrograde, with delays, missed connections, and last-minute changes being common. While this can be frustrating, preparing in advance and embracing flexibility can help turn these challenges into memorable experiences.

1. **Plan for Extra Time and Flexibility**: During Mercury Retrograde, it's wise to build in extra time for travel, allowing for potential delays, longer check-ins, or changes in plans. Booking flights, buses, or trains with flexible options can provide peace of mind, as can having alternative routes or backup plans in place.
2. **Double-Check Reservations and Documents**: Mercury Retrograde can lead to issues with bookings, reservations, and travel documents. Double-check all travel details, confirm reservations, and ensure that you have all necessary documents before heading out. It's also helpful to have digital and physical copies of tickets, identification, and accommodation confirmations.
3. **Embrace Flexibility and Pack Essentials**: Unexpected travel changes are common during Mercury Retrograde, so embrace flexibility and pack essentials that can make delays more comfortable. Bringing snacks, entertainment, chargers, and other comfort items can make waiting times more bearable. Try to see delays as an opportunity to relax, read, or people-watch, reframing disruptions as part of the adventure.
4. **Stay Calm and Keep a Sense of Humor**: Mercury Retrograde can sometimes feel like a cosmic prank, but approaching travel mishaps with a sense of humor can make them easier to handle. Remember that everyone is affected by delays, and a calm, lighthearted attitude can help diffuse tension. Sharing a laugh with fellow travelers or making the best of a delay can transform a frustrating situation into a positive experience.

Navigating Technology and Online Shopping During Mercury Retrograde

Technology is known to act up during Mercury Retrograde, with issues ranging from connectivity problems and device malfunctions to data loss. This period can also affect online shopping, making it a time to approach digital transactions with caution.

1. **Back Up Important Data and Files**: Mercury Retrograde is infamous for causing computer crashes, data loss, and device malfunctions. Back up important files, photos, and documents, especially if you're working on something important or planning holiday presentations. This practice will give you peace of mind and prevent the frustration of losing valuable information.
2. **Double-Check Online Orders**: Online shopping during Mercury Retrograde can lead to issues such as duplicate orders, wrong items, or delivery delays. When placing holiday orders, double-check the details, shipping address, and item specifications to minimize errors. Following up on orders and monitoring delivery status can also help avoid unpleasant surprises.
3. **Expect Minor Glitches with Communication Apps**: Video calls, messaging apps, and email may experience glitches during Mercury Retrograde, which can be frustrating when

trying to coordinate holiday gatherings. Be patient if you experience connectivity issues, and have alternative methods of communication (such as phone calls) ready in case digital platforms act up.

4. **Avoid Large Technology Purchases**: If possible, avoid buying large or expensive tech items during Mercury Retrograde, as these purchases may be more prone to defects, delays, or the need for returns. If you must make a technology purchase, review return policies, warranties, and purchase protections to ensure you're covered in case issues arise.

Embracing Reflection and Revisiting the Past

While Mercury Retrograde is often associated with challenges, it also provides a powerful opportunity for introspection, reflection, and revisiting past relationships or unfinished business. This period encourages us to slow down, look inward, and reassess our choices, making it an ideal time to focus on personal growth and healing.

1. **Reflect on Past Holiday Experiences**: Mercury Retrograde invites us to look back and learn from the past, making the holiday season a wonderful time to reflect on previous celebrations, lessons learned, and cherished memories. Take time to appreciate the growth and changes you've experienced, and consider how past holiday traditions can evolve to meet your current values and needs.

2. **Revisit Old Relationships or Reach Out to Loved Ones**: Mercury Retrograde can often bring people from the past back into our lives, making it an ideal time to reconnect with family, friends, or colleagues with whom you've lost touch. Reaching out with a holiday card, message, or phone call can rekindle meaningful connections and allow for healing or closure.

3. **Review Goals and Set New Intentions**: This period of introspection is ideal for evaluating personal goals, values, and aspirations. Reflect on what you accomplished over the past year, consider areas for growth, and set intentions that align with your true desires. Mercury Retrograde helps us focus on what truly matters, making it a perfect time to establish meaningful resolutions for the upcoming year.

4. **Practice Gratitude and Mindfulness**: Mercury Retrograde encourages us to slow down and appreciate the present, making mindfulness and gratitude practices especially powerful. Reflect on the people, experiences, and lessons that have enriched your life, and take time to express appreciation for them. These practices create a sense of peace and fulfillment, helping you approach the holidays with a calm and open heart.

Turning Mercury Retrograde Mishaps into Opportunities for Growth

While Mercury Retrograde can lead to unexpected disruptions, it also offers valuable lessons in adaptability, resilience, and patience. By embracing these challenges with an open mind, we can transform potential mishaps into moments of growth, humor, and connection.

1. **Embrace the Spirit of Adaptability**: Mercury Retrograde encourages us to remain flexible and open to change, especially when things don't go as planned. Embracing adaptability helps us respond calmly to disruptions, find creative solutions, and stay focused on what truly matters. Approach each challenge with a sense of curiosity, allowing unexpected events to shape your holiday experience in new and positive ways.

2. **Focus on the Present Moment**: When plans go awry, it's easy to feel frustrated or anxious about what could go wrong next. Practicing mindfulness and focusing on the present moment can help ground you, bringing a sense of calm and acceptance. By letting go of the need for control and embracing each moment as it comes, you can find joy in the unexpected and stay centered through changes.

3. **Laugh at the Little Mishaps**: Mercury Retrograde can sometimes feel like a cosmic comedy, with small mishaps piling up in ways that would be humorous if they weren't happening to you! Embracing humor can lighten the mood and turn inconveniences into funny stories. Laughing together at the "retrograde effect" can transform frustrations into shared memories that bond you with family and friends.

4. **Turn Delays into Opportunities for Reflection**: If travel delays or other interruptions give you unexpected free time, use it as a chance to pause, reflect, and reconnect with yourself. Whether journaling, reading, or simply sitting in quiet contemplation, this time can become a precious moment for introspection, helping you return to the holiday festivities with renewed perspective and appreciation.

Practical Tips for Navigating Mercury Retrograde During the Holidays

Incorporating mindful practices into your holiday celebrations can help you navigate Mercury Retrograde with grace, making the season more enjoyable and meaningful despite potential disruptions.

1. **Create a "Mercury Retrograde Kit"**: Assemble items that help you stay calm and organized, such as a notebook for lists, extra chargers, and travel essentials. Including small comforts like snacks, a book, or a stress-relief item can make it easier to handle delays or unexpected changes.

2. **Prioritize Clear and Honest Communication**: Make an effort to communicate with clarity and openness, avoiding assumptions or indirect language. If an issue arises, address it calmly and directly, focusing on understanding rather than confrontation. This approach minimizes misunderstandings and helps keep relationships harmonious.

3. **Embrace Minimalism in Holiday Planning**: Simplify your holiday plans, focusing on the activities and traditions that truly matter to you. By reducing complexity, you reduce the likelihood of disruptions, allowing you to approach the holidays with greater ease and focus.
4. **Practice Patience and Compassion**: Mercury Retrograde can affect everyone, so approach others with patience and understanding, especially if they seem stressed or overwhelmed. Compassionate communication fosters an atmosphere of mutual support, making it easier for everyone to navigate challenges together.

Final Thoughts: Embracing Mercury Retrograde as Part of the Holiday Journey

Mercury Retrograde may bring miscommunications and mishaps, but it also offers valuable lessons in patience, adaptability, and perspective. By approaching this period with mindfulness, humor, and an open heart, we can turn potential disruptions into opportunities for connection, growth, and self-discovery. Mercury Retrograde reminds us that the essence of the holidays lies not in perfection but in presence, love, and the ability to find joy even when things don't go as planned.

This holiday season, let Mercury Retrograde inspire you to slow down, embrace the present moment, and approach each experience with an open mind. By celebrating the beauty of imperfection and finding peace amidst the unexpected, may you create a holiday experience that is both meaningful and memorable, filled with love, laughter, and a deeper appreciation for life's unpredictable journey.

Chapter 42: Venus Retrograde - Re-evaluating Relationships

Venus, the planet of love, beauty, and harmony, governs our relationships, values, and sense of aesthetics. When Venus goes retrograde—an occurrence that happens approximately every 18 months—it offers a powerful opportunity to reflect on and re-evaluate our connections with others, our values, and even our relationship with ourselves. Venus Retrograde encourages us to pause, reassess, and reexamine relationships from a fresh perspective, often bringing unresolved issues to the surface and prompting us to address lingering dynamics.

During Venus Retrograde, we may find ourselves reconsidering relationship priorities, evaluating long-held beliefs about love, and revisiting past relationships. While this period can be challenging, it offers the gift of insight, allowing us to understand what truly fulfills us in our connections with others and to align more closely with our authentic needs and desires. In this chapter, we explore the impact of Venus Retrograde on relationships, self-worth, and values, providing guidance on how to navigate this introspective period with grace, clarity, and self-awareness.

The Astrological Influence of Venus Retrograde

In astrology, Venus rules love, romance, aesthetics, attraction, and values. While direct, Venus governs how we connect, relate, and create beauty in the world, guiding us in areas of pleasure, intimacy, and harmony. When Venus goes retrograde, her energies turn inward, prompting us to reflect on and reassess these areas of life, often revealing hidden truths or unresolved issues within our relationships and values.

1. **Re-Evaluating Relationships**: Venus Retrograde is a period for reflecting on the health and authenticity of relationships. We are encouraged to examine whether our connections align with our true values and if they fulfill our emotional needs.

2. **Revisiting Past Relationships**: Venus Retrograde can bring old flames or unresolved dynamics back into our lives, either literally or emotionally. This period encourages closure and deeper understanding, allowing us to learn from the past and move forward with clarity.

3. **Assessing Self-Worth and Values**: Venus rules self-worth and the things we hold dear. During its retrograde period, we are called to evaluate our values and consider if our current life aligns with them. This introspection often extends to how we value ourselves and can prompt positive shifts in self-esteem and self-care.

4. **Reflecting on Beauty, Pleasure, and Aesthetics**: Venus governs aesthetics, so during retrograde, our tastes and preferences may shift. This period is a time to reconnect with our authentic sense of beauty and reevaluate what brings us true joy and pleasure, both in our environment and in our personal style.

Navigating Relationship Dynamics During Venus Retrograde

Venus Retrograde encourages us to take a closer look at our relationships, questioning how they contribute to our well-being and whether they truly align with our needs. This period is a time for honesty, compassion, and introspection, allowing us to assess relationship dynamics with fresh eyes.

1. **Assessing Relationship Health and Compatibility**: Venus Retrograde provides a powerful opportunity to assess the health of our relationships, including romantic partnerships, friendships, and family bonds. Reflect on whether each relationship feels balanced, supportive, and aligned with your values. Are your needs being met? Are you able to express yourself authentically? These questions can help clarify whether a relationship is worth investing in or if changes are needed.

2. **Re-Evaluating Boundaries and Expectations**: This period encourages us to revisit boundaries and expectations within relationships, ensuring they reflect our current values and needs. Consider if your boundaries are strong enough to protect your well-being and if your expectations align with what each relationship realistically offers. Venus Retrograde is an ideal time to adjust boundaries and communicate expectations with kindness and clarity.

3. **Reconnecting with Emotional Intimacy**: Venus Retrograde urges us to deepen emotional intimacy within our connections, moving beyond surface-level interactions to explore the heart of each relationship. Use this time to engage in open, honest conversations about feelings, dreams, and desires. By fostering emotional closeness, we strengthen relationships and create a foundation of trust and mutual understanding.

4. **Letting Go of Unhealthy Dynamics**: Some relationships may reveal patterns or dynamics that no longer serve us, such as codependency, control, or emotional distance. Venus Retrograde can bring these issues to light, allowing us to address them constructively. If certain relationships consistently drain energy or compromise well-being, this period may prompt us to release them with gratitude and compassion, creating space for healthier connections.

Revisiting Past Relationships and Unresolved Emotions

Venus Retrograde often brings people from the past back into our lives, either literally or through memories and emotions. This phenomenon serves a purpose: it allows us to revisit unresolved feelings, gain closure, and learn valuable lessons from previous relationships.

1. **Understanding the Purpose of Past Relationships**: Reflecting on past relationships during Venus Retrograde can help us understand why certain connections came into our lives and what they taught us. By recognizing the purpose and lessons of each relationship, we gain insight into our growth, needs, and desires, helping us approach future relationships with greater clarity and wisdom.

2. **Gaining Closure and Forgiveness**: Venus Retrograde is an ideal time to seek closure and practice forgiveness, whether through reconnecting with an old partner, writing a letter, or

engaging in a forgiveness ritual. Releasing resentment or regret can free us from past attachments, creating emotional space for new, healthier relationships.

3. **Learning from Patterns and Choices**: This period encourages introspection on our romantic patterns, choices, and behaviors. Reflecting on past relationships allows us to identify recurring dynamics and address any patterns that may not serve us. By recognizing these patterns, we can make conscious choices that lead to healthier, more fulfilling relationships in the future.

4. **Avoiding Rekindling Relationships Impulsively**: Venus Retrograde can stir up nostalgia, but it's essential to approach old relationships with caution. While reconnection may be healing, rekindling a past romance impulsively can lead to repeating old patterns. Use this time for reflection rather than making long-term decisions about past relationships.

Self-Worth and Values: Reflecting on Inner Alignment

Venus Retrograde is not only about relationships with others but also about our relationship with ourselves. This period encourages us to examine our sense of self-worth, reconnect with core values, and make choices that align with our authentic needs.

1. **Evaluating Self-Worth and Self-Respect**: Venus governs self-worth, making its retrograde an ideal time to reflect on how we value and treat ourselves. Consider if you prioritize your own well-being, honor your boundaries, and practice self-care. This period is an opportunity to strengthen self-respect and embrace choices that reflect your true worth.

2. **Reassessing Personal Values and Priorities**: Venus Retrograde encourages introspection on personal values, prompting us to consider if our current lifestyle and choices align with what we truly value. This could relate to relationships, career, lifestyle, or financial priorities. Reconnecting with core values brings clarity, guiding us toward a more fulfilling and purposeful life.

3. **Exploring Desires for Beauty, Pleasure, and Joy**: Venus Retrograde invites us to consider what genuinely brings joy and pleasure into our lives. Take this time to reconnect with hobbies, interests, and activities that nourish the soul, exploring new or forgotten sources of inspiration and beauty. This introspection often leads to a more authentic, fulfilling relationship with ourselves.

4. **Letting Go of External Validation**: Venus Retrograde is a time to release the need for external approval and embrace self-acceptance. Reflect on whether certain relationships, behaviors, or habits are driven by the desire to fit in or please others. By letting go of these influences, we strengthen our sense of self and create a life rooted in personal authenticity.

Beauty, Aesthetics, and Personal Style

Since Venus governs beauty, aesthetics, and style, its retrograde period is a time to reflect on how we express ourselves visually and creatively. This period can bring about shifts in taste, a desire for change, or a renewed connection with our unique sense of beauty.

1. **Re-Evaluating Personal Style and Aesthetics**: Venus Retrograde often prompts changes in taste or a desire to refresh personal style. Use this period to explore what feels authentic, reflecting your current self. Refrain from making permanent changes, like tattoos or drastic haircuts, as tastes may shift again once Venus turns direct.
2. **Exploring New Avenues of Creative Expression**: This period encourages creative exploration, whether through art, fashion, music, or design. Experimenting with new colors, textures, or styles allows for self-discovery and enhances self-expression. Venus Retrograde supports experimentation, making it an ideal time to try out creative pursuits without the need for perfection.
3. **Creating a Harmonious Living Space**: Venus's energy extends to our environment, making its retrograde an ideal time to evaluate our living space. Consider if your home reflects your personality and values. Rearranging furniture, adding elements of nature, or creating a designated space for relaxation and reflection can enhance harmony and comfort.
4. **Appreciating Natural Beauty and Simplicity**: Venus Retrograde encourages us to reconnect with simple, natural beauty. Instead of focusing on external appearances or materialism, we're drawn to appreciate nature, authenticity, and simplicity. Take time to enjoy natural surroundings, engage in activities that promote inner peace, and appreciate the beauty in everyday life.

Practical Tips for Navigating Venus Retrograde

Venus Retrograde can be a profound period of self-discovery, offering opportunities to strengthen relationships, reconnect with values, and cultivate self-worth. By approaching this period mindfully, we can navigate its challenges and embrace its transformative potential.

1. **Engage in Reflective Practices**: Journaling, meditation, or spending time in nature can help you connect with inner insights during Venus Retrograde. Reflect on relationships, values, and self-worth, using these practices to deepen self-understanding and clarify what truly matters.
2. **Reconnect with Loved Ones Intentionally**: This period is ideal for nurturing existing relationships, whether by spending quality time together, sharing open conversations, or expressing appreciation. Reconnecting in meaningful ways strengthens bonds and creates a foundation for deeper understanding.

3. **Reframe Relationship Challenges as Learning Opportunities**: Venus Retrograde can reveal areas of growth within relationships, prompting us to address unresolved issues. Approach these challenges with a willingness to learn and grow, viewing them as opportunities for healing, clarity, and transformation.

4. **Postpone Major Relationship Decisions**: During Venus Retrograde, it's wise to avoid making impulsive decisions, such as moving in together, getting married, or ending a relationship. While reflection is encouraged, decisions should be approached with caution, as clarity may come after Venus resumes direct motion.

5. **Embrace Self-Care and Self-Compassion**: Venus Retrograde invites us to prioritize self-worth, so engage in self-care practices that nourish body, mind, and soul. This could include spa days, gentle exercise, creative expression, or moments of solitude. Self-compassion helps us navigate relationship challenges with resilience and understanding.

Re-Evaluating Values and Financial Goals

Since Venus also rules finances and material possessions, this retrograde period can inspire us to reassess financial priorities, spending habits, and material goals. This introspection encourages us to align our financial decisions with our core values, creating a more balanced relationship with money.

1. **Reconsider Financial Goals and Priorities**: Reflect on whether your financial goals align with your true values. Are you saving for what brings fulfillment, or are you influenced by external expectations? Venus Retrograde is a time to reevaluate spending, investments, and savings with an emphasis on what genuinely supports your well-being.

2. **Practice Mindful Spending**: Use this period to assess spending habits and reflect on what brings authentic joy versus temporary satisfaction. Avoid impulsive purchases, especially in areas of fashion, beauty, or luxury, as tastes may shift after Venus turns direct. Focus on mindful, intentional purchases that reflect long-term value.

3. **Declutter and Reorganize Possessions**: Venus Retrograde is a wonderful time to declutter your environment, letting go of items that no longer serve you. Consider donating, selling, or repurposing possessions to create a more harmonious, clutter-free space. This process not only clears physical space but also fosters a sense of mental and emotional clarity.

4. **Reflect on Material Values and Sustainability**: Venus Retrograde invites us to consider how our material choices impact the environment and align with sustainable values. Reflect on ways to reduce consumption, support ethical brands, or engage in eco-friendly practices. This period encourages conscious consumption that reflects a commitment to integrity and respect for the planet.

Final Thoughts: Embracing the Transformative Potential of Venus Retrograde

Venus Retrograde offers a profound opportunity for introspection, healing, and growth in matters of love, self-worth, and values. While this period may reveal challenges within relationships or prompt shifts in priorities, it ultimately guides us toward greater authenticity, alignment, and fulfillment. By embracing Venus Retrograde with an open heart and a willingness to learn, we gain insight into what truly brings joy and meaning into our lives.

This holiday season, let Venus Retrograde inspire you to approach relationships mindfully, reconnect with your inner values, and strengthen your sense of self-worth. As you navigate this period of re-evaluation, may you find clarity, healing, and a deeper connection to what truly matters. Through reflection, self-care, and compassion, may Venus Retrograde guide you toward a holiday season filled with love, authenticity, and lasting joy, rooted in the power of genuine connection and self-acceptance.

Chapter 43: Mars Retrograde - Reassessing Holiday Goals

Mars, the planet of drive, ambition, and action, represents our capacity to pursue goals, assert ourselves, and overcome challenges. It is the planet of energy, courage, and determination, pushing us to achieve, compete, and take action toward our desires. When Mars goes retrograde—an event that happens approximately once every two years—its forward-moving energy slows, inviting us to pause, reflect, and reassess our actions and intentions. Mars Retrograde is a time to reconsider goals, examine motivations, and approach challenges with renewed patience.

During the holiday season, when goals, resolutions, and activities abound, Mars Retrograde's influence encourages us to slow down, reflect on our priorities, and focus on intentional action. Instead of rushing to accomplish everything, Mars Retrograde offers an opportunity to approach the season with mindfulness, resilience, and clarity. In this chapter, we explore how to navigate Mars Retrograde during the holidays, understanding its impact on goals, relationships, and personal energy, and how we can harness its lessons to create a fulfilling, intentional holiday experience.

The Astrological Influence of Mars Retrograde

In astrology, Mars is associated with our willpower, courage, physical energy, and drive to pursue goals. It governs how we assert ourselves, handle challenges, and approach competition. During Mars Retrograde, this outward-focused energy is turned inward, encouraging reflection rather than action, patience rather than impulsivity. While it may feel frustrating to slow down, Mars Retrograde's influence offers valuable insights, helping us examine our motivations, reassess our goals, and take more thoughtful actions.

1. **Reassessing Goals and Ambitions**: Mars Retrograde is a period for re-evaluating our ambitions and goals, questioning whether they align with our values and current needs. This introspection can clarify what truly matters and prevent us from pursuing goals that don't bring fulfillment.

2. **Pausing for Reflection and Patience**: Mars Retrograde encourages a slower pace, helping us practice patience, especially when things don't go as planned. This period teaches us to avoid impulsive actions and consider the long-term consequences of our choices.

3. **Reflecting on Motivation and Intention**: Mars governs motivation, so its retrograde is a time to examine why we pursue certain goals or activities. Reflecting on our intentions can bring clarity, allowing us to focus on meaningful pursuits rather than superficial desires.

4. **Approaching Conflict and Assertion with Mindfulness**: Mars also rules conflict and assertiveness, so during retrograde, it's wise to handle disputes thoughtfully and avoid confrontations. This period helps us approach challenges with a balanced perspective, promoting constructive problem-solving rather than impulsive reactions.

Reassessing Holiday Goals and Priorities

Mars Retrograde invites us to take a closer look at our holiday goals and priorities, questioning what truly brings meaning and joy to the season. Instead of rushing to achieve every task or fulfill every obligation, we are encouraged to reflect on what matters most and pursue goals that align with our values.

1. **Clarifying Holiday Intentions**: Mars Retrograde is an ideal time to set clear intentions for the holiday season, focusing on what you hope to experience and create. Ask yourself, "What does a fulfilling holiday season look like to me?" and "What experiences do I want to prioritize?" Clarifying your intentions can help you avoid overextending and ensure your efforts align with meaningful goals.

2. **Prioritizing Quality Over Quantity**: This retrograde period emphasizes the importance of quality over quantity. Instead of aiming to complete a long list of holiday tasks, focus on a few meaningful activities that bring joy and connection. Whether it's spending time with loved ones, preparing a special meal, or practicing gratitude, prioritize actions that enrich your holiday experience.

3. **Re-Evaluating Social Commitments**: Mars Retrograde encourages us to reflect on our social obligations and avoid overcommitting. Consider whether each event or gathering aligns with your holiday goals and personal energy. If certain commitments feel draining or unnecessary, don't hesitate to decline. This period supports mindful decision-making, allowing you to reserve energy for gatherings that bring joy and fulfillment.

4. **Balancing Tradition with Flexibility**: Mars Retrograde is a time to reconsider rigid traditions or expectations, allowing for more flexibility. Ask yourself if certain traditions still resonate, or if they need to be adapted to fit your current needs and values. Being open to modifying traditions can create a holiday experience that feels both meaningful and relevant.

Reassessing Motivations and Desires

During Mars Retrograde, we are called to examine the motivations behind our goals, questioning whether they stem from personal fulfillment or external expectations. This reflection helps us realign with what genuinely matters, empowering us to pursue holiday activities with greater authenticity and joy.

1. **Reflecting on the "Why" Behind Each Goal**: Mars Retrograde encourages us to ask "why" before taking action. Reflect on the motivations behind each holiday goal, whether it's gift-giving, organizing events, or personal resolutions. Understanding your "why" helps clarify if these goals align with your values or if they stem from societal pressure or obligation.

2. **Avoiding Competitive or Superficial Goals**: Mars is associated with competition, but during retrograde, we are encouraged to let go of the need to impress or compete. Avoid goals that are primarily driven by appearance, prestige, or comparison to others. Instead, focus on

actions that bring personal satisfaction and meaning, aligning your holiday experience with genuine values.

3. **Embracing Minimalism and Simplicity**: Mars Retrograde encourages simplicity, making it a wonderful time to let go of excess and focus on what truly matters. Embrace a minimalist approach to holiday celebrations, focusing on experiences, meaningful connections, and gratitude. This shift in focus creates a sense of peace and prevents burnout, allowing for a more centered holiday season.

4. **Reflecting on Long-Term Goals and Growth**: Mars Retrograde offers a chance to assess long-term aspirations beyond the holiday season. Use this time to consider if your current goals contribute to personal growth, fulfillment, or well-being. This period encourages us to approach goals with a balanced perspective, focusing on sustainable progress rather than immediate results.

Managing Personal Energy and Self-Care During Mars Retrograde

Mars Retrograde can impact our physical energy levels, as the planet's usual drive is turned inward. During this period, we may feel more tired, sluggish, or less motivated to take action. By honoring this shift and practicing mindful self-care, we can approach the holidays with greater resilience and well-being.

1. **Listening to Your Body's Needs**: Mars Retrograde is a time to slow down and pay attention to physical cues. If you feel tired or unmotivated, honor your body's need for rest rather than pushing yourself to meet every holiday goal. Listening to your body's signals prevents burnout and promotes physical and emotional well-being.

2. **Incorporating Rest and Relaxation into Holiday Plans**: This retrograde period encourages us to incorporate moments of relaxation into holiday activities, balancing action with rest. Whether it's setting aside time for reading, taking a walk in nature, or practicing meditation, small acts of self-care ensure that you remain energized and centered.

3. **Focusing on Gentle and Grounding Activities**: During Mars Retrograde, physical activity should be gentle and grounding rather than intense or competitive. Engage in calming practices, such as yoga, tai chi, or walking, which support energy flow without overexerting the body. These practices help release stress and keep you connected to the present moment.

4. **Managing Expectations and Accepting Limitations**: This period invites us to let go of perfectionism and accept that some holiday goals may not be realistic. Manage your expectations and recognize that it's okay to set boundaries and say no to excessive demands. Embracing limitations allows you to enjoy the holidays at a comfortable pace.

Navigating Conflicts and Communication with Patience

Since Mars governs assertiveness and conflict, its retrograde period encourages us to approach disagreements with caution, patience, and empathy. By navigating holiday conversations with mindfulness, we can prevent misunderstandings and foster harmony within our relationships.

1. **Avoiding Impulsive Reactions**: Mars Retrograde can heighten impulsive responses, so practice patience and take time to consider your words before responding in challenging situations. Pausing before speaking allows you to communicate thoughtfully, reducing the risk of unnecessary conflict.
2. **Fostering Empathy and Understanding**: During Mars Retrograde, we are encouraged to practice empathy and focus on finding common ground. Approach conversations with an open mind and make an effort to understand others' perspectives. This approach fosters positive interactions and minimizes potential friction.
3. **Re-Evaluating Assertiveness and Boundaries**: This period is an ideal time to reflect on how you assert yourself and set boundaries. Assess whether your communication style is balanced, respectful, and effective. Adjusting how you express yourself can strengthen relationships, creating an environment of mutual respect and understanding.
4. **Letting Go of Small Grievances**: Mars Retrograde encourages us to let go of minor annoyances or disagreements, especially during the holiday season. Focus on the bigger picture, and avoid dwelling on issues that don't truly matter. This period helps us practice forgiveness, patience, and compassion in our interactions with others.

Reflecting on Personal Growth and Holiday Resolutions

Mars Retrograde's introspective energy supports setting thoughtful, realistic resolutions for the new year. By reflecting on personal growth and taking time to understand what truly drives us, we can set intentions that contribute to long-term well-being and fulfillment.

1. **Setting Intentions for Sustainable Growth**: Mars Retrograde encourages setting resolutions that focus on sustainable progress rather than quick fixes. Reflect on areas where you'd like to grow and establish intentions that align with personal values and long-term aspirations. This approach fosters meaningful, achievable progress rather than temporary changes.
2. **Revisiting Past Resolutions and Adjusting Goals**: Use this period to review past resolutions and assess which goals brought fulfillment and which did not. Consider if there are unfinished goals worth revisiting, or if some may need adjusting to align with your current values and lifestyle. Reflecting on past experiences allows you to set goals with greater clarity.
3. **Focusing on Self-Improvement Rather Than Competition**: Mars Retrograde shifts focus from external achievements to internal growth. Rather than comparing yourself to others,

center your resolutions around personal improvement and self-awareness. This approach supports authentic growth, helping you create a holiday experience that reflects genuine values.

4. **Practicing Patience and Persistence**: Mars Retrograde teaches us the value of patience, reminding us that growth is a journey rather than a destination. Approach each goal with resilience, understanding that progress may come gradually. This mindset allows for steady advancement and helps you avoid feeling discouraged by setbacks.

Practical Tips for Navigating Mars Retrograde During the Holidays

Mars Retrograde can be challenging, especially during the holiday season when energy, goals, and expectations are high. By embracing mindful practices and prioritizing self-care, we can navigate this period with resilience and grace.

1. **Create a Realistic Holiday Schedule**: Instead of trying to accomplish every task or attend every event, create a manageable schedule that prioritizes meaningful activities. Focus on a few key events or goals that bring joy and connection, and be willing to let go of non-essential tasks.

2. **Reflect on Goals and Adjust Accordingly**: Mars Retrograde is a time to reassess goals, so use this period to reflect on which holiday intentions truly matter. Consider adjusting plans that feel unrealistic or overly demanding, focusing instead on what aligns with your energy and values.

3. **Practice Gratitude and Mindfulness**: Mars Retrograde invites us to slow down, so practice gratitude for small moments, and take time to appreciate the beauty of the season. Engaging in mindfulness practices helps you stay grounded, present, and connected, creating a peaceful holiday experience.

4. **Seek Out Restorative Activities**: Embrace restorative activities, such as meditation, journaling, or time in nature, to maintain balance and prevent burnout. These practices encourage relaxation and help you release tension, ensuring that you remain centered and calm throughout the holiday season.

Final Thoughts: Embracing Mars Retrograde as a Time for Mindful Reflection

Mars Retrograde offers an opportunity to pause, reflect, and re-evaluate our goals, relationships, and sense of purpose. While this period may challenge our usual pace and drive, it ultimately encourages us to approach life with mindfulness, patience, and authenticity. By embracing Mars Retrograde's lessons, we can cultivate resilience, reconnect with our true motivations, and create a holiday season that is balanced, meaningful, and aligned with our core values.

This holiday season, let Mars Retrograde inspire you to slow down, reflect on what truly matters, and approach each moment with intention. By focusing on quality, authenticity, and inner growth, may you create a holiday experience that resonates with peace, connection, and purpose. As you navigate this period with mindfulness, may you find joy in the present, clarity in your goals, and strength in your journey of personal growth.

Chapter 44: Jupiter Retrograde - Reconnecting with Traditions

Jupiter, the planet of expansion, wisdom, and abundance, is associated with growth, optimism, and the pursuit of higher knowledge. Often seen as the "Great Benefic" in astrology, Jupiter encourages us to expand our horizons, explore new ideas, and find meaning in life's experiences. However, when Jupiter goes retrograde—an event that occurs approximately once a year and lasts for about four months—its energy turns inward, prompting us to slow down, reflect, and reassess what truly brings joy and fulfillment. Instead of focusing on outward growth, Jupiter Retrograde invites us to connect with inner wisdom, revisit core beliefs, and rediscover the traditions and values that form the foundation of our lives.

During the holiday season, Jupiter Retrograde offers a profound opportunity to reconnect with traditions, family, and the values that bring meaning to our celebrations. Rather than seeking new experiences, this period encourages us to explore the richness of established customs, honoring the spiritual and cultural roots of the season. In this chapter, we'll explore how to embrace Jupiter Retrograde's reflective energy, reconnect with traditions, deepen relationships, and create a holiday experience filled with gratitude, purpose, and authenticity.

The Astrological Influence of Jupiter Retrograde

In astrology, Jupiter governs expansion, knowledge, and personal growth. It's the planet of philosophy, spirituality, and higher learning, influencing our beliefs, values, and pursuit of wisdom. When Jupiter goes retrograde, its energy encourages us to look inward, re-examining our beliefs, rediscovering our values, and embracing a more mindful, introspective approach to growth.

1. **Reflecting on Values and Beliefs**: Jupiter Retrograde encourages introspection on core beliefs, prompting us to question long-held values and reconnect with what brings meaning and joy. This period invites us to consider how our beliefs shape our lives and to align our actions with our true values.

2. **Reconnecting with Traditions and Cultural Roots**: Rather than seeking new horizons, Jupiter Retrograde emphasizes the importance of tradition, encouraging us to honor the customs and rituals that connect us to our heritage, culture, and family history. It's a time to deepen our connection with meaningful practices that have stood the test of time.

3. **Practicing Gratitude and Inner Fulfillment**: Jupiter Retrograde reminds us that true fulfillment comes from within. This period encourages us to cultivate gratitude for life's simple blessings, rediscover joy in small moments, and focus on inner abundance rather than external achievements.

4. **Reflecting on Spiritual Growth and Personal Wisdom**: As the planet of wisdom, Jupiter's retrograde period is ideal for spiritual reflection, introspection, and seeking personal growth. It encourages us to explore our inner landscape, reconnect with spiritual practices, and deepen our understanding of life's greater purpose.

Reconnecting with Family and Cultural Traditions

Jupiter Retrograde invites us to turn inward and reconnect with the traditions that have shaped our family history, culture, and sense of belonging. By embracing the customs and rituals of the past, we honor the wisdom of our ancestors and strengthen our connection to the collective spirit of the holiday season.

1. **Exploring Family History and Heritage**: Use Jupiter Retrograde as an opportunity to learn more about your family's history, cultural heritage, and traditional practices. Consider asking elders about family stories, researching cultural customs, or exploring genealogy. Understanding your roots provides a deeper sense of identity and brings meaningful context to holiday traditions.
2. **Reviving Lost Traditions**: This period is an ideal time to revisit traditions that may have faded over the years. Whether it's a specific dish, a unique holiday ritual, or an old family song, reviving lost customs can bring a renewed sense of connection to the past. By incorporating these traditions into holiday celebrations, you create a bridge between generations and keep the family's legacy alive.
3. **Celebrating Cultural Diversity in Holiday Traditions**: If your family or community includes a blend of cultural backgrounds, Jupiter Retrograde offers a wonderful opportunity to celebrate diversity by incorporating different customs into holiday celebrations. Honoring various cultural practices not only enriches the experience but also fosters understanding, unity, and respect for different backgrounds.
4. **Creating New Traditions Rooted in Personal Values**: Jupiter Retrograde encourages us to create traditions that reflect our values, beliefs, and evolving sense of purpose. Consider what brings you and your family a sense of fulfillment, joy, and connection. Whether it's volunteering together, engaging in spiritual practices, or focusing on gratitude, creating meaningful traditions enhances the holiday experience.

Reflecting on the Spiritual Significance of the Holiday Season

As the planet of spirituality and higher wisdom, Jupiter's retrograde period provides a powerful opportunity to explore the deeper meanings of the holiday season. This period encourages us to look beyond materialism and embrace the spiritual aspects of celebration, gratitude, and unity.

1. **Honoring the Season's Spiritual Roots**: Many holiday traditions have deep spiritual or religious roots, whether they involve the celebration of light, gratitude, renewal, or the triumph of love and hope. Jupiter Retrograde invites us to explore these spiritual aspects, connecting with the universal messages of peace, compassion, and kindness that transcend cultural boundaries.
2. **Engaging in Reflective Practices**: This period is ideal for reflective practices that deepen our connection to the season's themes, such as journaling, meditation, or reading spiritual

texts. Reflect on questions like, "What values do I wish to honor this season?" or "How can I bring more kindness and compassion into my life?" These practices help ground us in the true meaning of the season, fostering a sense of purpose and inner peace.

3. **Practicing Gratitude and Mindful Celebration**: Jupiter Retrograde reminds us to focus on gratitude, encouraging us to appreciate the people, experiences, and blessings that enrich our lives. Embrace moments of mindful celebration, savoring each experience and expressing appreciation for loved ones, the beauty of the season, and life's simple joys.

4. **Exploring Rituals of Renewal and Reflection**: Many holiday traditions are rooted in themes of renewal, forgiveness, and reflection. Consider incorporating rituals that align with these themes, such as lighting candles, practicing forgiveness, or setting intentions for the new year. These rituals honor the season's spiritual essence and bring a sense of closure, healing, and hope.

Embracing Inner Abundance and Redefining Success

Jupiter's influence is often associated with abundance, but during retrograde, this abundance is redefined, focusing on inner fulfillment rather than external achievements. This period encourages us to explore what brings true joy and to let go of superficial definitions of success.

1. **Focusing on Simple Pleasures and Joys**: Jupiter Retrograde reminds us that fulfillment comes from simple moments of joy, whether it's spending time with loved ones, enjoying a favorite meal, or participating in holiday traditions. Shift your focus from material success to the richness of life's everyday blessings, and find contentment in what you already have.

2. **Redefining Success and Letting Go of Materialism**: During the holidays, there's often pressure to meet societal expectations or display material success. Jupiter Retrograde encourages us to release these pressures and redefine success as inner peace, love, and meaningful connections. Let go of the need to impress or prove yourself, and focus on creating an experience that is genuine and heart-centered.

3. **Practicing Generosity and Kindness**: Jupiter's energy is expansive, making it a wonderful time to practice generosity and kindness. Embrace the spirit of giving by sharing your time, resources, or talents with others, whether through volunteering, acts of kindness, or thoughtful gestures. These actions create a ripple effect of positivity and bring a deeper sense of purpose to the holiday season.

4. **Setting Intentions for Inner Growth and Wisdom**: Jupiter Retrograde encourages us to focus on growth from within, setting intentions that support inner peace, wisdom, and compassion. Reflect on qualities you wish to cultivate, such as patience, empathy, or resilience, and create goals that align with these values. This focus on inner growth brings lasting fulfillment and aligns with the season's message of renewal.

Strengthening Relationships and Fostering Community

Jupiter's energy fosters unity, making its retrograde period an ideal time to deepen relationships and strengthen community bonds. By focusing on connection and shared values, we create a holiday experience that brings people together in meaningful ways.

1. **Prioritizing Quality Time with Loved Ones**: Jupiter Retrograde encourages us to focus on quality over quantity, making it a wonderful time to prioritize meaningful interactions with family and friends. Engage in activities that promote connection, such as storytelling, cooking together, or simply sharing a cup of tea. These moments create lasting memories and reinforce the bonds of love and friendship.

2. **Engaging in Family Storytelling and Sharing Traditions**: Family storytelling is a powerful way to honor heritage, share values, and create a sense of continuity. During holiday gatherings, invite family members to share stories, memories, and experiences that capture the spirit of the season. This practice fosters a sense of belonging and connects generations through shared history.

3. **Fostering a Sense of Community and Belonging**: Jupiter Retrograde reminds us of the importance of community and encourages us to foster a sense of unity. Consider organizing community-oriented events, inviting neighbors to join holiday celebrations, or volunteering with local organizations. Embracing community creates an atmosphere of support, kindness, and collective joy.

4. **Practicing Forgiveness and Reconciliation**: This period is a wonderful time to heal rifts, practice forgiveness, and reconnect with those from whom you may have drifted apart. Reach out to loved ones with whom you wish to reconcile, or practice forgiveness through meditation or journaling. Jupiter Retrograde encourages us to embrace compassion and understanding, allowing for renewed connections and healing.

Reflecting on Growth and Setting Intentions for the New Year

As the year comes to a close, Jupiter Retrograde invites us to reflect on our personal growth, celebrate lessons learned, and set intentions that align with our highest aspirations. This period encourages us to approach the new year with wisdom, clarity, and a renewed sense of purpose.

1. **Celebrating Achievements and Personal Growth**: Reflect on the past year, celebrating both accomplishments and the lessons learned through challenges. Take time to appreciate how far you've come, acknowledging growth in areas such as resilience, empathy, or self-awareness. This practice cultivates gratitude and prepares you for a meaningful transition into the new year.

2. **Reassessing Long-Term Goals and Aspirations**: Jupiter Retrograde is an ideal time to reassess long-term goals, ensuring they align with your values and authentic self. Consider if certain goals need adjustment, and focus on intentions that bring a sense of purpose, fulfillment, and joy. This reflection allows you to approach the new year with clarity and confidence.

3. **Setting Intentions for Personal and Spiritual Growth**: Instead of focusing solely on external achievements, Jupiter Retrograde encourages us to set intentions that support inner growth. Reflect on qualities you wish to cultivate, spiritual practices you wish to deepen, or relationships you wish to nurture. These intentions support a fulfilling journey of self-discovery and personal wisdom.

4. **Creating a Gratitude Ritual for the New Year**: Gratitude is a powerful way to connect with Jupiter's energy, bringing peace and abundance to our lives. Consider creating a gratitude ritual as part of your holiday celebrations, such as writing thank-you notes, creating a gratitude jar, or sharing what you're grateful for with loved ones. This practice fosters appreciation and sets a positive foundation for the year ahead.

Practical Tips for Embracing Jupiter Retrograde During the Holidays

Navigating Jupiter Retrograde during the holiday season can enhance your celebrations by bringing a sense of purpose, reflection, and meaningful connection. Here are some practical tips to help you embrace this introspective period:

1. **Plan Thoughtful Gatherings**: Instead of hosting large or extravagant events, focus on intimate, meaningful gatherings that foster connection. Consider low-key dinners, shared storytelling sessions, or reflective holiday rituals that allow everyone to feel seen and appreciated.

2. **Reflect on Holiday Intentions**: Take time to set intentions for the holiday season that align with your values and priorities. Focus on activities that bring joy, peace, and connection, and let go of obligations that feel inauthentic or draining. This approach helps you create a holiday experience that resonates with purpose and authenticity.

3. **Reconnect with Nature and Simplicity**: Jupiter's wisdom encourages simplicity and connection with nature, so consider spending time outdoors or incorporating natural elements into holiday decor. Nature walks, stargazing, or a simple bonfire can bring a sense of peace and grounding, connecting you with the beauty of the season.

4. **Practice Mindful Gift-Giving**: Jupiter Retrograde encourages us to focus on meaningful rather than material gifts. Consider giving experiences, handmade items, or acts of service, which reflect thoughtfulness and appreciation. Mindful gift-giving fosters a sense of connection and aligns with the season's spirit of gratitude.

Final Thoughts: Embracing Jupiter Retrograde as a Time for Reflection and Tradition

Jupiter Retrograde during the holiday season offers a unique opportunity to connect with tradition, reflect on core values, and celebrate the richness of life's simple joys. By embracing this period with mindfulness, gratitude, and an open heart, we create a holiday experience that honors the past, strengthens relationships, and fosters a deeper sense of purpose and belonging.

This holiday season, let Jupiter Retrograde inspire you to reconnect with cherished traditions, celebrate the beauty of community, and cultivate a spirit of gratitude and inner abundance. As you embrace the season with mindfulness and reflection, may you find joy in the present moment, wisdom in your journey, and peace in the simplicity of life's most meaningful connections. Jupiter Retrograde invites you to celebrate not only the season but the journey of growth, gratitude, and love that enriches every step along the way.

Chapter 45: Saturn Retrograde - Lessons in Festive Responsibility

Saturn, often referred to as the "taskmaster" of the zodiac, is the planet of discipline, structure, and responsibility. Known for teaching us through challenges, Saturn's influence brings life lessons that foster growth, resilience, and maturity. When Saturn goes retrograde—an event that happens annually and lasts for about four and a half months—its energy turns inward, prompting us to reflect on our commitments, reassess our responsibilities, and evaluate the structures we have built in our lives. Saturn Retrograde encourages us to confront our fears, make necessary adjustments, and strengthen our foundations.

During the holiday season, when obligations, traditions, and social expectations can feel overwhelming, Saturn Retrograde offers a valuable reminder to approach responsibilities with mindfulness, integrity, and patience. Instead of merely fulfilling holiday duties out of obligation, Saturn Retrograde invites us to find meaning in our commitments, respect boundaries, and honor the values that bring depth to our celebrations. In this chapter, we explore Saturn Retrograde's influence on holiday responsibilities, its lessons in setting boundaries, and how to embrace this period to cultivate a season grounded in purpose, balance, and thoughtful care.

The Astrological Influence of Saturn Retrograde

In astrology, Saturn represents discipline, structure, accountability, and long-term goals. It governs the rules and boundaries that shape our lives, encouraging us to work toward stability, security, and achievement. When Saturn goes retrograde, its influence turns introspective, inviting us to reassess our commitments, confront limitations, and approach responsibilities with greater mindfulness and integrity.

1. **Reflecting on Responsibilities and Commitments**: Saturn Retrograde encourages us to evaluate our responsibilities and ensure that our actions align with our long-term goals. This period is an ideal time to consider whether current obligations support personal growth and well-being or if adjustments are necessary.

2. **Setting and Honoring Boundaries**: Saturn governs boundaries, and during retrograde, we are encouraged to examine where boundaries may be lacking or excessive. This period allows us to practice self-respect and assertiveness, ensuring that we prioritize our own needs and honor our limits.

3. **Confronting Fears and Limitations**: Saturn Retrograde often brings our fears and limitations to the surface, prompting us to confront them with honesty and courage. By acknowl-

edging these fears, we build resilience and strengthen our ability to handle challenges with maturity and patience.

4. **Reflecting on the Importance of Integrity and Accountability**: Saturn emphasizes responsibility and integrity, reminding us to approach obligations with respect and purpose. During retrograde, this energy encourages us to uphold commitments that are meaningful and to release those that feel burdensome or inauthentic.

Reflecting on Holiday Responsibilities and Setting Priorities

Saturn Retrograde invites us to reassess our holiday responsibilities, focusing on obligations that truly align with our values and bring joy. Instead of overcommitting to every event or task, we are encouraged to approach holiday responsibilities mindfully, focusing on quality over quantity and finding fulfillment in meaningful traditions.

1. **Evaluating Holiday Obligations**: This period is an ideal time to examine holiday obligations and assess which ones genuinely enrich the season. Consider if certain commitments, like hosting large gatherings or organizing events, align with your current energy and goals. If obligations feel overwhelming, consider ways to simplify or delegate responsibilities to make the season more manageable.

2. **Prioritizing Meaningful Traditions**: Saturn Retrograde encourages us to focus on traditions that bring a sense of purpose and connection. Reflect on which holiday rituals hold deep meaning for you and your loved ones, and prioritize those that foster joy and unity. Let go of superficial traditions that feel like mere obligations, and center your holiday around practices that resonate with your heart.

3. **Balancing Family Expectations with Personal Needs**: Family expectations can be especially strong during the holidays, but Saturn Retrograde invites us to balance these with our own needs. Reflect on where family expectations may clash with personal well-being, and establish boundaries that honor both your values and those of your loved ones. This approach fosters a holiday experience that respects everyone's needs.

4. **Setting Realistic Goals and Avoiding Overcommitment**: Saturn's influence teaches us to approach goals with patience and realism, helping us avoid overcommitment during the busy holiday season. Set achievable goals for holiday tasks, such as gift shopping, decorating, or cooking, and be mindful of your limits. This approach prevents burnout and ensures that each responsibility is handled with care.

Honoring Boundaries and Practicing Self-Care

Saturn Retrograde emphasizes the importance of boundaries, making this period an ideal time to establish and honor limits within social and family settings. By respecting our boundaries, we create a holiday experience that supports well-being, reduces stress, and fosters authentic connection.

1. **Establishing Boundaries Around Social Gatherings**: Social obligations can be draining, especially during the holidays. Saturn Retrograde encourages us to set boundaries that protect our energy, ensuring that we attend gatherings that are meaningful and decline those that feel excessive. Prioritize quality interactions over quantity, creating space for genuine connections.

2. **Balancing Family Dynamics with Self-Respect**: Family gatherings can sometimes bring up challenging dynamics or old patterns. Saturn Retrograde encourages us to approach these situations with self-respect, setting boundaries that prevent emotional exhaustion or compromise. Practice assertiveness and avoid engaging in interactions that feel uncomfortable or unkind.

3. **Carving Out Time for Solitude and Reflection**: Saturn's retrograde period supports moments of solitude and introspection, which are essential for recharging during a busy season. Make time for activities that nurture your soul, whether it's reading, meditating, journaling, or simply resting. These moments of quiet help you stay grounded, centered, and prepared for holiday interactions.

4. **Prioritizing Physical and Emotional Well-Being**: Saturn emphasizes responsibility to oneself, reminding us to prioritize self-care during the holidays. Practice good sleep, balanced nutrition, and physical movement to maintain physical health. For emotional well-being, engage in practices that reduce stress, such as mindfulness, gratitude, or time in nature. This approach helps you manage holiday responsibilities with strength and resilience.

Confronting Fears and Letting Go of Perfectionism

Saturn Retrograde often brings up fears, limitations, and a tendency toward perfectionism, especially in areas of responsibility and expectations. By confronting these fears and releasing perfectionist tendencies, we can create a holiday season that is more relaxed, joyful, and grounded in self-compassion.

1. **Letting Go of Holiday Perfectionism**: Saturn Retrograde encourages us to release the pressure to create a "perfect" holiday experience. Instead of striving for idealized standards, focus on creating a season that feels authentic, simple, and enjoyable. Embrace the imperfections and remember that meaningful moments often arise from spontaneity and genuine connection.

2. **Addressing Fears Around Expectations and Judgments**: Fear of disappointing others or being judged can often shape our holiday decisions. Saturn Retrograde invites us to confront these fears, recognizing that we cannot please everyone and that our worth is not defined by others' opinions. Focus on what feels right for you, and approach holiday responsibilities with confidence and self-assurance.

3. **Embracing Flexibility and Adapting to Change**: Saturn's influence can sometimes make us resistant to change, but retrograde encourages us to embrace flexibility. Be open to adapting holiday plans if circumstances shift, and avoid becoming too rigid in expectations. This openness to change creates a more relaxed, resilient approach to holiday responsibilities.

4. **Celebrating Progress Over Perfection**: Saturn Retrograde teaches us that progress and growth are more valuable than perfection. Acknowledge the efforts you've made throughout the year, and celebrate the personal growth that has enriched your life. This mindset shifts focus from perfectionism to gratitude, allowing you to approach the holidays with peace and self-compassion.

Reflecting on the Meaning of Responsibility and Integrity

Saturn Retrograde emphasizes responsibility, integrity, and commitment, encouraging us to approach holiday obligations with authenticity and purpose. This period offers a chance to reflect on what responsibility means to us, aligning our actions with personal values and ensuring that each commitment holds true meaning.

1. **Reevaluating the Purpose Behind Each Responsibility**: Saturn Retrograde invites us to reflect on why we take on certain responsibilities, examining if they align with our values and bring joy. Ask yourself, "Why is this commitment important?" and "Does it add value to my holiday experience?" By focusing on purpose-driven responsibilities, we foster a season filled with intention and meaning.

2. **Upholding Integrity in All Interactions**: Saturn's influence reminds us to approach each interaction with integrity, honesty, and respect. Whether it's a family gathering, a community event, or a small act of kindness, approach each responsibility with sincerity and dedication.

Acting with integrity creates a holiday experience that is aligned with personal values and fosters trust within relationships.

3. **Practicing Accountability and Following Through on Promises**: Saturn encourages accountability, making it a time to follow through on promises with thoughtfulness and care. If you've committed to helping with holiday preparations, organizing an event, or supporting a friend, make sure you fulfill your promises. This commitment to follow-through creates a sense of reliability and trustworthiness.

4. **Releasing Responsibilities That No Longer Serve You**: Saturn Retrograde also encourages us to release responsibilities that feel burdensome or misaligned. If certain obligations no longer serve your growth or well-being, consider letting them go with gratitude. This act of release makes room for new experiences that reflect your current values and priorities.

Strengthening Family Bonds Through Structure and Stability

Saturn is associated with structure and stability, making its retrograde period an ideal time to create holiday experiences that foster unity and consistency within family bonds. By embracing structure, we create a foundation that supports meaningful traditions and fosters a sense of security and belonging.

1. **Establishing Consistent Family Traditions**: Saturn Retrograde encourages us to establish or reinforce traditions that bring a sense of stability to family gatherings. Whether it's a holiday meal, a storytelling session, or a gratitude ritual, consistent traditions create a comforting rhythm that strengthens family bonds and creates lasting memories.

2. **Supporting Family Members with Thoughtful Boundaries**: Boundaries contribute to family stability by ensuring that each person's needs are respected. Saturn Retrograde encourages us to set boundaries that allow family members to express themselves while maintaining harmony. Thoughtful boundaries foster respect and understanding within family relationships, supporting a peaceful holiday experience.

3. **Fostering Responsibility and Accountability in Shared Tasks**: Saturn Retrograde encourages a sense of shared responsibility, making it a wonderful time to involve family members in holiday preparations. Assign roles based on each person's strengths and interests, creating a collaborative environment where everyone contributes. This approach not only lightens the load but also fosters teamwork and mutual appreciation.

4. **Celebrating Elders and Family Legacy**: Saturn is associated with elders and ancestral wisdom, making this period ideal for honoring family history and legacy. Create moments to celebrate the contributions of older family members, listen to their stories, and acknowledge their role in shaping family traditions. This respect for legacy deepens the family bond and reinforces a sense of continuity.

Practical Tips for Navigating Saturn Retrograde During the Holidays

Saturn Retrograde's introspective energy offers valuable lessons in responsibility, patience, and mindful celebration. By embracing its influence, we can create a holiday experience grounded in integrity, purpose, and thoughtful care.

1. **Create a Mindful Holiday Checklist**: Instead of listing every possible task, create a checklist that focuses on responsibilities that bring joy, connection, and meaning. Prioritize the tasks that truly matter, and let go of those that feel unnecessary or draining. This approach ensures that your holiday responsibilities are manageable and fulfilling.
2. **Practice Patience and Avoid Overextending**: Saturn Retrograde encourages a slower, more deliberate pace. Practice patience, and avoid overextending yourself by taking on excessive commitments. Focus on completing each responsibility with care, rather than rushing to achieve everything at once.
3. **Honor Personal Boundaries in Social Settings**: Be mindful of personal boundaries, especially in social gatherings. If a situation feels overwhelming, take a moment to step away, or politely excuse yourself if necessary. Respecting your boundaries ensures that you remain centered and calm, allowing for meaningful interactions.
4. **Reflect on Personal Growth and Lessons Learned**: Use this period to reflect on the personal growth and lessons you've experienced over the past year. Acknowledge the challenges you've overcome, the strengths you've developed, and the insights you've gained. This reflection fosters gratitude, resilience, and a sense of fulfillment.

Final Thoughts: Embracing Saturn Retrograde as a Time for Purposeful Responsibility

Saturn Retrograde during the holiday season offers a unique opportunity to approach responsibilities with purpose, patience, and self-awareness. By embracing its lessons, we create a holiday experience that is grounded in integrity, respect, and meaningful connections. Saturn Retrograde encourages us to find balance, set thoughtful boundaries, and honor the values that enrich our lives and relationships.

This holiday season, let Saturn Retrograde inspire you to approach each responsibility with intention, honor your boundaries, and celebrate the meaningful connections that bring joy and fulfillment. As you navigate this period with mindfulness, may you create a holiday experience that resonates with peace, purpose, and genuine connection. Saturn Retrograde reminds us that true celebration lies not in the quantity of tasks completed but in the quality of the moments shared, the respect given, and the love nurtured in every interaction.

Appendix

Appendix A: Glossary of Astrological Terms

Astrology is a complex and layered field, filled with specific terminology that enriches our understanding of celestial influences and their impact on human life. This glossary provides definitions of key astrological terms, helping readers navigate the language of astrology and apply its principles with clarity. From planets and aspects to signs and retrogrades, this section explains foundational terms that are essential for interpreting astrology.

A

- **Affliction**: An aspect or position that is traditionally considered challenging or restrictive. Afflictions often highlight areas of difficulty or growth in a natal chart, as they reveal areas where life's challenges may require greater resilience or focus.
- **Air Signs**: Gemini, Libra, and Aquarius are the Air signs, known for their intellectual curiosity, sociability, and communicative qualities. They are associated with ideas, relationships, and mental exploration.
- **Angles**: The four main points of a natal chart—Ascendant (rising sign), Descendant, Midheaven (MC), and Imum Coeli (IC)—are called angles. These points are critical in interpreting personal and external influences in a chart.
- **Angular Houses**: Houses 1, 4, 7, and 10 in the natal chart. These are powerful houses associated with action, public life, and personal identity. Planets in angular houses are said to have a strong influence on an individual's life.
- **Anaretic Degree**: The 29th degree of any sign, often seen as a critical or "fated" degree, indicating completion, urgency, or significant life transitions.

A (continued)

- **Ascendant (Rising Sign)**: The sign rising on the eastern horizon at the exact moment of birth. The Ascendant represents how we appear to others, our outer personality, and initial impressions. It is one of the most personal aspects of the natal chart.
- **Aspect**: The angle formed between two planets in a natal chart. Aspects reveal the dynamic interactions between planetary energies, indicating areas of harmony or tension. Major aspects include conjunctions, sextiles, squares, trines, and oppositions.

B

- **Benefic Planets**: Traditionally, Jupiter and Venus are considered benefic planets because their influence is seen as positive and beneficial. They are associated with good fortune, growth, and harmony in a natal chart.

C

- **Cardinal Signs**: Aries, Cancer, Libra, and Capricorn. These signs are known for their leadership, initiative, and action-oriented qualities. They mark the beginning of each season and bring dynamic energy.
- **Cazimi**: When a planet is within 0°17' of the Sun, it is considered "cazimi," or "in the heart of the Sun," intensifying the planet's energy and bringing clarity and empowerment.
- **Chiron**: An asteroid known as the "wounded healer" in astrology. Chiron represents areas of wounding and healing, highlighting where we experience both pain and transformative growth.
- **Composite Chart**: A chart created by blending the positions of two individuals' planets to understand the dynamics of their relationship. This chart is often used to analyze compatibility and relationship patterns.
- **Conjunction**: An aspect where two planets are close together, usually within 0–10 degrees, amplifying each other's energy. Conjunctions can be harmonious or intense, depending on the nature of the planets involved.
- **Cusps**: The dividing lines between the houses in an astrological chart. A planet on a cusp is considered to be influenced by both adjacent houses or signs.

D

- **Decan**: Each sign is divided into three parts called decans, each spanning 10 degrees. Each decan provides a variation on the main qualities of the sign, adding depth and uniqueness to planetary placements.
- **Descendant (DSC)**: The point directly opposite the Ascendant on the natal chart, representing partnership, marriage, and how we relate to others in one-on-one relationships.

E

- **Earth Signs**: Taurus, Virgo, and Capricorn are the Earth signs, known for their practicality, stability, and grounding energy. Earth signs are associated with the physical world, material resources, and realistic approaches.
- **Eclipse**: A powerful event that occurs when the Sun, Moon, and Earth align, creating a solar or lunar eclipse. Eclipses are seen as times of sudden change, new beginnings, and heightened energy.
- **Ephemeris**: An astronomical table that shows the daily positions of the planets over a period of time. Ephemerides are essential tools for astrologers to track planetary movements and predict transits.

F

- **Fire Signs**: Aries, Leo, and Sagittarius are the Fire signs, characterized by passion, enthusiasm, and creativity. Fire signs are associated with action, inspiration, and confidence.

G

- **Grand Trine**: A rare and harmonious configuration in a natal chart where three planets form a trine (120-degree aspect) with each other, creating a triangle. Grand trines bring ease, balance, and natural talent in the elements involved.

H

- **Houses**: The twelve divisions of a natal chart, each representing different areas of life, such as career, relationships, and home. The house where a planet resides reveals how its energy will manifest in a person's life.

I

- **Imum Coeli (IC)**: The lowest point in the chart, often associated with the 4th house. It represents home, family, roots, and our inner self.

K

- **Karmic Astrology**: A branch of astrology that focuses on the soul's journey and past-life influences, often using points like the lunar nodes, Saturn, and Chiron to understand lessons and growth.

L

- **Lunar Nodes**: The North Node and South Node are points where the Moon's orbit intersects the ecliptic. They represent karmic lessons, with the North Node indicating areas for growth and the South Node showing past-life patterns or comfort zones.

M

- **Midheaven (MC)**: The point at the top of the chart, associated with career, public life, and ambitions. It represents our outer purpose and aspirations.

- **Mutable Signs**: Gemini, Virgo, Sagittarius, and Pisces are the Mutable signs, known for their adaptability, flexibility, and willingness to embrace change. They mark the transition between seasons and are associated with transformation.

N

- **Natal Chart**: A map of the sky at the exact moment of a person's birth, showing the positions of the planets, signs, and houses. The natal chart is the foundation of astrological interpretation and reveals insights into personality, strengths, and life path.

O

- **Opposition**: An aspect where two planets are 180 degrees apart, creating tension and balance. Oppositions often bring challenges that encourage growth and integration between opposing forces.

P

- **Planetary Return**: A significant event that occurs when a planet returns to the same position it held at the time of birth. Common returns include the Solar Return (annual) and the Saturn Return (every 29–30 years).

Q

- **Quincunx**: Also known as an inconjunct, it is an aspect where two planets are 150 degrees apart. Quincunxes often indicate areas of adjustment or integration between energies that seem incompatible.

R

- **Retrograde**: A period when a planet appears to move backward in its orbit from our perspective on Earth. Retrogrades encourage reflection, introspection, and revisiting past experiences, depending on the nature of the retrograde planet.

S

- **Square**: An aspect where two planets are 90 degrees apart, creating tension and challenge. Squares indicate areas of growth through overcoming obstacles and finding balance.
- **Stellium**: A grouping of three or more planets in a single sign or house, creating a concentrated area of energy. A stellium intensifies the themes of the sign or house involved.

T

- **Transit**: The current position of a planet in relation to the planets in a natal chart. Transits provide insights into how current planetary influences affect an individual's experiences, moods, and focus over time.
- **Trine**: A harmonious aspect where two planets are 120 degrees apart, creating an easy flow of energy. Trines bring natural talent, luck, and ease in the areas represented by the planets involved.

V

- **Venus Retrograde**: A period when Venus appears to move backward in the sky, bringing reflection in matters of love, beauty, and values. Venus Retrograde encourages reassessment of relationships and self-worth.

W

- **Water Signs**: Cancer, Scorpio, and Pisces are the Water signs, associated with emotion, intuition, and sensitivity. Water signs are often deeply connected to feelings, creativity, and compassion.

Y

- **Yod**: Known as the "Finger of God," a yod is a rare configuration where two planets form a sextile (60 degrees apart) and both form a quincunx to a third planet, creating a triangle. Yods indicate special challenges or missions, often bringing fated or transformative experiences.

Z

- **Zodiac**: The twelve constellations that make up the astrological year, each associated with specific qualities, elements, and ruling planets. The zodiac is the framework for astrological interpretation and understanding planetary influence.

This glossary provides an overview of essential astrological terms that offer insight into the language of astrology. Understanding these definitions helps to deepen your exploration of celestial influences, enabling a more nuanced and informed approach to astrology. Whether you're interpreting a natal chart or exploring the meaning of a planetary transit, these terms form the foundation of astrological wisdom and enhance your connection with the cosmos.

Appendix B: Calendar of Upcoming Celestial Events for Future Holiday Seasons

This calendar of celestial events highlights significant astronomical and astrological occurrences that will influence holiday seasons over the next several years. These events include planetary retrogrades, eclipses, meteor showers, and rare planetary alignments. Each event brings unique energy and significance, enriching the holiday season with opportunities for reflection, growth, and celebration. This appendix provides dates and descriptions of key celestial events, helping you plan festivities and rituals around these powerful cosmic influences.

2024

December 13–14, 2024 – Geminids Meteor Shower

- Peak viewing night for the Geminids, one of the most active and colorful meteor showers. The Geminids are known for bright, multicolored meteors, making them a stunning addition to winter celebrations. Viewing will be enhanced by a waning crescent moon, providing darker skies for an ideal spectacle.

December 15, 2024 – Mercury Retrograde Begins in Capricorn

- Mercury goes retrograde just before the holidays, affecting communication, travel, and planning. It's a period for reflection and careful preparation, as Mercury's influence may bring delays or misunderstandings. Double-check plans and embrace flexibility during this introspective time.

December 21, 2024 – Winter Solstice

- The Winter Solstice marks the longest night of the year and the official start of winter in the Northern Hemisphere. This event is celebrated in many cultures as a time of renewal and hope, symbolizing the return of the light as days begin to lengthen. It's a powerful time for intention-setting and gratitude rituals.

December 26, 2024 – Full Moon in Cancer

- This Full Moon highlights themes of home, family, and emotional connection. It's a nurturing influence, encouraging deeper bonds with loved ones. A wonderful night for reflective gatherings, the Cancer Full Moon invites warmth and emotional intimacy during the holiday season.

2025
December 12–13, 2025 – Geminids Meteor Shower

- The Geminids meteor shower will peak, with the New Moon allowing for excellent visibility of the meteor activity. This event offers a magical backdrop for holiday stargazing and moments of quiet reflection under a clear, dark sky.

December 18, 2025 – Saturn Retrograde Ends in Aries

- Saturn stations direct, marking a shift in energy and easing the restrictions felt during its retrograde. After a period of introspection and restructuring, Saturn direct in Aries inspires courage and action, making it an ideal time for finalizing holiday plans and setting future goals.

December 21, 2025 – Winter Solstice and Venus Retrograde in Scorpio

- Venus begins retrograde on the day of the Winter Solstice, intensifying focus on relationships, intimacy, and personal values. This retrograde encourages deep reflection on love and commitment, inviting us to reconnect with what truly matters in our connections with others.

December 29, 2025 – Full Moon in Gemini

- A communicative Full Moon that highlights the value of connection, curiosity, and learning. This Gemini Full Moon brings social energy, ideal for gatherings and lighthearted conversations. It's a good time for sharing stories, laughter, and creative exchanges with loved ones.

2026
December 12–13, 2026 – Geminids Meteor Shower

- The Geminids return with a peak during a waxing crescent moon phase, providing favorable conditions for viewing. These vibrant meteors will add an extra layer of wonder to the holiday season, perfect for outdoor gatherings and quiet moments of celestial awe.

December 18, 2026 – New Moon in Sagittarius

- A New Moon that encourages fresh starts, optimism, and adventure. This Sagittarius New Moon is perfect for setting intentions for travel, learning, and personal growth in the year ahead. It's an inspiring time to reflect on dreams and aspirations with a sense of hope and excitement.

December 21, 2026 – Winter Solstice

- The Winter Solstice once again marks the beginning of longer days. This powerful time for rituals of renewal and gratitude brings a sense of balance and harmony, encouraging reflection on the year's lessons and hopes for the future.

December 25, 2026 – Mars Retrograde Begins in Leo

- Mars goes retrograde in Leo, bringing a period of introspection regarding personal ambitions, courage, and self-expression. This retrograde can encourage a reassessment of goals and creative pursuits, urging us to focus on authenticity rather than external validation.

2027
December 13–14, 2027 – Geminids Meteor Shower

- The Geminids meteor shower will peak with a New Moon, ensuring ideal dark skies for a breathtaking display. This celestial event provides a stunning opportunity for holiday stargazing, reminding us of the beauty and vastness of the universe.

December 15, 2027 – Uranus Retrograde Ends in Gemini

- Uranus stations direct, bringing a forward movement to innovative ideas, technology, and communication. This change may inspire fresh perspectives and new approaches, making it an excellent time to embrace open-mindedness during holiday gatherings.

December 21, 2027 – Winter Solstice

- As the longest night of the year, the Winter Solstice is a time to honor the transition from darkness to light. It's a perfect occasion for quiet reflection, meditation, and gatherings that emphasize warmth, unity, and peace.

December 27, 2027 – Full Moon in Leo

- This expressive Full Moon in Leo brings celebratory energy, ideal for sharing joy, laughter, and creativity with others. It's a wonderful time for gatherings that celebrate individuality, as well as for artistic and festive activities that bring people together.

2028
December 13–14, 2028 – Geminids Meteor Shower

- The Geminids will peak under the light of a waxing crescent moon, providing a stunning meteor show. This event is a yearly favorite, adding celestial beauty to holiday gatherings and inspiring awe and wonder.

December 16, 2028 – Mercury Retrograde Begins in Capricorn

- Mercury Retrograde begins just before the holidays, bringing a period of reflection on communication, organization, and travel plans. This retrograde period invites us to approach holiday planning with extra care, ensuring patience and flexibility.

December 21, 2028 – Winter Solstice

- The Winter Solstice, marking the return of longer days, is a time for gratitude, introspection, and hope. Celebrate this turning point with rituals that honor the light's return, such as candle lighting, meditation, and setting intentions for the year ahead.

December 24, 2028 – Mars Conjunct Saturn in Aquarius

- Mars and Saturn come together in Aquarius, creating a powerful alignment that emphasizes discipline, innovation, and resilience. This conjunction encourages purposeful action and the potential for progress in personal or community-oriented goals.

December 30, 2028 – Full Moon in Cancer

- The Cancer Full Moon brings emotional warmth and a focus on home, family, and connection. It's a nurturing influence, ideal for heartfelt gatherings and activities that honor family traditions and personal bonds.

2029
December 13–14, 2029 – Geminids Meteor Shower

- The Geminids will peak with favorable viewing conditions under a waning crescent moon. This annual display of colorful meteors will bring magic to the holiday sky, perfect for contemplative or shared moments of stargazing.

December 20, 2029 – New Moon in Sagittarius

- This New Moon invites a fresh start, with an emphasis on optimism, adventure, and learning. Sagittarius energy encourages us to dream big, making it an ideal time for setting intentions related to growth, exploration, and self-discovery.

December 21, 2029 – Winter Solstice

- The Winter Solstice marks the arrival of winter and the gradual return of light. This powerful time for gratitude and reflection encourages us to look inward, honor the year's lessons, and set meaningful intentions for the future.

December 24, 2029 – Venus Conjunct Pluto in Capricorn

- Venus and Pluto align, bringing an intense focus on love, transformation, and depth in relationships. This conjunction encourages introspection around emotional attachments, creating a holiday atmosphere that emphasizes sincerity, healing, and transformation.

December 31, 2029 – Full Moon in Virgo

- The Virgo Full Moon brings a grounding, practical energy to close the year. It's a wonderful influence for organization, reflection, and planning, making it a fitting time to release what no longer serves and set thoughtful intentions for the new year.

These upcoming celestial events offer moments for reflection, renewal, and celebration during the holiday seasons of the next several years. Each event, whether an eclipse, retrograde, or solstice, brings unique energy that enhances the spirit of the season, inviting us to align with the cycles of the cosmos. Embrace these powerful influences, letting them inspire gatherings, rituals, and moments of gratitude, as the universe adds its own magic to our holiday traditions.

Appendix C: Tips on Observing Celestial Events and Identifying Zodiac Symbols in the Night Sky

Observing the night sky can be a captivating way to connect with the cosmos, especially when aligning it with astrological insights. This guide provides practical tips for observing celestial events, recognizing zodiac constellations, and understanding how to make the most of your stargazing experience. From selecting the best tools and locations to identifying major constellations and planning for optimal viewing, this appendix serves as a comprehensive resource to deepen your connection to the stars.

1. Essential Tips for Observing Celestial Events

Observing celestial events, whether meteor showers, lunar phases, or planetary alignments, requires a bit of preparation. Here's how to optimize your experience:

Choose an Ideal Location

- **Find a Dark Sky Site**: Light pollution from cities obscures visibility, so head to areas with minimal artificial lighting. Parks, mountains, beaches, or designated dark-sky preserves are excellent options.
- **High Altitude is Helpful**: If possible, view from higher elevations where atmospheric interference is reduced, providing a clearer view of celestial objects.
- **Away from Trees and Buildings**: A wide, open space allows for an unobstructed view of the sky, which is especially useful for events that occur close to the horizon.

Timing is Everything

- **Check Local Moon Phases**: A full moon can wash out many celestial objects, while a new moon provides darker skies ideal for stargazing.
- **Plan Around Peak Viewing Times**: Celestial events like meteor showers have peak times (often after midnight), so check online resources to determine the best time for viewing.
- **Allow Your Eyes to Adjust**: Give your eyes 15-30 minutes to adapt to the darkness, avoiding phone screens or artificial lights that can disrupt your night vision.

Gather the Right Equipment

- **Binoculars**: These are a great starting point for beginners. They enhance your view of the moon, planets, and certain star clusters.
- **Telescope**: For a closer view of planets, galaxies, and nebulae, consider investing in a telescope. Small, beginner-friendly telescopes offer excellent introductory views of planets and the moon.
- **Star Charts and Apps**: Physical star charts or astronomy apps like Stellarium and SkySafari help you identify constellations and planets in real-time.

- **Red Flashlight**: A red flashlight preserves night vision, allowing you to read charts or adjust equipment without disrupting your ability to see faint objects.

2. Tips for Observing Specific Celestial Events

Each type of celestial event has unique considerations that can make or break the experience. Here are some tips for key events:

Meteor Showers

- **Find the Radiant Point**: Meteor showers have a radiant point, often located in a specific constellation (e.g., the Perseids in Perseus, the Geminids in Gemini). While meteors can be visible across the sky, they'll often appear to originate from this point.
- **Watch with the Naked Eye**: Telescopes and binoculars restrict your field of view. The naked eye is best for catching quick streaks of light across the sky.
- **Lie Down and Relax**: Bring a reclining chair or blanket so you can comfortably lie back and scan the sky, giving you a full view.

Eclipses (Solar and Lunar)

- **Solar Eclipses**: Never look directly at a solar eclipse without protective eyewear. Use eclipse glasses or a solar filter for telescopes. Pinhole projectors and solar viewing boxes offer safe, indirect ways to observe a solar eclipse.
- **Lunar Eclipses**: These are safe to view with the naked eye. For a detailed view, use binoculars or a telescope to see the moon's features as it enters the Earth's shadow, turning shades of orange and red during a total eclipse.

Planetary Alignments and Conjunctions

- **Check App or Star Chart**: Planetary alignments and conjunctions can be tricky to spot without guidance. Use an app to find the exact positions of the planets and track their movement over several nights.
- **Look Near the Horizon**: Conjunctions often occur close to the horizon, so find a location with an open view and begin observing shortly after sunset or before sunrise.

New and Full Moons

- **New Moons**: While not visible, new moons are ideal for observing other celestial bodies due to the darker sky. Plan stargazing trips around new moon nights to enhance visibility of faint objects.
- **Full Moons**: Observe the surface details of the full moon with binoculars or a telescope. Though full moons make it harder to see stars, they are excellent for lunar observation, revealing mountains, craters, and the "seas" or maria.

3. Identifying Zodiac Constellations in the Night Sky

The zodiac constellations form the backdrop for the sun's path, known as the ecliptic. Each zodiac constellation is visible during different times of the year. Here's how to identify each zodiac sign in the night sky:

Aries (The Ram)

- **Best Viewing**: October to December
- **Location**: Look in the northern hemisphere above Taurus. Aries is a small, faint constellation with three main stars forming a curved line.
- **Notable Stars**: Hamal (the brightest star in Aries) and Sheratan.

Taurus (The Bull)

- **Best Viewing**: November to February
- **Location**: Look for a "V"-shaped cluster of stars with the bright orange star Aldebaran marking the bull's eye. Taurus is near Orion, making it easy to locate.
- **Notable Features**: The Pleiades (a nearby open star cluster) and the Hyades cluster.

Gemini (The Twins)

- **Best Viewing**: December to March
- **Location**: Above and to the left of Orion, Gemini's two bright stars, Castor and Pollux, make it easily identifiable.
- **Notable Features**: The stars Castor and Pollux represent the heads of the twins, with other stars trailing down to form their bodies.

Cancer (The Crab)

- **Best Viewing**: January to April
- **Location**: Between Gemini and Leo, Cancer is faint, so look for a dark sky. It appears as a dim, spread-out constellation.
- **Notable Features**: The Beehive Cluster (M44), visible with binoculars or a telescope.

Leo (The Lion)

- **Best Viewing**: February to May
- **Location**: Look for a backward question mark or "sickle" shape representing the lion's head, with the bright star Regulus marking its heart.
- **Notable Features**: Regulus, the lion's heart, and the Sickle asterism.

Virgo (The Maiden)

- **Best Viewing**: April to July
- **Location**: Virgo lies beneath Leo, identifiable by its brightest star, Spica.
- **Notable Features**: Spica, the brightest star in Virgo, and clusters of galaxies visible with telescopes.

Libra (The Scales)

- **Best Viewing**: May to August
- **Location**: Between Virgo and Scorpius. Libra's stars form a shape reminiscent of a set of scales.
- **Notable Features**: Zubenelgenubi and Zubeneschamali, the two main stars, which represent the balance beam.

Scorpius (The Scorpion)

- **Best Viewing**: June to September
- **Location**: Look for a distinctive curved line of stars with a bright red star, Antares, marking the heart of the scorpion.
- **Notable Features**: Antares and the "sting" of the scorpion's tail curving below.

Sagittarius (The Archer)

- **Best Viewing**: July to October
- **Location**: Near Scorpius, Sagittarius is shaped like a teapot and is close to the center of the Milky Way.
- **Notable Features**: The "Teapot" asterism and the nearby galactic center, which appears as a bright section of the Milky Way.

Capricornus (The Sea Goat)

- **Best Viewing**: August to November
- **Location**: Found between Sagittarius and Aquarius, Capricornus appears as a faint triangle of stars.
- **Notable Features**: Its faint stars form a shape resembling an arrowhead or goat's head.

Aquarius (The Water Bearer)

- **Best Viewing**: September to December
- **Location**: Near Capricornus, Aquarius appears as a series of faint, scattered stars.
- **Notable Features**: Known for its diffuse appearance; the star Sadalsuud is the brightest in the constellation.

Pisces (The Fish)

- **Best Viewing**: October to January
- **Location**: Look below Andromeda. Pisces consists of two faint groups of stars connected by a string of stars, forming two fish swimming in opposite directions.
- **Notable Features**: Alrescha, a notable double star in Pisces.

4. Additional Tips for Identifying Zodiac Constellations

- **Use the Ecliptic**: The ecliptic is the sun's path across the sky and runs through all twelve zodiac constellations. If you're trying to identify zodiac constellations, locate the ecliptic to guide your search.
- **Seasonal Constellations**: Zodiac constellations are seasonal, and each is best visible during certain months of the year, as listed above. Check your location's visibility based on the season to know which constellations to look for.
- **Star Hopping**: Use bright stars or nearby constellations as reference points. For example, Orion is a good starting point for locating Taurus and Gemini, while Leo can help you find Virgo.

5. Best Practices for Stargazing and Observing Zodiac Constellations

- **Go During a New Moon**: New moons provide darker skies, perfect for observing faint constellations and zodiac symbols.
- **Check Weather Conditions**: Cloud cover can obstruct the view, so choose a clear night for stargazing.
- **Use a Star Chart or App**: Apps like Stellarium, SkySafari, and Star Walk provide real-time guidance, showing you the current positions of zodiac constellations and planets.
- **Be Patient and Enjoy the Journey**: Observing celestial bodies requires patience. Allow yourself to enjoy the process, taking in the beauty of the night sky as you search for constellations.

By understanding how to observe celestial events and recognize zodiac constellations, you can deepen your appreciation for the cosmos and connect meaningfully with the astrological influences in the night sky. Whether during a meteor shower or beneath the light of a full moon, these tips offer guidance to enhance your celestial experience and foster a profound sense of wonder.

Appendix D: Resources for Further Reading on Astrology and Celestial Events

To further explore astrology and celestial events, this appendix offers a comprehensive list of recommended books, websites, apps, and educational resources. Whether you're interested in understanding the basics of astrology, tracking celestial movements, or diving into advanced astrological theory, these resources provide valuable knowledge and insights to deepen your connection with the cosmos.

Books on Astrology
Beginner-Friendly Books

1. **"The Only Astrology Book You'll Ever Need" by Joanna Martine Woolfolk**
   - This classic book introduces astrology basics, including natal chart interpretation, sun signs, and planetary placements. With clear language and visuals, it's an accessible guide for those new to astrology.
2. **"Astrology for the Soul" by Jan Spiller**
   - Focused on the concept of the lunar nodes, this book is ideal for readers interested in exploring karmic and spiritual astrology. Jan Spiller's work offers insights into life purpose, growth, and the soul's journey.
3. **"Parker's Astrology" by Julia and Derek Parker**
   - Known for its comprehensive approach, this illustrated guide covers the essentials of astrology, including chart interpretation, aspects, houses, and transits. It's an excellent resource for beginners and intermediate readers.
4. **"Astrology Made Easy" by Yasmin Boland**
   - Boland's book breaks down astrology in an easy-to-understand format, covering planetary placements, sun signs, and the major houses. A great starting point for those interested in personal astrology and self-understanding.
5. **"You Were Born for This: Astrology for Radical Self-Acceptance" by Chani Nicholas**
   - A modern approach to astrology, this book focuses on self-acceptance and personal empowerment through astrology. Chani Nicholas combines astrology with insights on purpose, relationships, and self-discovery.

Intermediate to Advanced Astrology Books

1. **"The Inner Sky" by Steven Forrest**
   - Forrest's work focuses on psychological astrology, exploring how the planets and signs reflect different aspects of personality and inner growth. This book is ideal for those seeking a deeper understanding of the emotional and psychological layers in astrology.
2. **"Planets in Transit" by Robert Hand**
   - Considered one of the best resources on transits, this book provides detailed interpretations of planetary movements and how they affect the natal chart. It's a valuable reference for intermediate and advanced students.

3. **"The Astrological Houses: The Spectrum of Individual Experience" by Dane Rudhyar**
   - Rudhyar's book delves into the significance of the twelve houses, exploring how each house relates to different life experiences. His approach combines psychological and spiritual astrology, offering a nuanced perspective.
4. **"Aspects in Astrology" by Sue Tompkins**
   - A detailed examination of planetary aspects, this book explores how different planetary interactions affect personality, relationships, and life experiences. It's a valuable resource for interpreting the aspects within a natal chart.
5. **"Horoscope Symbols" by Robert Hand**
   - Another work by Robert Hand, this book focuses on the symbolism and archetypes within astrology, covering signs, planets, houses, and aspects. It's recommended for those interested in exploring astrology's symbolic depth.

Books on Celestial Events and Astronomy

1. **"NightWatch: A Practical Guide to Viewing the Universe" by Terence Dickinson**
   - This beginner-friendly guide provides practical information on stargazing, telescope usage, and identifying celestial objects. It's a go-to resource for observing celestial events and understanding the basics of astronomy.
2. **"The Backyard Astronomer's Guide" by Terence Dickinson and Alan Dyer**
   - Known for its stunning visuals and in-depth explanations, this guide covers the essentials of stargazing, telescope use, and identifying stars, planets, and galaxies. It's perfect for amateur astronomers and astrology enthusiasts who enjoy observing the night sky.
3. **"Astrophotography for the Amateur" by Michael A. Covington**
   - This book offers detailed guidance on capturing celestial events and objects through photography. It's ideal for anyone interested in documenting their stargazing experiences.
4. **"Turn Left at Orion" by Guy Consolmagno and Dan M. Davis**
   - A practical guide for observing stars, planets, and other celestial phenomena, this book is easy to follow and features star charts, making it a helpful resource for beginners and those exploring celestial events for the first time.
5. **"The Universe Today Ultimate Guide to Viewing the Cosmos" by David Dickinson and Fraser Cain**
   - A complete guide to viewing the cosmos, this book includes information on observing planets, meteor showers, eclipses, and other celestial events. It's accessible for beginners and provides practical tips for maximizing stargazing experiences.

Websites for Astrology and Celestial Events
Astrology Websites

1. **Astro.com (Astrodienst)**
   - One of the most trusted astrology websites, offering free natal chart generation, detailed reports, and resources on transits, synastry, and personal forecasts. A valuable tool for beginners and seasoned astrologers alike.
2. **Cafe Astrology**
   - Known for its user-friendly explanations, Cafe Astrology offers resources on natal charts, planetary transits, retrogrades, and compatibility. This site is ideal for beginners and intermediate astrologers.
3. **AstroSeek**
   - A free astrology platform that offers a range of tools, including natal chart calculators, transits, synastry charts, and solar returns. It also has interactive tools for exploring zodiac compatibility and timing techniques.
4. **Chani Nicholas**
   - This website, managed by astrologer Chani Nicholas, provides horoscopes, workshops, and courses focused on astrology for self-care, empowerment, and social change.
5. **The Astrology Podcast**
   - An informative platform for astrology podcasts, covering everything from natal charts to horary astrology. Hosted by astrologer Chris Brennan, it's ideal for those wanting to delve into astrology on a deeper level.

Astronomy and Celestial Event Websites

1. **Time and Date**
   - This site provides accurate dates, times, and viewing details for celestial events like eclipses, moon phases, meteor showers, and solstices. It's a comprehensive tool for planning your stargazing sessions.
2. **NASA's Skywatching Page**
   - Offers monthly guides for celestial events and provides information on upcoming eclipses, meteor showers, planetary oppositions, and more. NASA's resources are detailed and scientifically accurate.
3. **The Sky Live**

- An interactive site that provides real-time tracking of planets, stars, and other celestial bodies. It includes visibility forecasts, moon phases, and star charts to enhance your night sky observations.

4. **Stellarium Web**
   - An online planetarium where you can view a virtual map of the sky from your location. It shows real-time positions of stars, planets, and constellations, making it perfect for locating zodiac constellations.

5. **International Dark-Sky Association (IDA)**
   - A site dedicated to reducing light pollution and preserving night skies. IDA offers information on dark-sky locations, which are ideal for stargazing and observing celestial events in clear, dark skies.

Mobile Apps for Astrology and Celestial Events

1. **Co-Star**
   - A personalized astrology app that provides daily horoscopes, insights based on your birth chart, and compatibility readings. It's known for its modern approach and accessibility for astrology enthusiasts.

2. **The Pattern**
   - The Pattern uses astrology to deliver insights on personality, relationships, and timing. Its algorithm interprets astrological data in a user-friendly way, making it a popular app for self-discovery.

3. **Time Passages**
   - A comprehensive astrology app that allows users to explore natal charts, transits, and compatibility. It includes detailed descriptions of aspects, houses, and planetary placements.

4. **SkySafari**
   - A powerful app for stargazing, allowing you to locate and identify celestial objects in real-time. SkySafari includes descriptions, interactive simulations, and guides to help with locating zodiac constellations.

5. **Stellarium Mobile**
   - The mobile version of the popular Stellarium software, this app offers an interactive sky map that helps users identify stars, constellations, planets, and zodiac symbols with ease.

6. **Night Sky**
   - Known for its augmented reality feature, Night Sky allows you to point your phone at the sky to identify stars, planets, and constellations. It's a valuable tool for beginners and offers detailed information on celestial events.

7. **Star Walk 2**
   - A user-friendly app that provides real-time information on celestial objects, constellations, and upcoming events. Star Walk 2 also includes alerts for meteor showers, eclipses, and other celestial events.

Online Courses and Educational Resources

1. **Astrology University**
   - Offers a wide range of astrology courses for all levels, from beginner to advanced. Topics include natal chart interpretation, transits, synastry, and specialized techniques like horary and predictive astrology.

2. **Kepler College**
   - An accredited astrology school offering online courses and certification programs in astrology. Kepler College is ideal for students interested in formal, structured learning.

3. **The Astrology School (Chris Brennan)**
   - Run by astrologer Chris Brennan, The Astrology School offers online courses and resources on Hellenistic astrology, natal chart interpretation, transits, and other topics.

4. **Coursera – Astronomy: Exploring Time and Space (University of Arizona)**
   - This free online course explores astronomy basics, celestial phenomena, and the universe's structure. It's perfect for astrology enthusiasts looking to understand the science behind celestial events.

5. **Khan Academy – Cosmology and Astronomy**
   - Khan Academy's free courses provide an introduction to cosmology and astronomy, covering topics like stars, galaxies, and the universe's history. A helpful resource for foundational knowledge on celestial events.

6. **LearnAstrology.com**
   - Offers online courses, resources, and articles for those interested in studying astrology independently. It covers various topics, including birth charts, horoscopes, and advanced astrological techniques.

7. **The AstroTwins' Online Astrology Classes**
   - Known for their accessible style, The AstroTwins offer courses for beginners covering natal charts, planetary aspects, and timing. Their resources are ideal for those looking to integrate astrology into daily life.

Podcasts for Astrology and Celestial Insights

1. **The Astrology Podcast**
   - Hosted by Chris Brennan, this podcast covers a wide range of topics, from the basics of astrology to advanced techniques, interviews with experts, and discussions of current astrological events.
2. **Astrology with Andy**
   - Focuses on the practical side of astrology, featuring interpretations of famous individuals' charts, relationship insights, and guidance on personal growth.
3. **Ghost of a Podcast (Jessica Lanyadoo)**
   - Astrologer Jessica Lanyadoo combines astrology with guidance on self-care and relationships. Each episode covers a mix of astrology, psychology, and intuitive advice.
4. **Big Sky Astrology Podcast**
   - Hosted by April Elliott Kent, this podcast provides an accessible overview of current transits, moon phases, and planetary movements, with an emphasis on practical astrology.
5. **Astrology University Podcast**
   - Features guest astrologers and covers topics in modern and traditional astrology, including forecasts, discussions on zodiac signs, and advanced techniques.

These resources provide a solid foundation for anyone looking to deepen their understanding of astrology and celestial events. Whether you're a beginner exploring your natal chart, an astronomy enthusiast wanting to observe the night sky, or an advanced student studying the nuances of transits and aspects, these books, websites, apps, and courses will guide your journey and enhance your connection to the cosmos.

<u>Message from the Author:</u>

I hope you enjoyed this book, I love astrology and knew there was not a book such as this out on the shelf. I love metaphysical items as well. Please check out my other books:

-Life of Government Benefits

-My life of Hell

-My life with Hydrocephalus

-Red Sky

-World Domination:Woman's rule

-World Domination:Woman's Rule 2: The War

-Life and Banishment of Apophis: book 1

-The Kidney Friendly Diet

-The Ultimate Hemp Cookbook

-Creating a Dispensary(legally)

-Cleanliness throughout life: the importance of showering from childhood to adulthood.

-Strong Roots: The Risks of Overcoddling children

-Hemp Horoscopes: Cosmic Insights and Earthly Healing

- Celestial Hemp Navigating the Zodiac: Through the Green Cosmos

-Astrological Hemp: Aligning The Stars with Earth's Ancient Herb

-The Astrological Guide to Hemp: Stars, Signs, and Sacred Leaves

-Green Growth: Innovative Marketing Strategies for your Hemp Products and Dispensary

-Cosmic Cannabis

-Astrological Munchies

-Henry The Hemp

-Zodiacal Roots: The Astrological Soul Of Hemp

- **Green Constellations: Intersection of Hemp and Zodiac**

-Hemp in The Houses: An astrological Adventure Through The Cannabis Galaxy

-Galactic Ganja Guide

Heavenly Hemp

Zodiac Leaves

Doctor Who Astrology

Cannastrology

Stellar Satvias and Cosmic Indicas

<u>Celestial Cannabis: A Zodiac Journey</u>
AstroHerbology: The Sky and The Soil: Volume 1
AstroHerbology:Celestial Cannabis:Volume 2
Cosmic Cannabis Cultivation
The Starry Guide to Herbal Harmony: Volume 1
The Starry Guide to Herbal Harmony: Cannabis Universe: Volume 2
Yugioh Astrology: Astrological Guide to Deck, Duels and more
Nightmare Mansion: Echoes of The Abyss
Nightmare Mansion 2: Legacy of Shadows
Nightmare Mansion 3: Shadows of the Forgotten
Nightmare Mansion 4: Echoes of the Damned
The Life and Banishment of Apophis: Book 2
Nightmare Mansion: Halls of Despair
<u>Healing with Herb: Cannabis and Hydrocephalus</u>
<u>Planetary Pot: Aligning with Astrological Herbs: Volume 1</u>
Fast Track to Freedom: 30 Days to Financial Independence Using AI, Assets, and Agile Hustles
<u>Cosmic Hemp Pathways</u>
How to Become Financially Free in 30 Days: 10,000 Paths to Prosperity
Zodiacal Herbage: Astrological Insights: Volume 1
Nightmare Mansion: Whispers in the Walls
The Daleks Invade Atlantis
Henry the hemp and Hydrocephalus

10X The Kidney Friendly Diet
Cannabis Universe: Adult coloring book
Hemp Astrology: The Healing Power of the Stars
Zodiacal Herbage: Astrological Insights: Cannabis Universe: Volume 2
<u>Planetary Pot: Aligning with Astrological Herbs: Cannabis Universes: Volume 2</u>
Doctor Who Meets the Replicators and SG-1: The Ultimate Battle for Survival
Nightmare Mansion: Curse of the Blood Moon
<u>The Celestial Stoner: A Guide to the Zodiac</u>
Cosmic Pleasures: Sex Toy Astrology for Every Sign
Hydrocephalus Astrology: Navigating the Stars and Healing Waters
Lapis and the Mischievous Chocolate Bar

Celestial Positions: Sexual Astrology for Every Sign
Apophis's Shadow Work Journal: **:** A Journey of Self-Discovery and Healing
Kinky Cosmos: Sexual Kink Astrology for Every Sign
Digital Cosmos: The Astrological Digimon Compendium
Stellar Seeds: The Cosmic Guide to Growing with Astrology

Apophis's Daily Gratitude Journal

Cat Astrology: Feline Mysteries of the Cosmos
The Cosmic Kama Sutra: An Astrological Guide to Sexual Positions
Unleash Your Potential: A Guided Journal Powered by AI Insights
Whispers of the Enchanted Grove

Cosmic Pleasures: An Astrological Guide to Sexual Kinks
369, 12 Manifestation Journal
Whisper of the nocturne journal(blank journal for writing or drawing)
The Boogey Book
Locked In Reflection: A Chastity Journey Through Locktober
Generating Wealth Quickly:
How to Generate $100,000 in 24 Hours
Star Magic: Harness the Power of the Universe
The Flatulence Chronicles: A Fart Journal for Self-Discovery
The Doctor and The Death Moth
Seize the Day: A Personal Seizure Tracking Journal
The Ultimate Boogeyman Safari: A Journey into the Boogie World and Beyond
Whispers of Samhain: 1,000 Spells of Love, Luck, and Lunar Magic: Samhain Spell Book
Apophis's guides:
Witch's Spellbook Crafting Guide for Halloween
<u>Frost & Flame: The Enchanted Yule Grimoire of 1000 Winter Spells</u>
<u>The Ultimate Boogey Goo Guide & Spooky Activities for Halloween Fun</u>
Harmony of the Scales: A Libra's Spellcraft for Balance and Beauty
The Enchanted Advent: 36 Days of Christmas Wonders

Nightmare Mansion: The Labyrinth of Screams
Harvest of Enchantment: 1,000 Spells of Gratitude, Love, and Fortune for Thanksgiving
The Boogey Chronicles: A Journal of Nightly Encounters and Shadowy Secrets
The 12 Days of Financial Freedom: A Step-by-Step Christmas Countdown to Transform Your Finances
Sigil of the Eternal Spiral Blank Journal
A Christmas Feast: Timeless Recipes for Every Meal
Holiday Stress-Free Solutions: A Survival Guide to Thriving During the Festive Season
Yu-Gi-Oh! Holiday Gifting Mastery: The Ultimate Guide for Fans and Newcomers Alike
Holiday Harmony: A Hydrocephalus Survival Guide for the Festive Season
Celestial Craft: The Witch's Almanac for 2025 – A Cosmic Guide to Manifestations, Moons, and Mystical Events
Doctor Who: The Toymaker's Winter Wonderland
Tulsa King Unveiled: A Thrilling Guide to Stallone's Mafia Masterpiece

Pendulum Craft: A Complete Guide to Crafting and Using Personalized Divination Tools
Nightmare Mansion: Santa's Eternal Eve
If you want solar for your home go here: https://www.harborsolar.live/apophisenterprises/

Get Some Tarot cards: https://www.makeplayingcards.com/sell/apophis-occult-shop

<u>Get some shirts: https://www.bonfire.com/store/apophis-shirt-emporium/</u>

<u>Instagrams:</u>
@apophis_enterprises,
@apophisbookemporium,
@apophisscardshop
Twitter: @apophisenterpr1 Tiktok:@apophisenterprise
Youtube: @sg1fan23477, @FiresideRetreatKingdom
Hive: @sg1fan23477

Podcast: Apophis Chat Zone: https://open.spotify.com/show/5zXbr-CLEV2xzCp8ybrfHsk?si=fb4d4fdbdce44dec

Newsletter: https://apophiss-newsletter-27c897.beehiiv.com/

Get printable holiday budget planners: apophisenterprisesllc.org/Apophis-emporium-shop /ols/products/holiday-budgeting-packageprintable

www.ingramcontent.com/pod-product-compliance
Lightning Source LLC
Chambersburg PA
CBHW081358130726
47998CB00011B/2997